T0176530

MODEL-BASED TESTING
ESSENTIALS

MODEL-BASED TESTING ESSENTIALS

Guide to the ISTQB® Certified Model-Based Tester Foundation Level

ANNE KRAMER
BRUNO LEGEARD

Published by John Wiley & Sons, Inc., Hoboken, New Jersey
Published simultaneously in Canada

All names of products and companies used in this book may be trademarks of their corresponding owners. In particular, the following terms and abbreviations are registered trademarks: BPMN™, Hewlett-Packard®, HP®, ISTQB®, IQBBA®, iSQI®, MATLAB Simulink®, Microsoft® Windows®, Model Driven Architecture®, MOF®, Object Management Group®, OMG®, RUP®, Sparx® Systems Enterprise Architect®, Stateflow®, UML®, Unified Modeling Language™, XMI®.

For general information on our other products and services or for technical support, please contact our Customer Care Department within the United States at (800) 762-2974, outside the United States at (317) 572-3993 or fax (317) 572-4002.

Wiley also publishes its books in a variety of electronic formats. Some content that appears in print may not be available in electronic formats. For more information about Wiley products, visit our web site at www.wiley.com.

Library of Congress Cataloging-in-Publication Data

Names: Kramer, Anne, (Software engineer) author. | Legeard, Bruno, author.
Title: Model-based testing essentials : guide to the ISTQB certified
    model-based tester foundation level / Anne Kramer, Bruno Legeard.
Description: Hoboken, New Jersey : John Wiley & Sons Inc., [2016] | Includes
    bibliographical references and index.
Identifiers: LCCN 2015035751 | ISBN 9781119130017 (cloth)
Subjects: LCSH: Computer software–Testing–Examinations–Study guides. |
    Model-based reasoning–Examinations–Study guides. | International
    Software Testing Qualifications Board–Examinations–Study guides. |
    Electronic data processing personnel–Certification.
Classification: LCC QA76.76.T48 K73 2016 | DDC 005.3028/7–dc23 LC record available at
http://lccn.loc.gov/2015035751

Set in 10/12pt, Times-Roman by SPi Global, Chennai, India.

Printed in the United States of America

10 9 8 7 6 5 4 3 2 1

DEDICATION

To our families

CONTENTS

FOREWORD BY GUALTIERO BAZZANA

When I was asked by my dear friend Bruno Legeard to provide a foreword to the "Model-Based Testing Essentials" book that he was authoring together with Anne Kramer, I was very pleased because this was a sort of flashback that reminded me of when I was younger, so much younger than today, and was preparing my PhD dissertation, which was based on automatic test generation for telecommunication systems based on SADT and SDL models further transformed into Petri Nets.

This is just a small witness of the fact that the concept of model-based testing (MBT) has been in existence for many years; nowadays methods, techniques, and tools have matured to a point at which MBT is ready for widespread adoption in many domains, starting from the ones that have historically taken advantage of such approach (e.g., aerospace, railway and telecommunications) to others, such as automotive, in which systematic structured testing techniques have been more and more applied in the last years and MBT has quickly become a *de facto* standard.

In my capacity of ISTQB® President, I am very happy to welcome this book that will greatly help professionals in taking the exam for ISTQB® Model-Based Tester certification; as a matter of fact, ISTQB® has approved for general market availability in October 2015 the Model-Based Tester syllabus, which is available for free download from our website (www.istqb.org) and that is the basis around which this book has been prepared, constituting an excellent study guide to the ISTQB® Certified Model-Based Tester.

ISTQB® stand for International Software Testing Qualifications Board, a not-for-profit association, which has gained the status of world's leading organization for Software Testing Certification, by running over 560,000 exams as of June 2015.

Our mission is to continually improve and advance the software testing profession by defining and maintaining a Body of Knowledge that allows testers to be certified based on best practices, connecting the international software testing community, and encouraging research.

In this context, the ISTQB® portfolio of certifications has recently been expanded in order to complement the historically "Core" certifications (Foundation, Advanced Test Manager, Advanced Test Analyst, Advanced Technical Test Analyst, Expert) with a set of certifications dedicated to Agile Testing and a brand new cluster of "Specialist" modules, whose goal is to cover specific topics/domains in a vertical way, using a drill-down/deep-dive approach.

The "Model-Based Tester" syllabus and certification is the first of several Specialist modules to be brought to market; it complements the Core Foundation as a Specialist module and it provides a practical and easy entry to the MBT approach.

The ISTQB® Glossary of software testing terms defines Model-Based Testing as "Testing based on or involving models"; by studying this book, testers will learn how to use models to drive test analysis and design, as well as how to take advantage of the models for other testing activities such as test implementation and reporting. In so doing, you will be able to improve the effectiveness and efficiency of the test process.

So, my thanks to the ISTQB® Working Group members who developed the ISTQB® MBT certification and to Anne and Bruno for providing a thorough and pragmatic study guide to it, which I am sure will be appreciated by the software testing professionals worldwide.

Gualtiero Bazzana
ISTQB® President

FOREWORD BY ROBERT V. BINDER

Although I have long contended that all testing is model based, the nature of tools and models defines substantially different approaches to software testing. After some 20 years of research and practice in automated model-based testing over thousands of projects around the world, a broad, substantial, and proven body of knowledge has been established. I have been fortunate to play a role in this evolution as a developer and user of several model-based testing tools and as the author of three dozen test design patterns (each a model.)

During these two decades, software and computing technology has become indispensable for modern life and is increasingly shaping it. Although it has become easier to produce software, it has not become any easier to be sure that our creations are always well-behaved. Model-based testing has shown that it can better meet the quality challenges of present-day systems than the wishful thinking that is often used as a testing strategy.

We know how to select, deploy, develop, and integrate model-based testing tools. We know how to create test models for all kinds of application domains and technology stacks. We know how to adapt development, testing, and maintenance processes to make best use of model-based testing, in both agile and traditional life cycles. Perhaps most important, we have learned when model-based testing is practical and when it is not.

These have been pioneering years with attendant successes and failures. Some once promising approaches and explorations have fallen away. The curiosity and energy of open-source developers and researchers have shown how formalized relationships may be realized as useful tools. Technology entrepreneurs have created a small but ever-better stream of product offerings, each testing market acceptance and rejection. Large and small organizations have tried model-based testing. Many have found it useful enough to take the difficult path of institutionalizing it.

These pioneers had to learn by trial and error, reading available publications, and sometimes plunging into the depths of research reports. They and their organizations have had to accept the risk that such experimentation brings.

I believe that in the next 5–10 years, model-based testing can become as routine and widely used as testing with open source tools such as Selenium or Junit. Credible and practical education in model-based testing will be critical for this transition.

Until now, a practitioner, manager, or agilist wondering what model-based testing is really all about had to work hard to get an answer. That meant attending an annual conference such as UCAAT and/or taking a risk to experiment with a pilot project. That pioneer would have to work out how model-based testing fit with their understanding of software development and testing, and finally how it could be socialized in their organization.

With the publication of *Model-Based Testing Essentials*, readers have a credible, practical, and complete introduction to and guidance for using model-based testing. This book distills hard-won knowledge in a systematic presentation of topics needed to use and deploy model-based testing. I believe it will not only be a useful guide to prepare for the ISTQB® exam, but a valuable handbook for new and experienced practitioners alike.

Robert V. Binder
Carnegie-Mellon University Software Engineering Institute, Pittsburgh
November 2015

PREFACE

Testing our products gives us confidence that they perform as intended. If we do not find any bugs, then everything should be fine … or not? What, if we do not really have confidence in the test itself? Are we sure we test the parts that are really important? Is our test complete and, if we think so, are we able to prove this? What about the cost of testing? Is it possible to spare time or money in the testing phases?

Questions like this brought the testing community to think about using models for testing purposes, and to develop a new testing approach called model-based testing (MBT). The initial idea of MBT dates back to 1970s, but its industrial application on a larger scale started only during the last decade. Today, the community of MBT adepts is growing constantly and the topic attracts more and more attention. Therefore, the International Software Testing Qualifications Board (ISTQB) decided to issue a new certification scheme, the "ISTQB Certified Tester Foundation Level – Model-Based Tester Certification."

The ISTQB standard glossary of terms used in software testing [1] defines MBT as "testing based on or involving models." By model, we mean a somehow formal or structured representation of the system under test, its environment, or the test itself, which directly supports test analysis and design activities, but also test planning and control, implementation and execution, and reporting activities.

Why MBT is worth reading a book or attending a training course? In 2014, we performed a user survey among MBT practitioners and asked them about their expectations regarding MBT (see Figure 1). [1]

---

[1] See Ref. [3] for the complete results of the survey and Ref. [4] for a detailed analysis.

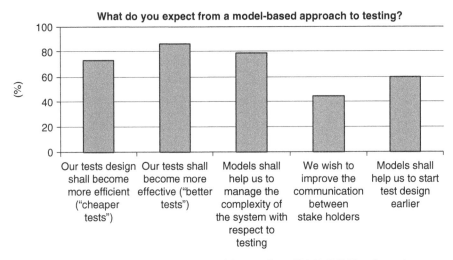

Figure 1   Expectations of MBT practitioners (from 2014 MBT User Survey).

The top four expectations clearly relate to the questions we asked about testing practices in the beginning of this section:

- Better tests
    We expect that MBT will help us to increase the effectiveness of our test process, for example by discovering more bugs during the various test cycles.
- Cheaper tests
    We are interested in automated test generation to reduce the costs of test creation and maintenance and, thus, to increase the overall efficiency of our test process.
- Managing complexity
    Models are abstract representations of some existing or planned reality. They proved to be very helpful in system architecture and design. Using them in the test process should help us to keep the overview and to focus on what matters for our test objectives.
- Start test design earlier
    One of the major promises of MBT is early requirements validation. We can start the modeling activities long time before the system under test exists in reality. Thus, MBT should help us in implementing the ISTQB good practice of early testing.

This book will show you how MBT can fulfill these expectations based on the current state of the practice in this area as taught in the ISTQB Model-Based Tester – Foundation Level certification syllabus. Furthermore, we focus on essential aspects of model-based testing in practice. Beyond the syllabus, we provide additional information on MBT and share with you our personal experience with the technique.

> *The 2014 MBT User Survey*
>
> *In 2012, Robert V. Binder conducted the first survey among MBT practitioners to collect data and experience on the usage of model-based testing [2]. One year later, we started an independent initiative at ETSI's User Conference on Advanced Automated Testing. The 2013 survey was more technical and aimed at validating a common MBT classification scheme. Finally, we decided to join both initiatives and started the 2014 MBT User Survey.*
>
> *The survey was open from mid-June 2014 to early August 2014. One hundred model-based testing practitioners answered, providing a relevant picture of the current state of the practice in the MBT area. We wanted to learn how MBT users view the efficiency and effectiveness of the approach, what works, and what does not work. The results are publicly available [3]. For a detailed analysis, please refer Ref. [4].*

THE ISTQB CERTIFIED TESTER FOUNDATION LEVEL – MODEL-BASED TESTER

There are many different approaches to model-based testing. Some adepts place their expectations in complete automation, both of test case generation and test execution. Others use the models mainly to describe the test idea and to generate test cases for manual execution. All those approaches are valid and have their advantages, but without a structured introduction to the topic, newcomers are rapidly lost. This is where the ISTQB certification scheme helps.

The ISTQB MBT certification extends the ISTQB Certified Tester Foundation Level and provides additional skills to professional testers. The qualification scheme addresses people having reached the first level of achievement in their software testing career, including testers, test analysts, test automation engineers, test managers, as well as system and software developers and architects. It may also be beneficial for anyone who wants a deeper understanding of software testing and of the use of models for test generation, such as project managers, quality managers, product managers, business analysts, and business process experts. In general, an ISTQB Certified Model-Based Tester has acquired the necessary skills to contribute successfully to MBT projects in a given context.

Figure 2 provides a summary of the ISTQB MBT syllabus content. The syllabus is divided into five chapters, covering the introduction of MBT (Chapter 1), the main phases of the MBT process (Chapters 2–4), and the evaluation and deployment of an MBT approach (Chapter 5).

The syllabus covers 36 learning objectives at different cognitive levels of knowledge (so-called K-levels):

- 9 at level K1 (Remember),
- 22 at level K2 (Understand),
- 5 at level K3 (Apply).

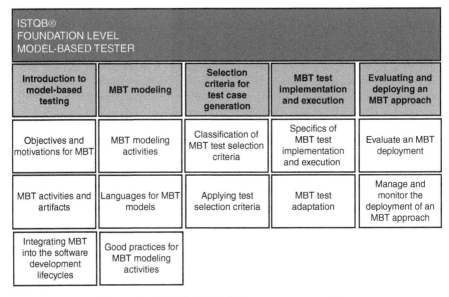

Figure 2   ISTQB MBT syllabus – content overview.

In addition, the syllabus includes 10 MBT-specific terms, which are equally part of the examination.

Throughout this book, we provide you with the required knowledge to pass successfully the ISTQB MBT certification. Various exercises invite you to practice modeling and test generation activities. If you are not interested in passing the exam, you may skip them, but if you are, beware of the fact that they are essential to reach cognitive level K3.

HOW THIS BOOK IS ORGANIZED?

This book consists of 12 chapters plus 3 appendices. We tried to stay as close as possible to the structure of the ISTQB MBT syllabus. However, for pedagogic reasons, there are some exceptions from this rule. To make the mapping easier for you, each chapter of this book starts with a reference to the corresponding syllabus section(s).

In Chapter 1, we introduce the topic of model-based testing and tell you what you can realistically expect from this test approach.

In Chapter 2, you find the definition of the MBT-specific terms that are part of the ISTQB MBT examination. Moreover, we define additional terms used in this book to make sure we all understand them in a similar way. Section 2.3 is very important. We present the two simple graphical modeling languages proposed by the ISTQB MBT syllabus. Unless stated otherwise, all example models in this book respect the rules of one of those two sample languages.

Chapter 3, then, goes to the root of the matter. We explain how a test process employing MBT looks like, including its activities, actors, and roles, as well as its input and output, and its integration into the global software development lifecycle.

Modeling being a core activity in MBT, three chapters of this book deal with this topic. Chapter 4 points out some fundamental aspects you should consider before starting to write an MBT model.

Chapter 5 presents a variety of different modeling languages. It shall enable you to select the most appropriate language for your particular application focus. In addition, we provide some general information on MBT modeling tools.

In Chapter 6, we present common good modeling practices and draw your attention to typical mistakes and pitfalls. Unlike the other sections of Chapter 6, Section 6.8 is not based on the syllabus. Instead, it contains a longer list of recommendations regarding modeling practices from other sources including our personal experience.

In Chapter 7, we have a short glimpse on classic test design techniques as taught in the ISTQB Certified Tester Foundation Level course. We see how MBT relates to those techniques, which it does not replace, but supports.

Chapter 8 is entirely dedicated to test case selection. We present a taxonomy of selection criteria, examples for their practical application, pros and cons, and report some recommendations. The last section of this chapter briefly deals with automated test generation in general.

Next to test generation comes test implementation and execution, which is the topic of Chapter 9. We explain the specifics of MBT test implementation, the dependencies on modeling and test generation activities, and the additional steps required to automate the generated test cases.

Chapter 10 is the last chapter having a direct correspondence in the ISTQB MBT syllabus. It deals with the introduction of MBT in a company. It is not the classic "Do a pilot first" stuff. Instead, we focus on very specific aspects of MBT. How do the objectives of your organization influence the choice of an MBT approach? Where do the cost factors originate and where may we expect financial benefits? We present metrics to measure success and good practices to apply. In a section on tool support, we consider MBT tools supporting test generation activities and their integration with other tools.

In Chapter 11, we present three radically different case studies illustrating the daily work with MBT.

The last chapter summarizes the book with an overall positive conclusion. MBT is worth trying! Finally, in the appendices you will find the solutions of the exercises, a short quiz to test your understanding, and some additional information.

ACKNOWLEDGMENTS

We are very pleased to thank the colleagues from whom we received valuable help and contributions for this book. We are grateful to the reviewers of the initial drafts of the book for their helpful comments and suggestions: Regina Weickmann,

François Guerin, Vincent Guillard, Véronique Hamel, and Norbert Kastner. As part of the ISTQB Model-Based Tester Working Group, we had many debates and influential interactions during all the periods of developing the ISTQB syllabus with the colleagues in the working group. We want to thank all the other members of the author team: Stephan Christmann, Lars Frantzen, Armin Metzger, Thomas Müller, Ina Schieferdecker, Stephan Weißleder, and also Natasa Micuda, who managed the exam material and Stephan Schulz, who managed the review process of the syllabus.

Special thanks to Arnaud Bouzy and Elizabeta Fourneret for providing material for the use cases, respectively, in Sections 11.1 and 11.3 and to Abbas Ahmad for the TTCN-3 example.

Finally, we acknowledge the strong support we had from our families during the writing of this book. Anne particularly thanks her husband, Hansgerd, and her daughter, Alice, for their enormous patience, the unceasing encouragement, and their loving support, which made this book possible. Bruno thanks his wife, Oumhanie, and children Anissa, Loïc, Fabien, and Maëva, for their constant support, love, and understanding.

Anne Kramer – Erlangen
Bruno Legeard – Besançon
July 2015

1

INTRODUCTION TO MODEL-BASED TESTING

This chapter covers the learning objectives of syllabus Section 1.1 – "Objectives and Motivations for MBT."

1.1 WHY DO WE NEED NEW APPROACHES TO TESTING?

In the earliest days of software testing, developers just made sure the program was running correctly. Debugging and testing were the same. The notion of testing as a separate activity came up in 1957. Unlike debugging, testing assures that the software really solves the problem [5]. Since then, "Software Tester" became a profession along with special qualification schemes such as the ISTQB Certified Tester.

The significance of testing directly correlates with the complexity of software applications and, thus, constantly increases. Software systems become not only larger, but also more interoperable. They support extensive workflows on various platforms. Product variants also add to complexity. Ideal for marketing, because they allow you to target different market segments, they are a hell to test! As a result, we have a huge number of test cases to execute and, rapidly, lack the overview. We are no longer able to answer questions such as "What shall be tested?/What has been tested?" or "Which tests are important?/What may be left out?" "How do you want to check completeness of large document-based test specifications?" Besides, the documentation of the test idea is lost amidst the detailed test instructions. Thus, though being the authors, we later do not remember why we tested something the way we did.

Model-Based Testing Essentials–Guide to the ISTQB® Certified Model-Based Tester Foundation Level,
First Edition. Anne Kramer and Bruno Legeard.
© 2016 John Wiley & Sons, Inc. Published 2016 by John Wiley & Sons, Inc.

The industrial demands regarding time-to-market and cost reduction constantly increase and definitely affect testing. Testing less not being an option, we need faster and better tests. "Better" means improved objectivity, repeatability, and transparency. This is where model-based testing (MBT) comes in. The main idea is to formalize and automate as many activities related to test case specification as possible and, thus, to increase both the efficiency and effectiveness of testing. Instead of writing a test case specification with hundreds of pages, we draw a model (called an *MBT model*) and, then, use a tool to generate the tests. In the manager's dreams, it is even simpler. We reuse models from software design and obtain the corresponding test cases simply by pressing a button. However, as we discuss in this book, MBT is not just reusing development models and working with a tool, but an entire new approach to test design and test implementation.

There is another, psychological motivation for MBT. Let us face the truth: being a software tester is still not as prestigious as it should be. Testing is perceived as a destructive activity [6]. Testers try to find bugs, looking for flaws. Even worse, they really find them! In addition, they constantly complain about imprecise or inexistent requirements. Testers ask uncomfortable questions and expect an answer. They work so well that testing quite often becomes more expensive than expected. Testing is one of these cost factors (known as "cost of quality") managers try to reduce, and nobody really knows, how expensive it would have been without testing ("cost of poor quality"). It is very difficult to measure quantitatively what the tester's work is worth.

By writing MBT models, the tester applies a technique also used in requirements analysis and development to manage complexity by abstraction. As we discuss later, modeling is not so different from coding. If testers are able to do this, they are on equal terms with the developers and communication becomes easier. Ideally, the developer perceives the tester's work as helpful rather than as criticism. In addition, an MBT model visualizes the complexity of testing. For those who decide on budgets, the risk of leaving out specific scenarios becomes far more obvious than in a traditional, document-based approach.

1.2   WHAT IS MODEL-BASED TESTING?

The idea of MBT is ingeniously simple. If we had to summarize this book in one sentence, our recommendation would be the following: "Draw pictures whenever possible to explain what you are doing or going to do, and use it to create and maintain your testware." This is what modeling is all about, at least if we think about graphical models (i.e., diagrams). There is also a brief section on textual modeling languages in this book. Some MBT approaches combine graphical and textual representations, either to visualize the textual model in a diagram or to complete the graphical model with textual information.

Writing models is nothing magic. We do it instinctively. If a process becomes too complicated to explain, we draw a flowchart. If we want to describe how the different components of a larger system relate to each other, we draw a block diagram. Both the flowchart and the block diagram help us in structuring and visualizing complex issues.

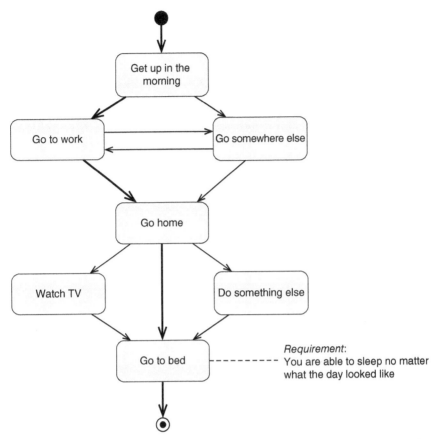

Figure 1.1 Test of a normal working day with some variations (activity diagram; Note: Throughout this book, we use the simplified modeling languages defined in the ISTQB MBT syllabus [13] (see Section 3.3). However, you should be aware that this is only one out of many possible notations. Depending on the selected modeling language, notation paradigm, and tool support, the same MBT model may look different).

Now, everybody who has tried knows that testing really is a complex issue. So why not use models to describe what we want to test and how we are going to do it?

Figure 1.1 shows an example of a very simple model. It describes a normal working day we all know well enough. We get up in the morning, go to work, back home, and straight into bed. In France, they have a nice expression for this kind of life, which is "Métro, boulot, dodo" (literally "subway, work, sleep"). The bold arrows in the figure indicate this typical working day. Fortunately, some variants exist. If we are not too tired, we watch TV or do something else before going to bed. Sometimes we do not directly go to work or we may go somewhere else for lunch and then get back to work. Depending on the path you take through the model there are small variations in this daily routine.

What has the model in Figure 1.1 to do with testing? Imagine that the person whose day we described in the model is the system under test. The requirement we have to check is that the system is able to sleep no matter what variation of the daily routine it went through. Thus, each path through the model corresponds to a sequence that we could test, that is, a potential test case. Unfortunately, if we do not put any limit to the back and forth between working place and somewhere else, we obtain an infinite number of possible paths, corresponding to an infinite number of test cases. Performing an infinite number of tests is neither possible nor does it make sense. In most cases, the worker mostly leaves his working place just once to get some lunch. We should definitely test this situation!

For the model in Figure 1.1, this means that we neglect repeated loops. This leads us to 18 different sequences, corresponding to 18 test cases.

Exercise 1   *Find the 18 possible sequences in Figure 1.1 under the assumption that repeated loops are not allowed.*

Now, imagine a slightly different situation. If the person works in sales, he or she will probably perform several trips per day to visit some customers. This is not covered by our 18 test cases. However, is it necessary to test two, three, four, five … trips per day? Probably not. Usually, it is sufficient to prove that the system works for the longest sequence. Maybe, five trips per day is a reasonable upper limit to test in a 19th test case.

There is something important to understand from this simple example. It is one thing to draw a model and a second thing to obtain test cases from it. This is very different from traditional test design where you only write down those test cases you want to execute (even if, in the end, there may be no time for them). We have to think about what we really want to test, and it strongly depends on the system under test and its context which sequences we should select. Of course, similar considerations influence traditional test design, but they are far more explicit in MBT. We use the term "test selection criteria." Those criteria guide us in the selection of tests we want to generate from our MBT model.

It is only a small step from Figure 1.1 to our first test case derived from an MBT model. All we have to do is to follow a path from start to end and to collect the information in between. The test case "Métro, boulot, dodo" (the bold path in Figure 1.1) looks like Table 1.1.

TABLE 1.1   Our First Test Case Generated from a Model

Test Case – Normal Working Day 01
Get up in the morning Go to work Go home Go to bed *Requirement:* You are able to sleep no matter what the day looked like passed □   failed □

Figure 1.1 looks like a simple description of the system under test we could find in our requirements specification, but it is only a start. Testers can be very mean. It is their task to find errors. They try to push the system under test to its limits. A tester will probably try 100 trips back and forth to work. Even more, he will not stay with the model in Figure 1.1. Instead, he will add additional arrows and check, whether it is possible to watch TV at work or to sleep somewhere else. He will discuss the enriched model with developers and other stakeholders and discover that there is an undocumented requirement that the system does not snore. This is already the first step toward quality (and a restful night).

Even if this is not the most efficient way to do MBT, a simple model similar to the one in Figure 1.1 helps already a lot, especially if you have to test complex systems. It is a bit like writing a mind map. In the beginning, you do not know where to start, but during the modeling process, you start seeing the abstraction layers. In addition, you can discuss the test design with others and show them the picture. You draw the model to clarify, to document, and to discuss the test idea.

To perform MBT on a higher maturity level, we need additional information on how the tests stimulate the system and what they exactly check. Using a modeling tool, we are able to add a detailed description to each action in a way that they are contained in the model, but invisible in the picture. As a human, we can only see them in a separate window, for example, if we double-click on the action, but a test case generator will be able to collect them into a test case. One question, however, remains. Which paths through the model shall we test and which paths may we leave out? Tools can help by selecting paths according to given criteria, but even then, we have to decide about the criteria that we wish to apply. There will be a larger section dealing with test selection criteria later on.

1.3 BENEFITS OF MBT

MBT positively affects the efficiency and effectiveness of testing on several aspects. On one hand, MBT models help in managing complexity, improve communication between testers and other project stakeholders, and foster common understanding of requirements. On the other hand, they provide us with better control on generated test cases and with the option to automate test design and implementation activities. Finally, MBT models are a kind of knowledge management.

1.3.1 MBT Models Provide an Overview and Help in Managing Complexity

The biggest advantage of using models to describe tests is the fact that they help in keeping the overview on what is actually tested. The hackneyed saying in this context is "a picture is worth a thousand words." The estimation on how many words fit on a page A4 vary between 250 and 500. Since test specifications are usually not so dense, let us be conservative and assume an average of 250 words. Thus, one picture of an MBT model replaces four pages of document-based test specification. Exaggerated? Not necessarily. It depends on the model.

TABLE 1.2   Our First Test Case with Detailed Test Instructions

Test Case – Normal Working Day 01 (Extended Version)

- Switch off the alarm clock
- Get out of the bed
- Take a shower
- Get some breakfast
- Brush teeth
- Dress for work
- Leave the house

- Take the car
- Drive to work
- Search a parking lot
- Memorize location
- Go to office

- Leave the office
- Search the car on the parking deck
- Drive home
- Park the car
- Enter the house

- Brush teeth
- Undress for the night
- Check the alarm clock
- Switch off the lights
- Go to bed

Requirement: You are able to sleep no matter what the day looked like
passed □   failed □

Take the example in Figure 1.1. We decided to derive 19 test cases from the model, all of them being at least as long as the one in Table 1.1, which is one-fifth of A4. Thus, this simple model already corresponds to roughly four pages of text, but the test case does not even clearly describe what to do. With more detailed test descriptions, the generated test case may look like the one in Table 1.2. The text nearly tripled in size, but the picture remains the same. In addition, the MBT model separates the conceptual test design from technical test implementation details. This is why models help in keeping the overview – and the best is – the use of models for testing purposes is not limited to a specific test objective or to a specific application domain! We use models to test the business processes and rules of a large enterprise IT system, as well as models for load testing of a graphical user interface of a web application. Obviously, the various MBT models look extremely different, but the underlying concept is the same.

By using MBT models instead of prose, we introduce a higher level of abstraction in test design. Just compare Figure 1.1 with Table 1.2. The picture shows the context of our tests far better than the textual description. Possibly, our test strategy requires extended tests for critical parts. If you show the MBT model to an expert (e.g., a software developer), he will be able to tell you, in which part of the model (and, thus, of the system) the tests will probably detect more problems than in the other parts, because the part implements a new feature or because it is more complex than the rest.

1.3.2 MBT Models Help Communicating

For a moment, put yourself in the shoes of the developer: The project deadline approaches. You still have to implement some features and there is a bug you are unable to locate. Of course, you are stressed – and this is exactly the moment when the tester starts asking uncomfortable questions. "What happens to the data entered beforehand, if I press Cancel? Does 'Cancel' always take me back to the start screen? Are you sure?"

Next, try the tester's shoes. You still have some time, but from experience you know that you should start writing the tests, now. The requirements are not as bad as they could be. Of course, some points remain unclear, especially regarding the Cancel button. Unfortunately, all the system-matter experts are currently under stress. They do not have much time for you. How can you bring your understanding of the requirements and your questions to the point?

Draw a picture! If this becomes too complicated, draw several pictures. If you use a tool, you can construct so-called hierarchical models with different abstraction layers. Thus, you may discuss the general workflow with the product manager and the implementation details with the developer, showing each of them the part of the model that corresponds to his level of understanding. The model fosters a common perception and understanding of the requirements and helps identifying misunderstandings.

A common scenario from personal experience

From time to time, customers ask for an exemplary MBT model for a feature that is usually not too complex. We call this an MBT prototype. The scenario that follows is always the same. Based on the existing documentation we construct the model. If questions arise, we comment them in the model. When we present the model to the customer the discussion starts … between the customer representatives. Most often, the group does not have the same understanding of the feature and, sometimes, we really detected an inconsistency in the specification or an unspecified behavior.

(Anne Kramer)

1.3.3 MBT Models Validate Requirements

Writing good requirements is extremely difficult. You may spend a lot of time in formulating and reviewing them, but the ultimate check takes place when you start working with them. Only then, you will see how good they are in reality.

Obviously, the first to work with the requirements are the developers. Somehow, but they steer around most problems regarding unclear requirements. Either they are more inventive or they have shorter communication channels than testers. (The latter is definitely true, if the test is outsourced.) The next to work with the requirements are the testers. Good testers are rigorous. They despair of unclear or conflicting requirements because it is their task to prove that the software conforms to those requirements. Quite often, testers detect major problems in the requirements that the developer must fix. Thus, the earlier the testers start their work the better it is.

With MBT, it is not necessary to know all implementation details to start writing tests. In a top-down modeling approach, the first version of the MBT model has a high level of abstraction and does not yet contain any detailed test descriptions. It describes the main features to be tested, the checks to perform, and their order. The checks usually refer to the requirements. In Figure 1.1, this is the feature "You are able to sleep no matter what the day looked like." We still do not know anything about the detailed instructions in Table 1.2, but we may start thinking about possible ways to keep the system awake. (A real bad horror shocker on TV would do.)

Of course, you do not necessarily need to write a model for these preliminary thoughts. However, it is an excellent way to validate requirements early, especially if the requirements are in prose. The earlier you start with MBT modeling activities, the earlier you will be able to share your thoughts with business analysts and developers, to generate test cases and to perform them. This helps implementing the "early testing" principle. If you start the MBT modeling activity at the end of the requirements analysis phase, you may even have the chance to resolve unclear or conflicting requirements before they are implemented wrongly – and, as we all know by now, the earlier you find a defect, the faster, easier, and cheaper it is to fix.

1.3.4 MBT Models Visualize Tests

Classic document-based test specifications easily count several hundreds of pages. Reviewing them is a hard task. People's concentration has its limits. They are certainly able to check the consistency within one test case, but it is very hard to check, whether each test aspect has been fully covered.

Show them the model! It represents your idea of the tests. You can show them the paths you decided to take and those you left out, and explain your reasons. Even better: the model helps you to remember your own thoughts and decisions when asked in a few months.

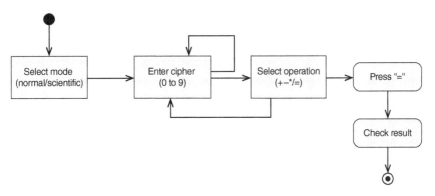

Figure 1.2   A well-known application (activity diagram).

Try yourself by doing Exercise 2. How well do you understand the model in Figure 1.2 without any explanation?

Exercise 2   *The model in Figure 1.2 describes the test of a commonly known application. Do you recognize the system under test? What exactly shall be tested?*

The figures are easier to understand than lengthy textual descriptions and to discuss with non-technical stakeholders, for example, business analysts. Again, this facilitates communication and helps in validating requirements at an early stage of the project.

1.3.5   Model-Based Test Generation Is Well Supported by Tools

All the above-mentioned advantages are due to the MBT model itself. They do not depend on any tool support apart from a model editor. However, only a test case generator will provide you with the full advantages of MBT, that is, the possibility of automation.

Various model-based test generators are available on the market. They differ a lot regarding the required input and the generated output. In one aspect, however, they are alike. Test generators are cheaper, faster, and more precise than humans are. They can do all the work that requires precision, but no particular intelligence. For example, they may traverse all paths through the model, gathering information on the way and create an output like Table 1.2.

Of course, someone has to draw the MBT model. The big advantage is that we only have to do it once and the generator replicates the information automatically. The generator may even create several test suites from the same model using different test selection criteria. In traditional test design, the tester spends only a small part of his time on the initial test design, that is, the test idea. The rest is writing and/or implementing test cases. In MBT and with a test case generator, we reverse this ratio. The tester spends the majority of time on analyzing the behavior of the system under test and imagining possible test scenarios and much less on deriving test cases thanks to automated test generation. The improved efficiency is a major argument in favor of tool support, especially in the maintenance phase of the tests.

Once we have the model, we may generate different sets of test cases from it, depending on the test objectives. We already practiced this in Section 1.2 when we derived 18 test cases corresponding to the different variations of a normal working day in office, plus one additional test case for the continuously traveling sales representative. Again, appropriate tool support considerably facilitates the task of test case selection.

Apart from test case generation, tools also support other test-related activities, such as documenting traceability between test cases and requirements, documenting the test approach or generating test scripts and interfaces for automated test execution. In our first model describing the test procedure for a normal working day (Figure 1.1 in Section 1.2), we linked the requirement to the action that checked its fulfillment. The test case generator may automatically include this information to all generated test cases and/or generate a separate traceability matrix from the model, thus keeping both test specification and traceability matrix permanently synchronized. A picture of our model together with the applied test selection criteria documents our test approach in a test plan. Finally, test case generators usually provide interfaces to (or include features of/are part of) test management tools. Altogether, MBT supports all kinds of automation in the testing process.

1.3.6 MBT Models Document Knowledge and Helps in Sharing It

Imagine the following scenario: Project A is finished. The first version of your product is out in the market. Most developers and testers left the team to go for new opportunities. Then, Project B starts. The target is to develop an enhanced version of the same product with some new features and a low-cost variant of the hardware.

From a testing perspective, we have to ensure that the existing features still work as before. In addition, we will have to add new tests to verify the enhancements in version 2. In a traditional document-based approach, you would probably keep the existing test specification, possibly adapt it a bit and write completely new test cases for the new features. However, this is not the most efficient way to work. First, it will be difficult to test the new features in combination with the old ones without duplicating parts of the test procedure specification. Second, the number of test cases will constantly increase leading to longer and longer execution times. Third, you have no idea why the existing test cases are written the way they are.

As stated before, models document the test idea. For new testers, it is easier to understand both the system under test and the test approach by looking at the figure, rather than by reading long documents. They may then reuse the model, or parts of it,

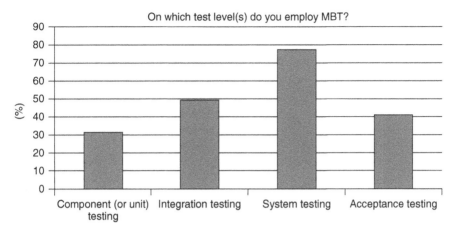

Figure 1.3   Test levels reported by MBT practitioners (from 2014 MBT User Survey).

and adapt it to their specific needs. If well done, it is possible to set up model libraries, which is a very efficient form of knowledge management all testers benefit from. Modeling helps the testers to understand what they describe and, thus, to acquire continuously new competencies and domain knowledge.

By the way, most developers and test automation engineers hate writing documents. To lesser extent, they even hate reading them. They accept the visual representation of the same content in a model far better than the textual representation.

1.3.7   MBT Covers Many Test Objectives, Test Levels, and Test Types

First, MBT more or less addresses all test levels. In the 2014 MBT User Survey, we asked MBT practitioners, on which test level(s) they employ MBT [4].[1] They reported all test levels (see Figure 1.3), even if we observe a tendency toward model-based integration testing (50%) and a clear trend toward model-based system testing (77%).

Similarly, MBT is not limited to specific application domains (see Figure 1.4). In this book, we focus on software testing, partly due to our personal background and partly, because software testing is so complex.

Regarding the type of testing, a large majority of MBT practitioners (97%) employ models for functional testing, but MBT also supports other types of testing such as performance, security, and usability testing (see Figure 1.5).

Finally, MBT supports all kind of test objectives depending on the selected modeling language, the subject and focus of the MBT model and various test selection criteria, as discussed later in this book.

---

[1] We limited the survey question to the four test levels defined in Ref. [6]. System integration testing (e.g., end-to-end testing) is located somewhere between the system and acceptance testing.

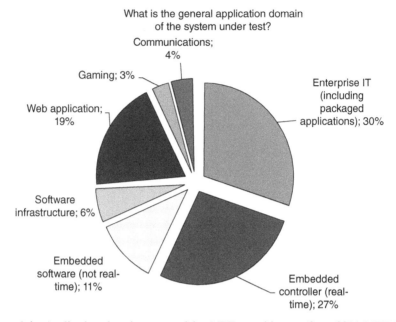

Figure 1.4   Application domains reported by MBT practitioners (from 2014 MBT User Survey).

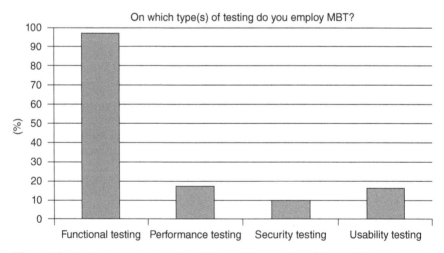

Figure 1.5   Testing types reported by MBT practitioners (from 2014 MBT User Survey).

1.4   PITFALLS OF MBT

MBT provides benefits but with a cost. In this section, we sum-up several drawbacks and pitfalls of MBT.

1.4.1   Introducing MBT Is a Change

MBT requires some "rethinking." Many people call it a paradigm shift. From a formal point of view, the expression "paradigm shift" does not exactly fit in this context (see box "Why MBT is not a paradigm shift?"). MBT does not overthrow traditional test design, but extends and supports classic test design techniques such as equivalence partitioning, boundary value analysis, decision table testing, state transition testing, and use case testing.

   Nevertheless, MBT is a change. The need for explicit test selection criteria is one example. The MBT model represents a set of possible tests, but it is neither feasible nor reasonable to generate and/or execute all of them. The MBT model in Figure 1.1 represents an infinite number of possible test cases. Somehow, we have to select, because "more tests" is not a synonym for "better tests." This is definitely different from document-based test design. There, you would never write down a test scenario you do not intend to execute.

Why MBT is not a paradigm shift?

Thomas Kuhn developed the concept of "paradigm shift" in his book "The Structure of Scientific Revolutions" [7]. A paradigm corresponds to the core concepts that we use to analyze and explain the world. It provides model problems and solutions to the scientists. Kuhn claimed that scientific progress is not evolutionary, but rather revolutionary. From time to time, a scientific discipline passes through a state of crisis because of significant anomalies that are observed, but may not be explained by the current paradigm. During such a crisis, new ideas come up and eventually end up in a new paradigm that fits better.

   Initially restricted to natural science, the expression "paradigm shift" has become very popular. Nowadays, we use it in various contexts. (If you are further interested in that topic, please refer to Robert Fulford's column on the misuse to the word "paradigm" [8].)

   MBT is not a paradigm according to the definition of Kuhn. MBT models are not in contradiction with "traditional" test specifications described in natural language, even if MBT requires a different way of thinking and testers with higher qualification. Instead, we should consider MBT as an add-on providing a higher level of abstraction and the additional possibility of automated test case generation.

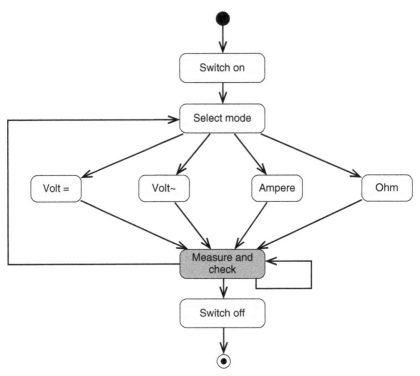

Figure 1.6 MBT model describing the measurement modes of a multimeter (activity diagram; Note: In this figure, we highlight the action where the verification takes place (rounded gray rectangle)).

Even the test cases themselves look different. Figure 1.6 shows the different measurement modes of a multimeter (direct and alternating voltage, electric current, and resistance). Theoretically, we may obtain an infinite number of test cases from this model. In practice, we will limit ourselves to a set of test cases following some logic we have in mind, which corresponds to the test objectives in this particular project. For example, we may derive one test case per measurement mode, each of them checking repeated measurements in the selected mode, plus one test case checking all four modes one after the other in a single sequence. The logic in mind is called "full coverage" of the measurement modes, but with limited effort. We made sure that each model element is reached at least once and add one test case to cover possible switches between measurement modes. The selection of the sequences depends on the algorithm the MBT tool uses for test generation. In the extreme, we may end up with one very long sequence checking everything in a row.

Psychologically, this is not always easy to accept. In fact, you delegate part of the work to the tool and, as is always the case with delegation, you should accept the other person's way of working, as long as the results meet the goals (in this case the test objectives).

Sometimes, the tool will even generate test cases you never thought of. From the multimeter example in Figure 1.6, you may derive test cases with many mode switches and many consecutive measurements in the same mode. The tool will propose an order of actions, which is probably not the one you would have obtained in manual test design. Of course, the fact that the tool uncovers unusual scenarios is rather an advantage than a disadvantage, but it definitely needs getting used to (see box "Play the game").

Last, but not least, introducing MBT to an existing test process is comparable to any other organizational change project. It concerns everybody involved in development and quality assurance, introduces new tools, forces testers to learn new and rather formal modeling languages, and so on. Section 10.1 addresses the question how to overcome such potential obstacles. In short, changes take time and should be well prepared. Never underestimate human resistance against change.

Play the game

Once upon a time, I had to review an MBT project to analyze the effort savings. It was a large IT project developed by an outsourced team in a context of legacy code migration. The testing team was skilled and mastered the tool chain well, including the newly introduced MBT tool.

Then, I discovered that the MBT models were developed to produce test cases based on detailed test case specifications, meaning already designed test cases. This seems wonderful and easy to do: from the test case specifications, you draw your MBT model, and then generate the corresponding test cases including the test implementation. However, it is not as easy as it seems to be. Since they wanted to reproduce precisely the test design they had already, they struggled with the MBT tool (which could be any tool of this kind) and finally did not obtain the expected effort gains.

Why did they stick to the existing test design? They could have changed and written their MBT model from scratch, for example, starting from the requirements to avoid fixing themselves on an existing test design. The answer is simple.

Managing changes in an organization is a process. They initially thought that MBT is just like using a new test editor. But it is not. MBT impacts your test process, and you have to play the game to get the benefits.

(Bruno Legeard)

1.4.2   MBT Is Not for Free

Do you speak model? Probably not. Unlike a natural language, we do not learn modeling languages at school, at least not to the same extent. Even with a degree in computer science, you are not immediately able to construct a model exactly the way it should be for MBT, because that way strongly depends on the MBT tooling. You speak model, but with an accent, the tool cannot understand.

Changes need time. The most pessimistic prediction was given by Max Planck: "A new scientific truth does not triumph by convincing its opponents (…), but rather because its opponents eventually die, and a new generation grows up that is familiar with it" [9]. You will need some time and possibly even some training to learn the handling of the modeling tool, the modeling language and the specific aspects the test case generator brings in. Moreover, you have to buy these tools. The initial costs represent a potentially high initial threshold. To convince your sponsor you should have an idea regarding expected costs and savings.

In the literature, you will find only few quantitative data evaluating MBT in industrial contexts and comparing the use of MBT with other testing approaches (see, e.g., Refs. [10, 11] in some embedded system domains). Many companies perform a pilot project to obtain those quantitative figures. Unfortunately, they are often reluctant to publish the results to avoid disseminating internal data. In addition, the figures strongly relate to a specific context and are only of limited use for other companies.

Therefore, we recommend that you perform your own pilot project. Define and record your own metrics to measure the efficiency of MBT in your context and compare them with data recorded in similar projects in your company. Of course, you need to ensure this similarity. Person-hours, number of requirements, types and number of features, and number of product variants are a good basis for comparison.

When comparing the costs, be careful about nonrecurrent cost (such as training cost) and manage other threats to validity of the comparison. If done thoroughly, you can succeed in obtaining reliable data for your own organization. They will help you to estimate MBT return on investment and to take a decision regarding MBT deployment. Chapter 10 in this book provides you with clear criteria for measuring return-on-invest, managing and evaluating the success of MBT introduction.

1.4.3 Models also Have Bugs

With appropriate MBT tooling, it is quite easy to react on changes such as late requirements or new information. You just change some part in the model and press a button. The test case generator will then propagate all changes to the test cases without creating additional effort. Unfortunately, the test case generator also propagates all errors within the model to the generated test cases.

You will realize that writing and maintaining a complex model is difficult, too. Once you introduce conditions that govern the generation of paths, writing an MBT model gets close to programming. Whenever you program something, you introduce bugs. Thus, we must literally "debug" our model.

Even without logical conditions, the model is not necessarily correct, just because it is a graphical representation as you can see in Figure 1.7. The model describes three possible states of a CD player: STOP, PLAY, and PAUSE. For simplicity, we neglected the states ON, OFF, and STANDBY. You can switch from STOP to PLAY, from PLAY to PAUSE – and vice versa. You can also switch directly from PAUSE to STOP, but the transition from STOP to PAUSE is wrong. The model describes a situation that does not correspond to reality. Based on the model, the test case generator produces erroneous test cases, which will definitely fail during execution.

Therefore, it is extremely important to review the model thoroughly. Most modeling tools provide features to verify the formal correctness of a model. Model

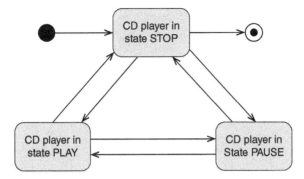

Figure 1.7 Example of an MBT model with bug (state diagram of a CD player; Note: In this figure, we use a different modeling language. Rounded rectangles represent states instead of actions (see Section 3.3)).

simulators support dynamic checks to validate the model. We deal with the question of MBT model quality in detail in Section 6.1.

1.4.4 MBT Can Lead to Test Case Explosion

A popular counter-argument against MBT is test case explosion. To understand this effect, look at Figure 1.8. It shows the data transfer with a messaging app. Four friends communicate in a chat room. There is no rule regarding the order of the chats received

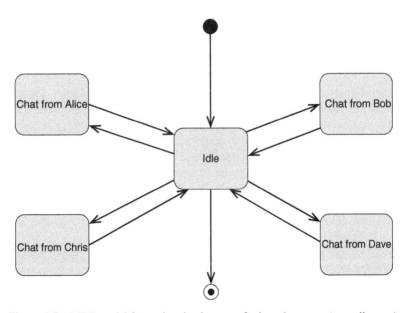

Figure 1.8 MBT model for testing the data transfer in a chat room (state diagram).

TABLE 1.3   Number of Possible Variations of the Messages in the Chat Room

Total Number of Chats	Number of Variations	Maximum Number of Chats Per Person	Number of Variations
0	$4^0 = 1$	0	1
1	$4^1 = 4$	1	65
2	$4^2 = 16$	2	7,365
3	$4^3 = 64$	3	Out of memory
4	$4^4 = 256$		

by the system. Whoever wants to write may do it, even if it is several times the person in a row.

The model itself looks harmless, but the number of possible variations (meaning possible combinations of chats) increases exponentially with the total number of chats (see left hand-side of Table 1.3).

The situation becomes even worse if we decide to limit the number of chats per person rather than the total number of chats. In other words, each person may write 0 to n messages, n being the maximum number of messages we fixed. You can see the increasing number of variations at the right-hand side of Table 1.3. Between zero chats (system just idle) to a maximum of two chats per person, there are already three orders of magnitude. This is why we speak of "test case explosion." The table also shows the effect of the rapidly increasing number of test cases. Tools run out of memory and test manager despair.[2]

Technically speaking, limiting the total number of chats is equivalent to limiting the path length, whereas limiting the maximum number of chats per person corresponds to limiting the number of loops in the model.

Somehow, we have to limit the number of test cases and select a subset, which fits our test objectives. For example, with stress testing in mind, we may want to consider both extremely short and extremely long communications. Here, appropriate tool support is crucial. Still, do not expect the tool to do the thinking for you. The tool will provide you with some more or less intelligent algorithms to select the paths, but it cannot decide which paths are more important to test than others are.

Test case explosion definitely is an issue in MBT. The good news is that there are ways to avoid or at least reduce this effect. The test selection criteria presented in Section 8.1 are a powerful weapon against test case explosion, but it is also possible to adapt the MBT models, as discussed in Section 8.2. Figure 1.9 illustrates a third solution. Here, the MBT model itself is considerably simpler, but completed by external test data.

---

[2]For mathematical cracks who want to calculate the number of variations with maximum three chats, please contact us. We will send you the formulas.

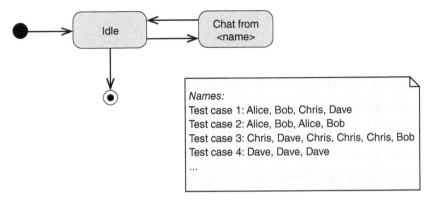

Figure 1.9 Limiting test case explosion by combining the model with external test data (state diagram).

1.5 WHAT CAN YOU REALISTICALLY EXPECT?

MBT divides the testing community. On one hand, we have a more or less well-founded reserve against a change in our established test approach. On the other hand, the expectation regarding increased efficiency and effectiveness of testing are high, and in some cases even disproportionate. The aim of this book is to give a realistic idea on what we can achieve with MBT, how we may do it, and where the limitations are.

We started using models in early 2000s and we are still so convinced of their advantages that we write a book on this topic. However, we must also admit that we went through the trough of disillusionment that is typical of technological hypes [12] (see Figure 1.10).

MBT is not a miraculous solution of all problems. Using models for testing purposes has many advantages, but it does not replace classic test design techniques. You have to know the traditional test design techniques such as boundary value analysis to be able to put them into an MBT model. Therefore, if your company struggles with those basic techniques, introducing MBT will not solve them. Still, modeling helps testers to "improve their understanding of the domain to perform tests more effectively and efficiently" [13].

Similarly, MBT is much more than buying a good tool. Of course, tooling plays a very important role in obtaining the full degree of efficiency MBT promises, but as the old saying goes: "A fool with a tool is still a fool." We discuss in Chapter 3 how MBT impacts the entire test process.

Last, but not least, MBT is not equivalent to complete test automation. If you currently execute your tests manually, it is not a good idea to switch from classic paper-based testing to MBT and from manual to automated tests in one step. As we discuss in Chapter 9, test automation is a challenge on its own.

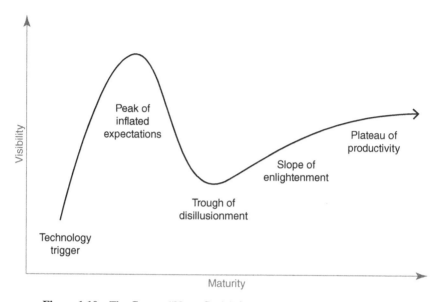

Figure 1.10   The Gartner "Hype Cycle" for technological innovations [12].

Thus, the decision to introduce MBT should be well thought out, based on clear goals and measurable objectives and, finally, receive full management support. Section 6.6 provides an overview on possible tool support for modeling activities, whereas Chapter 10 explains how to introduce MBT in your company. Introducing changes step-by-step with measurable (and monitored) intermediate goals is clearly recommended for any test process improvement.

2

WHAT YOU SHOULD KNOW ABOUT MBT BEFORE STARTING

Before we go into details of how to construct and use model-based testing (MBT) models in practice, it might be a good idea to clarify some fundamental terms such as model and MBT first. Unless stated otherwise, all definitions of terms in this chapter stem from the ISTQB standard glossary of terms used in software testing [1]. Bear with us if the following section is a bit theoretic, but if you strive to obtain the ISTQB MBT certificate, you should learn the definitions (in quotes) by heart.

2.1 ISTQB MBT GLOSSARY TERMS USED IN THIS BOOK

This section covers the terms referenced by the syllabus and defined in the ISTQB standard glossary of terms used in software testing.

Obviously, the most important term to know is "model-based testing." The definition provided by ISTQB is as simple as it is convincing. The term "model-based testing" designates any kind of "testing based on or involving models." As "model-based testing" is a rather long term, we usually refer to it by the acronym "MBT." Another term we already encountered in the previous chapters is "MBT model." It stands for "any model used in model-based testing."

An MBT model does not necessarily describe the system, but may focus on the system's environment or describe the test itself. The best-known example of a pure "environment model" is the so-called usage model that describes the user behavior. A pure test model, as defined by the ISTQB glossary, is "a model describing testware

Model-Based Testing Essentials–Guide to the ISTQB® Certified Model-Based Tester Foundation Level, First Edition. Anne Kramer and Bruno Legeard.

that is used for testing a component or a system under test." It may describe the set of commands a manual tester or an automated test script performs to check the system under test.

In practice, models used for MBT are usually not so easy to classify. Most of them are not pure system, test, or environment models, but some mixture of these three subjects. This is exactly the reason why we use the universal term "MBT models."

In Section 1.4.4, we discussed about "test case explosion." The ISTQB glossary defines test case explosion as the "disproportionate growth of the number of test cases with growing size of the test basis, when using a certain test design technique." The authors even added an additional explanation: "Test case explosion may also happen when applying the test design technique systematically for the first time." We deal with test case explosion and techniques to avoid this effect later in this book.

To meet the test objectives, and to avoid test case explosion, we have to apply the so-called "test selection criteria," that is, "criteria used to guide the generation of test cases or to select test cases in order to limit the size of a test." Some examples of test objectives are as follows:

- At a minimum, test all high-priority requirements of your product.
- For each use case, test at least the main scenario.
- For the input data, test all possible combinations of equivalence partition values.
- Perform a load test to check the product performance using a variety of possible test sequences.

Section 8.1 of this book presents various test selection criteria and explains which criterion fits which test objective. Technically, many of those criteria are based on coverage of model elements. We will encounter terms such as full transition coverage, later. Full transition coverage means that each arrow in the figure is reached at least once. If we miss one arrow out of five, we obtained only 80% transition coverage. In general, "model coverage" designates "the degree, expressed as a percentage, to which model elements are planned to be or have been exercised by a test suite." In this case, the model elements are the coverage items. By definition, a "coverage item" is "an entity or property used as a basis for test coverage, e.g., equivalence partitions or code statements".

Some syllabus terms refer to the way the generated test cases are executed. From our experience, most companies employ a "model-based testing approach whereby test cases are generated into a repository for future execution." We call this approach "offline MBT." It is opposed to "online MBT" (also called "on-the-fly" MBT). The latter is defined as a "model-based testing approach whereby test cases are generated and executed simultaneously." Online MBT definitely requires tool support, whereas the degree of automation in offline MBT varies from company to company, ranging from purely manual test case generation and execution to completely automated approaches.

When test execution automation is part of the MBT project, test actions generated from the MBT model are implemented through a "test adaptation layer." This term denotes "the layer in a test automation architecture which provides the necessary code to adapt test scripts on an abstract level to the various components, configuration or interfaces of the SUT."

What is a test case?

During my work as a consultant I realized, that there are not only plenty of different ways to specify and perform tests, but also huge differences in the testing vocabulary. I particularly remember one customer with whom we discussed for more than an hour, before it crossed somebody's mind that we used the term "test case" in different ways. For me, the test case was a set of steps and verification points grouped together in an MS Excel sheet. For the customer, each of those lines was one test case.

The ISTQB standard glossary of terms used in software testing [1] curtails this Babylonian confusion. According to the glossary, a test case is "a set of input values, execution preconditions, expected results and execution postconditions, developed for a particular objective or test condition, such as to exercise a particular program path or to verify compliance with a specific requirement." Consequently, a "test" is "a set of one or more test cases" [14].

A test case does not contain detailed execution instructions. For this, we have the test procedure specification. According to the ISTQB glossary, a test procedure specification is "a document specifying a sequence of actions for the execution of a test." It is "also known as test script or manual test script."

This brings a third term up. A test script is "commonly used to refer to a test procedure specification, especially an automated one" [1].

(Anne Kramer)

2.2 OTHER TERMS TO KNOW

2.2.1 What Do We Mean by "Model"?

The term "model" has several meanings. A miniature car is a model, but definitely not the type we derive test cases from. The catwalk model will probably not be of any help, either, unless she – or he – graduated in computer science. Unfortunately, the ISTQB standard glossary of terms does not define the term model. The reason behind is that this glossary does not contain terms that have already been defined elsewhere (i.e., outside the software testing world). Therefore, we have to look at other certification schemes. Good sources for modeling questions are certification schemes for requirements engineering. Depending on the syllabus, a model is defined as "a system of assumptions, concepts and relationships between them allowing to describe (model) in an approximate way a specific aspect of reality" [15] or as "an abstraction of existing reality or a plan for reality to be created" [16].

Miniature cars (or at least some of them) are small-size representations of real cars that respect form, proportion, and color. Still, it is only part of the truth, as it neglects many aspects inside the car. This is why we speak of "abstraction." The same applies to models in software engineering. They represent an abstraction of existing software or a plan for a new one, but they never describe everything in one model (this would be the software itself). Either they concentrate on specific aspects neglecting the rest or they combine aspects to form a condensed overview. Remember the flowchart and the block diagram mentioned in the introduction. The flowchart concentrates on the temporal order of actions, while the block diagram is a condensed overview where each block represents some complex subsystem.

Apart from these "representation" and "reduction" properties, models have a third property: they are pragmatic [17]. We draw them for a specific purpose, for example, to specify the interaction between different software modules.

It is very important to understand this pragmatic property of MBT models. For example, MBT models used at acceptance-level testing differ from MBT models used at system-level testing. They focus on different aspects with a different level of abstraction (generally more detailed in the case of system testing than acceptance testing).

2.2.2   What Is a "Modeling Language"?

People that do not speak the same language are restricted in their communication. This is also true for modeling and, consequently, we speak of "modeling languages." A modeling language defines how to write and read a model written in this language. To understand the language, we have to learn its syntax and semantics. The syntax defines the form, that is, what signs or symbols we use to represent information, as well as their relations and order. We call this set of signs or symbols following a well-defined syntax the "notation." The semantics defines the meaning of the symbols.

Figure 2.1 shows two South African road signs and illustrates how important it is to know both syntax and semantics of a language. Even to a European reader the syntax is clear. Road signs have some two-dimensional shape with a border, a background color, and some symbols inside. The semantics is already less clear to Europeans. Having subconsciously the Vienna Convention on Road Signs and Signals [18] in mind, we know that the equilateral triangle is a danger warning and that the circular shape is probably a prohibitory sign. As for the symbols, Europeans may only guess their meaning. We do not know the full semantics on the South African road sign

Figure 2.1   South African road signs.

"language." (The circular sign stands for "No unauthorized vehicles," the triangular sign says "Give way ahead.")

The most famous modeling language is the Unified Modeling Language (UML), a standard published by the Object Management Group [19], followed by the Business Process Modeling Notation (BPMN), another standard of the Object Management Group, but other modeling languages also exist. In addition, some modeling languages propose several notations to describe different aspects of the system or the test. Both the flowchart and the block diagram can be expressed in pure UML, but using different notations. As discussed in Chapter 5, we may choose among a variety of different modeling languages and notations.

2.2.3   Graphical Versus Textual Models

Up to now, all models in this book were graphical models. Depending on the specific graphical notation, they may differ with regard to the symbols used and the meaning that these symbols have, but they all use graphical elements to represent information. However, an MBT model can be also a pure textual model.

Textual models do not contain any graphical elements, but include specific keywords from the modeling language and mathematical symbols such as plus ($+$), minus ($-$), and equals ($=$). Textual languages vary by their degree of formalism.

The pseudocode in Figure 2.2 shows an excerpt of a textual MBT model written in the formal modeling language B. The model serves to test the conformance of SIM cards[1] to their specification. B is an example of a formal textual modeling language, which can be used to formalize system specifications and to develop MBT models.

The excerpt describes the behavior of the "VERIFY_PIN" interface provided by the SIM card. The interface is called each time you enter your personal identification number (PIN) to authenticate yourself on your cell phone. In fact, it is nothing else than the standard login example. MAX_TRY is the number of bad attempts, after which your PIN is blocked. If the session is already blocked, the return value is 9,840. If the PIN is ok, the PIN counter is reset to MAX_TRY, the session is enabled, and the return value is set to 9,000. Otherwise, the return value depends on the counter. If it was the last attempt, the counter is set to 0, the session is blocked and disabled, and the return value is set to 9,840. If you still have some attempts left, the PIN counter is decremented and the return value is set to 9,804, which corresponds to "Try again."

Figure 2.3 shows another example of a textual MBT model. The so-called decision table formalizes some business rules a bank follows for accepting or refusing consumer credits. The credit is granted, if its duration is between 12 and 48 months, its amount is below $25,000 and if the applicant uses it to purchase either domestic appliance or consumer electronics. Otherwise, the bank refuses to loan money.

The decision table in Figure 2.3 also describes behavioral aspects of the system under test, but in a tabular way.

Many MBT approaches combine graphical and textual models.

---

[1]A subscriber identification module (SIM) card is an integrated circuit used in a cell phone. It stores the international mobile subscriber identity and the related key securely and supports identification and authentication of subscribers.

```
...
sw <-  VERIFY_PIN(code) =
        PRE
              code : CODE
              counter : MAX_TRY
        THEN
              IF (blocked_status = blocked)
              THEN
                    sw := 9840
              ELSE
                    IF (pin = code)
                    THEN
                          counter:= MAX_TRY || permission_session
                                  := true || sw := 9000
                    ELSE
                          IF (counter = 1)
                          THEN
                                counter := 0 || blocked_status
                                        := blocked ||
                                permission_session := false ||
                                        sw := 9840
                          ELSE
                                counter := counter - 1 || sw := 9804
                          END
                    END
              END
        END
```

Figure 2.2   Example of a textual model, using the formal modeling language B.

◇ p_credit_duration: CREDIT_DURATION	◇ p_credit_amt: CREDIT_AMT	◇ p_good_category: GOOD_CATEGORY	◇ message: MESSAGE	◇ Requirements
BETWEEN_12_48_MONTH	INF_25000	DOMESTIC_APPLIANCE	CREDIT_ACCEPTED	category domestic appl.
BETWEEN_12_48_MONTH	INF_25000	SOUND_VIDEO_GAME	CREDIT_ACCEPTED	category home
		else	CREDIT_REFUSED	uncovered good category
INF_12_MONTH			CREDIT_REFUSED	duration too small
	else		CREDIT_REFUSED	credit amount out of range
SUP_48_MONTH			CREDIT_REFUSED	duration too large

Figure 2.3   A decision table as MBT model element.

> ### The MBT umbrella
>
> *The European Telecommunications Standards Institute (ETSI) defines "model-based testing" as "an umbrella of approaches that generate tests from models" [20]. The term "umbrella" is well chosen in this context. The term unites a variety of approaches, all using models for testing purposes.*

2.2.4   Diagram Versus Model

When we speak about "a model," we do not only refer to one single picture, but to a collection of so-called diagrams. It is important to understand the difference between

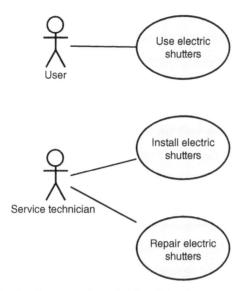

Figure 2.4 Example of a diagrammatic model describing the use cases of electric shutters (use case diagram).

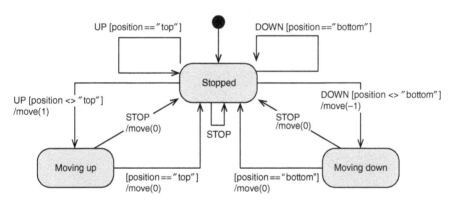

Figure 2.5 Internal states of an electric shutter (state diagram).

"model" and "diagram." For example, consider the use case diagram in Figure 2.4. It shows us, who does what with the system under test, in this case an electric shutter. However, this is only one possible view on the system. Figure 2.5 shows another diagram that describes the internal states of the shutter itself. A third diagram possibly focuses on the timing behavior of the shutter, a forth one on the control flow. All those diagrams together with their subdiagrams form one model.

This distinction between diagram and model is not specific to MBT. In software architecture, these diagrams are called "views." Architectural views have become good development practice and should have a firm place in any software architecture documentation template.

However, keep in mind that there is an important difference between models for system design and those for testing purposes. MBT models reflect the test objectives. It is quite common to have several diagrams in an MBT model. These diagrams may even partly describe the same functionality, once in detail and once on a higher abstraction level, where several detailed steps are resumed into one.

2.3   THE MODELING LANGUAGES USED IN THIS BOOK

In Chapter 5, various different modeling languages used for MBT are discussed. Each of those languages has its adepts and the discussion, which language to use, can become quite dogmatic. In the end, the choice strongly depends on the system under test, the features to be tested, and your company's culture, meaning the way people think. We have seen MBT models that respected UML to the dot and others that were just flowcharts describing what to do. In the first case, the authors believed that the formalism was an important aspect that helped getting things straight. In the second case, "too much UML" was considered as a disadvantage because it hampered communication with nontechnical stakeholders. The good news is that there is no right or wrong. Whatever helps you structuring your tests should be welcome. Just do it the way that fits you best.

Still, we should agree on a common way to write and read the models in this book. We need a kind of "modeling Esperanto"; a language, which is sufficiently simple to understand it in a few minutes, but still sufficiently comprehensive to describe the most frequently occurring aspects in testing. Fortunately, the ISTQB MBT syllabus defines two graphical modeling languages: one for workflows and one for state/transition diagrams.

Those languages are, respectively, subsets of corresponding UML diagrams:

- The first one is a subset of UML activity diagrams.
- The second one is a subset of UML state machines.

Strictly speaking, UML activity diagrams and state machines are two notations of one modeling language (and not two different modeling languages). However, the distinction between "modeling language" and "notation" is slightly confusing. For the sake of simplicity, we align this book with the ISTQB MBT syllabus, which favors the term "language."

2.3.1   A Simple Graphical Modeling Language for Workflows

The simple modeling language for workflows defined in appendix A of the ISTQB MBT syllabus contains elements from UML activity diagrams and describes sequences of actions in a flow. Diagrams in this modeling language have a start and an end node, and everything else happens in between following the indicated order.

Figure 2.6 shows the model elements of this simple modeling language for workflows. It contains all elements defined in Ref. [13], but it is only a schematic

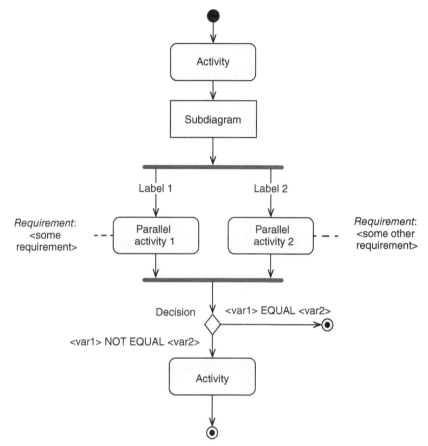

Figure 2.6 Model elements of a simple graphical modeling language for workflows (activity diagram).

representation. Figure 2.7 shows a concrete example. This model describes the well-known game "musical chairs." Apart from some particular elements, the figure should be self-explaining.

Both start and end are represented by black circles. To distinguish them, the end node is smaller with an additional circle around. Theoretically, a diagram may contain several end nodes, but in the example shown in Figure 2.7, there is only one. The game is over when there is only one seated player left.

Rounded rectangles indicate the actions to take. The arrows represent the flow. They indicate the order in which the actions are performed. Diamonds indicate decisions. If it improves readability, diamonds may also serve to merge the flows from different decisions.

For better understanding, we can annotate decisions and arrows with text (the so-called labels), the latter even with logical expressions. This includes mathematical expressions and Boolean operators. In Figure 2.7, "yes" and "no" are examples

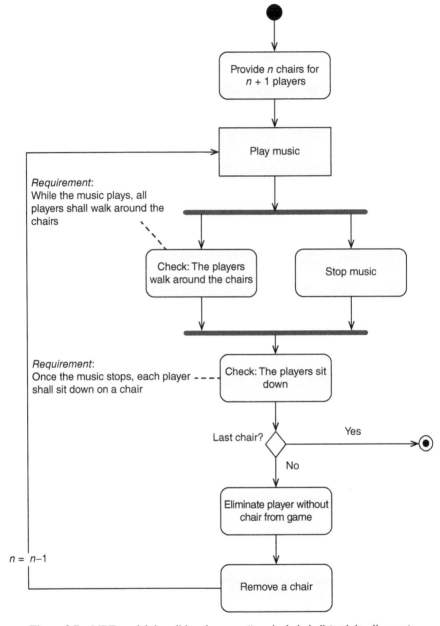

Figure 2.7 MBT model describing the game "musical chairs" (activity diagram).

of labels, and "$n = n - 1$" is an example of arithmetic. We could also replace the labels by the Boolean expressions "n EQUAL 1" and "n NOT EQUAL 1."

Activity diagrams are the most intuitive diagrams because they are nothing more than flowcharts, if you do not go into many UML details. Up to now, we used only common flowchart elements. However, we require some additional model elements to describe specific situations. Two of those are the horizontal bars, which indicate the start and end of parallel activities. In the example of the musical chairs, the players walk around the chairs. In parallel, the game master stops the music. The diagram does not indicate any time relationship between the action performed by the players and the action performed by the game master. The game master may stop the music at any moment. In UML, the first horizontal bar is called "split" and the second bar "join." Before continuing after the join bars, all parallel activities must have finished. The players must not sit down before the music stops.

If the diagram becomes too complicated, we have to split it up into subdiagrams, represented by sharp-cornered rectangles. Subdiagrams are very useful to separate different levels of abstraction. The subdiagram "Play music" in Figure 2.7 describe in detail, how the game master enters the CD into the player, select a song and starts playing. It would be very confusing to have those details in the top-level diagram.

Last, but not least, we should be able to establish a relationship between the requirement we want to test and the part of the MBT model, where the requirement is verified. In the simple graphical modeling language defined by the ISTQB MBT syllabus, the requirement identifier is simply linked to the model element by a dashed line.

2.3.2 A Simple Graphical Modeling Language for State Diagrams

State diagrams are event-based, that is, each change from one state to another (called "transition") is triggered by an event. We already saw an example in Figure 2.5 for the internal states of the electric shutters. Figure 2.8 shows the model elements for the simple modeling language for state diagrams defined in the ISTQB MBT syllabus. Some model elements are identical both in representation and in meaning with activity diagrams. We have black circles for start and end, diamonds for decisions and merge of decisions, text linked by a dashed line for requirements. Sharp-cornered rectangles represent subdiagrams.

However, there is a huge difference in the main elements: the rounded rectangles represent states and the arrows transitions. This is a completely different concept. In state diagrams, the actions are on the arrows – either as trigger or as resulting action. To distinguish the trigger from guard conditions, the guard is indicated in brackets. Thus, the complete syntax on an arrow is "trigger [guard]/action."

To understand this, have a look at Figure 2.9. It shows the state diagram for e-mails. The reception of an e-mail immediately triggers the SPAM filter. If the system recognizes it as spam, it moves the e-mail directly to the recycle bin. The new e-mail

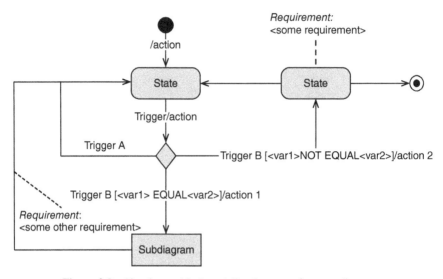

Figure 2.8 Simple graphical modeling language for state diagrams.

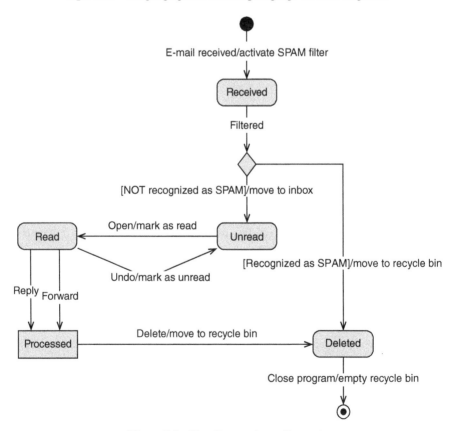

Figure 2.9 E-mail states (state diagram).

state is "Deleted." Otherwise, the system moves the e-mail to the Inbox and sets it in state "Unread." If the user opens the e-mail, it is marked as read and set to state "Read," but the user may also undo this action, setting the e-mail back to state "Unread." Both actions "Reply" and "Forward" bring the e-mail to the state "Processed." However, the state "Processed" is more complicated. We have different symbols for reply and forward. In addition, the e-mail content is copied into a new e-mail and so on. Therefore, we have a subdiagram for the state "Processed."

Exercise 3 *What happens to the e-mail described in Figure* 2.9 *if we close the program? Does the model in the figure correctly describe all possible situations?*

State diagrams are very popular in system design, because they really help getting things clear on an implementation level. However, they can become much more technical than the two examples we have seen until now, especially if error management is taken into account.

3

PROCESS ASPECTS OF MBT

This chapter covers the learning objectives of syllabus Section 1.2 "MBT Activities and Artifacts in the Fundamental Test Process" and Section 1.3 "Integrating MBT into the Software Development Lifecycles."

For simplicity, we call any test process implementing an MBT approach an "MBT process."

3.1 MBT AND THE FUNDAMENTAL TEST PROCESS

As an ISTQB Certified Tester, we know that testing is more than just writing and executing tests. Figure 3.1 shows the fundamental test process as defined in the Certified Tester – Foundation Level (CTFL) syllabus [6]. The first step involves planning the testing activities. Then, we analyze the test basis and design test cases before we implement end execute them. Afterward, we have to assess the results by addressing several questions. Have we fulfilled the plan? Do we need more tests? Have we documented the results and are they as expected? Defining these exit criteria is part of the test planning activity; their implementation related to the phase "Evaluation of exit criteria and reporting." Finally, we have to clean up, archive all test-related artifacts, identify the lessons-learned, and perform other test closure activities. In parallel, we have to keep an eye on progress and check regularly whether we still stick to the plan.

Model-Based Testing Essentials – Guide to the ISTQB® Certified Model-Based Tester Foundation Level, First Edition. Anne Kramer and Bruno Legeard.
© 2016 John Wiley & Sons, Inc. Published 2016 by John Wiley & Sons, Inc.

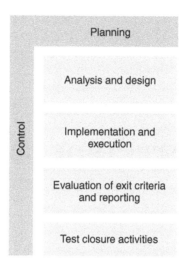

Figure 3.1   ISTQB fundamental test process.

Figure 3.1 insinuates a sequential process, but this is only partly true. The activities of the fundamental test process may overlap or take place concurrently. In addition, the entire process is iterative and incremental.

At a first glance, we may think that deploying model-based testing (MBT) in a project just influences test analysis and design activities without changing anything in the test process in place. This is not true. Of course, test analysis and design change if we use MBT models, but MBT actually influences almost all testing activities, as discussed in the following sections.

3.1.1   Test Planning and Control

The major output of the test planning activities is a documented test plan. It describes the test objectives, the test approach, the activities and techniques, the test environment, and many more. If we want to deploy an MBT approach, we have to explain this in the test plan. The ISTQB MBT syllabus also recommends providing a rationale for its use.

In addition, the test plan has to consider MBT-specific activities. This relates to task description, schedule, effort estimation, tools, and resources. Do not forget configuration management activities for MBT models and other MBT artifacts. You will work with several versions of your MBT model during the project, as well as during the maintenance phase afterward. Changes should be controlled and defects in the model documented. Possibly, you should also include some MBT training in your test plan to ensure tester qualification. If MBT is still new to your team, lack of training might introduce additional risks. In contrast, using models in test design clearly reduces the risk of misunderstanding the requirements.

Test control activities include the definition and monitoring of MBT-specific metrics and key performance indicators (KPIs), for example, requirements coverage. We deal with metrics and KPIs measuring effectiveness, efficiency, and quality of MBT in Section 10.4.

3.1.2 Test Analysis and Design

Test analysis and design is definitely the part of the fundamental test process that changes most in an MBT approach. It contains two activities that are not present in classic test design: modeling and test generation.

Instead of writing test specifications in prose, we create, modify, and review MBT models. We have to draw diagrams respecting modeling guidelines; create subdiagrams whenever useful to structure the model, to avoid redundancies, and to prepare reuse; link requirements to model elements; and so on. Test generation from models does not exist at all in a document-based test approach. We have to define test selection criteria, generate the test cases, and verify the output. If applicable, the generated tests are exported into a test management tool.

Modeling completely changes the way we analyze the test basis. We do not just read the requirements specification and try to understand it; we "translate" it into a model. This is much more effective than the classic approach and provides early feedback to system design. If we reuse existing models from requirement analysis or system design, the test generation activity will possibly detect inconsistencies in the model, because a test generator is much more rigorous than a human reviewer is.

Some modeling tools allow to archive and version diagrams (as opposed to the entire model). This allows you to have several authors for one MBT model.

3.1.3 Test Implementation and Execution

It strongly depends on the characteristics of the MBT approach, how far the test implementation activity is changed. It is possible to generate test procedure specifications for manual execution or test scripts for automated test execution from the MBT model, if the required information is accessible to the MBT tool. The MBT tool can also generate or link test data to abstract test cases.

If you apply keyword-driven testing, the MBT model defines the keywords, whereas the implementation is part of the test adaptation layer. In this case, test script implementation does not change at all, but test design does. This approach has a considerable advantage: the model author stays on a rather high level of abstraction and discusses on this level with other stakeholders such as business analysts, while the test script developer writes the code. This separation of tasks corresponds to two roles defined by ISTQB on Certified Tester Advanced Level: test analyst (model author) and test automation engineer (test script developer).

Test execution itself is less affected by MBT, unless you apply online execution. However, MBT opens completely new possibilities to govern tests. In fact, the

MBT model itself is a tool that supports test management activities. You can use project-driven test selection criteria, for example, to define regression tests or to select high-priority test cases.

Change management is important. The MBT model will probably change once you execute the first tests. Either the model detected a bug and the bug fix requires a different test or the model itself turns out to be incorrect. As mentioned before, testing is an iterative and incremental process.

3.1.4   Evaluation of Exit Criteria and Reporting

Typical exit criteria are "all tests executed" and "all tests passed or explained." In terms of MBT, we speak about "planned coverage reached," where coverage may refer to requirements coverage as well as model or data coverage. The principle, however, remains the same. We measure testing progress and define criteria when we may stop testing.

Traceability of requirements to model elements and, thus, to test cases is a very important part of the documentation. It allows us to pronounce a verdict for a requirement and to analyze the impact of remaining defect or new changes. If the defect affects low-priority functionality, it is easier to justify why we can live with it. The good news is that MBT automates the management of bidirectional traceability between generated tests and requirements. If you reference the requirements in the MBT model, you are able to monitor the MBT modeling activities, for example, by generating requirements coverage reports.

Some MBT tools allow you to mirror the test execution results back into the model. This is extremely helpful, because faults tend to cluster and it can be quite difficult to find out, which part of the system causes the problem.

3.1.5   Test Closure

MBT impacts even test closure activities. First, you have to archive all artifacts. Second, lessons learned from the current project may help to improve in the future. It is a good idea to inspect the modeling guidelines regularly. Third, you should prepare the reuse of MBT models, for example, in case of a software product line. Build a model library and establish a scheme that allows you to find a diagram again later.

In a project review, MBT-specific metrics and KPIs help to assess the efficiency and effectiveness of the MBT approach.

3.2   THE TYPICAL MBT PROCESS

We just learned that most activities in an MBT process are also present in a classic test process, even if they involve models instead of prose. The major difference lies in the modeling activity and the steps required to obtain executable tests from the MBT model, which are the next topic of this section.

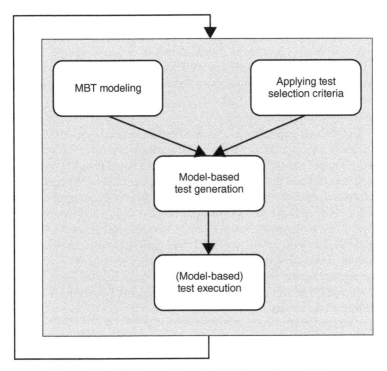

Figure 3.2   Workflow with typical MBT-specific activities.

3.2.1   MBT-Specific Activities

Figure 3.2 depicts typical MBT-specific activities in a testing workflow.
   We distinguish four main activities:

1. *MBT modeling*
      MBT modeling has the purpose of making the test explicit. The resulting
   MBT model is a structured representation of the aspects we want to verify.
   It describes the control and observation points (or verification points) of the
   system, the expected dynamic behavior or workflows to be tested, equivalence
   classes, and logical operators for test data, but possibly also concrete values.
   The model elements are linked to requirements in order to ensure bidirectional
   traceability between the requirements on one side and model elements, as well
   as generated tests on the other side. MBT models must be sufficiently precise and complete to allow automated generation of tests from those models,
   including the test oracle (i.e., the expected results).

2. *Applying test selection criteria*
      There is usually a large (if not infinite) number of possible tests that can be
   generated from an MBT model. Therefore, the tester has to apply test selection

criteria to cherry-pick the appropriate tests, or to ensure a certain degree of coverage of specific items. Common coverage-based selection criteria are requirements coverage, coverage of model elements, or data coverage. They strongly relate to well-known test design techniques such as equivalence partitioning, state transition testing, or use case testing (see Chapter 8 for more details on test selection criteria).

3. *Model-based test generation*

Usually, test generation is an automated process using an MBT tool. The test generator takes the MBT model and the chosen test selection criteria as input and produces test cases, but also test data and possibly test scripts (depending on the model and the tool). The test cases generated by the tool are typically sequences of actions with input parameters and expected output values for each action. They are easy to understand by humans and should be sufficiently complete to be understood and performed by a manual tester. In the context of automated test execution, the MBT tool generates automated test scripts. To execute them, the tester has to perform another activity. He has to implement the test adaptation layer to enable fully automated execution of the generated test scripts. The test adaptation layer implements keywords or function calls defined in the model.

4. *(Model-based) test execution*

Model-based test execution is not necessarily very different from classic test execution, which is the reason why we put the brackets. The generated tests are executed either manually or within an automated test execution environment. In both cases, we challenge the system under test and obtain a verdict for each test case. Some tests pass and some fail.[1] Failed tests indicate a discrepancy between the actual behavior of the system under test and the expected results described in the MBT model. We have to investigate them to decide whether the failure is caused by misbehavior of the system, by an error in the model and/or the requirements or by an error in the test adaptation layer. In all cases, we have to fix the problem, unless we decide to live with it. Test result analysis and test script debugging are an important part of the test execution task. If we are able to trace the error back into the MBT model, we have a better overview on the context the error occurs in. We can also tell from the MBT model, which test cases will fail too, because they traverse the same model element and, thus, avoid unnecessary test execution.

It is good practice to perform those activities iteratively and incrementally. This means that the modeling activity starts with a basic MBT model containing few model elements, but apt to generate a small number of useful test cases using some simple test selection criteria. Once those first test cases have been validated, the tester extends the MBT model to cover more requirements, generates an extended set of test cases, and so on. The MBT process should implement this iterative and incremental

---

[1]Other possible outcomes are "not tested," "not applicable," or "error," where error indicates a problem with the test setup (usually a problem in the startup or shutdown routine of automated test scripts).

approach, regardless of the software development lifecycle it is integrated into. It helps to guarantee full alignment with the test objectives and to keep MBT modeling activities efficient (modeling only what is useful for the test objectives).

While the activities presented in this section are typical for MBT, their methodological implementation varies a lot. For example, if MBT is used for customer acceptance testing, the generated test cases correspond to roughly described scenarios guiding the end user in his manual validation activities. If MBT is combined with keyword-driven testing, the generated tests are similar to manually designed test scripts with action-words. Besides those two cases, we have MBT approaches producing test cases with detailed instructions for manual testers, or automated test scripts with code instead of keywords. At the end of the book, we present several case studies to illustrate the MBT workflow in different approaches (see Chapter 11).

3.2.2 Roles in the MBT Process

Figure 3.3 shows another view of the typical MBT process. Unlike Figure 3.2, which was a simplified representation of the MBT workflow focusing on main MBT activities, Figure 3.3 focuses on the artifacts and roles involved.

This typical MBT process involves four main roles:

1. *Test managers*

    Test managers are involved in the planning, monitoring, and control of testing activities and tasks. They devise the test objectives (in our case the

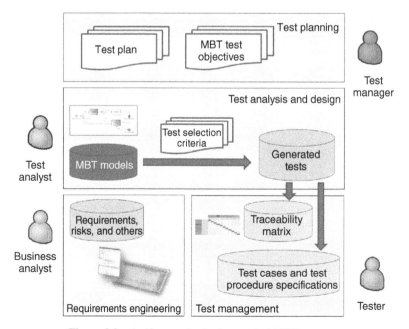

Figure 3.3 Artifacts and roles in a typical MBT process.

PROCESS ASPECTS OF MBT

42

MBT test objectives) and monitor the progress using MBT output artifacts such as the traceability matrix.

2. *Business analysts (or subject matter experts)*

The business analysts are the reference regarding the requirements of the system under test and related business processes and needs. They communicate with the test analysts to clarify the specifications and testing needs. In agile development processes, they may play the role of the product owner. They define the user stories and attend sprint meetings to ensure that the MBT models conform to the evolving user stories. With their domain knowledge, they are able to understand dependencies between different modules and the impact of those dependencies on the models. Thus, they provide useful inputs to test analysts during MBT model reviews.

3. *Test analysts*

Test analysts interact with customers and business analysts on behalf of the requirements to be covered. They design the MBT model(s), use a test generation tool to automatically generate tests and, finally, produce a repository of test suites that will satisfy the project's test objectives. Test analysts are also responsible for reviewing manual test cases generated through models and validating the correctness and coverage of the tests.

4. *Testers*

Testers are responsible for manual test execution on the basis of the test repository. The tester's input is the test repository generated by the test analysts from the MBT models.

We distinguished between test analysts and testers. Test analysts own MBT models and are responsible for the quality of the test repository in terms of coverage of the requirements and detection of defects. Therefore, their interaction with business analysts is crucial. In the other direction, test analysts interact with testers to facilitate manual test execution. This interaction process is highly iterative. In smaller project organizations, the same person quite often endorses the roles of test analyst (authoring MBT models) and tester (executing the tests).

Figure 3.3 illustrates an MBT process with manual test execution, but MBT is used with automated test execution as well (see Figure 3.4). In an MBT approach with automated test execution, we encounter a fifth role:

1. *Test automation engineers*

The test automation engineers are responsible for connecting the generated tests to the system under test for automated test execution. They start from the specification of the test adaptation layer and the keywords used in the MBT model and implement them.

Of course, these two variants of a typical MBT process may coexist in a single process targeting both manual and automated test execution. For example, generated tests may be executed manually first, and for the next version of the software, a subpart can be automated for regression testing purpose. If a test management system is used, test

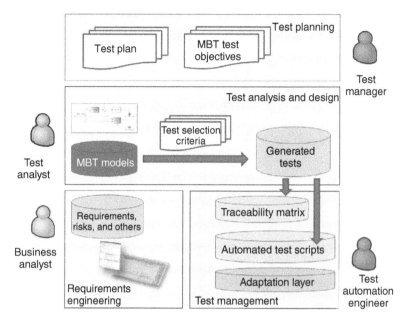

Figure 3.4   MBT process with automated test execution.

cases, test procedure specifications, and automated test scripts are stored in the central test repository of the test management tool. Indeed, automated test generation governs the documentation of the test repository. This includes documentation of the test design steps, requirements traceability, test scripts, and other documentation, which is automatically derived from the MBT model. Thus, maintaining the test repository is synonymous to maintaining the MBT models and regenerating tests from those models.

To summarize, MBT does not introduce new roles, but changes the tasks of existing roles. It is important to prepare the test team when introducing the new approach. They have to accept the method and be convinced of its advantages. If not, it is quite probable that MBT introduction will fail.

3.2.3   Input and Output of the MBT Process

Figure 3.3 introduces various input and output artifacts to be considered in the MBT process.

Relevant input artifacts are as follows:

- test plan and MBT test objectives (from the planning phase);
- requirements (from the requirements engineering phase);
- risk mitigations (from risk analysis);
- existing models (either from other development activities or from previous MBT projects);

- known defects and tester experience (found/acquired in previous projects);
- guidelines and any other information (oral or documented) relevant for testing purposes (e.g., priorities).

The output artifacts of an MBT process can be either manually designed or automatically generated. Typical output artifacts are as follows:

- MBT models, which are either enhancements of reused models from system design or dedicated MBT models;
- test selection criteria based on the test objectives;
- generated tests, test cases, test data and possibly test procedures specifications (see section below);
- generated traceability documentation (traceability matrix) documenting the bidirectional relationship between requirements and tests;
- test plan sections describing the test scope or the targeted test coverage (test selection criteria);
- test suites, test execution schedules, and other artifacts relevant for test management (e.g., all tests requiring specific test equipment), provided that the MBT model contains this information;
- test metrics (e.g., actually achieved requirements coverage).

A customized MBT process for automated test execution introduces two additional artifacts:

- Automated test scripts, automatically generated as part of the MBT testware. These scripts are either structured using a keyword approach or call upon test automation libraries.
- The test adaptation layer, developed by the test automation engineer to implement each keyword called in the test scripts in order to make them fully automated (see Chapter 9 for more information on this matter).

Writing a test adaptation layer is good practice in test automation engineering (with or without MBT). It helps to separate test design activities from test coding activities.

MBT input and output artifacts in a nutshell

- *Input artifacts are possibly all test basis used in the traditional test process (meaning all documents from which the requirements of a component or system can be inferred) and also all outputs from test planning activities (including test policy, test strategy, test plan, etc.).*
- *Output artifacts are either developed during the MBT process (MBT models, test selection criteria, test adaptation layer) or generated (test cases, test procedure specifications, test scripts, traceability matrix, etc.).*

3.2.4   Generated Artifacts

The diversity of MBT approaches can be quite confusing and makes it difficult to identify the "best" approach to take. Therefore, let us have a closer look at the generated artifacts.

The most prominent generated output from MBT models are, of course, test cases. Still, there are huge differences regarding the degree of detailing, abstraction, and automation of the generated test cases.

3.2.4.1   Test Cases With or Without Test Scripts   Obviously, if you do not put detailed descriptions regarding test execution in the model, the generated test cases cannot contain them either. Test cases obtained from those models document the test design. They form a sort of blueprint for the test procedure specifications or test scripts, which we have to write separately.

In this case, the model must not be too stringent, which has the advantage of being rather easy to maintain. Unfortunately, any change in the model probably requires changes in one or several test scripts. This is where inconsistencies come in and where most maintenance effort is spent. MBT models with this low level of details are still useful to validate requirements early, but they do not yield the full benefits of automated test generation.

On the other extreme, you can generate complete manual or automated test scripts, if the MBT model contains the required information.[2] Here, the model is more precise and requires particular care, especially, if arithmetic expressions are used. In UML, these logical expressions are called "guard conditions." They are very helpful to exclude inconsistent paths. For example, the expected result for the bus schedule test in Figure 3.5 depends on the value of "period" determined by the precondition. (Note, that it depends on the tool whether and how variables are set and evaluated. In the example illustrated by Figure 3.5, there are hidden fields provided by the modeling tool, which we can use to set the variable "varPeriod" to "daytime," "evening," or "night.")

You can certainly imagine how easy it is to introduce a "bug" in the model. Possibly, there is copy/paste error in one of the preconditions so that the same value for "varPeriod" is set twice to "daytime" and never to "night." In addition, the case-sensitive comparison may fail due to erroneously set capital initials in "Daytime," "Evening," or "Night." Even simply typos screw the comparison up. If this happens, we must "debug" the model.

3.2.4.2   Test Scripts for Manual or Automated Execution   Let us say we opt for complete generation of detailed test scripts. Again, what you get out of the generation process depends on what you put in. As has been mentioned before, we only see part of the information the diagrams elements may contain in Figure 3.5. Depending on the modeling tool, more or less additional attributes are available that are not visible

---

[2]In the case of keyword-driven testing, the MBT model contains the keywords, the test adaptation layer the translation of those keywords into code and the MBT tool puts those information together in test scripts.

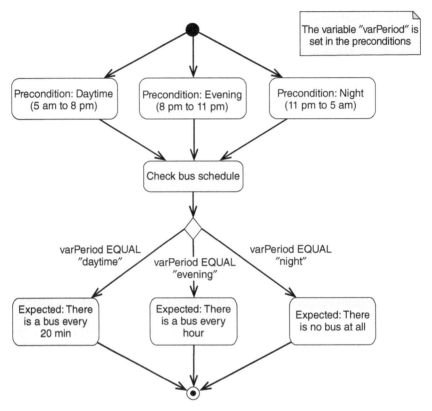

Figure 3.5 Logical expressions excluding inconsistent paths (activity diagram).

in the graphical presentation. We may use these attributes to add more text or, if appropriate, calls to the adaptation layer code. The test case generator collects this information all along the selected path through the model and concatenates them to build the test script.

Figure 3.6 shows an example of the Microsoft Windows calculator. We may select between the two modes "normal" and "scientific." Then, we type a more or less arbitrary combination of ciphers and operations. The corresponding detailed steps are hidden in subdiagrams (indicated by the rectangle in the diagram). In the end, we type "=" and check the result (using a test oracle, which is implemented somewhere else). From the same model, we may generate instructions for manual test execution or test scripts for automated execution, if we previously entered the information in the model.

Figure 3.7 shows the subdiagram "Select operation (+−*/=)" together with an example of a manual test instruction (to the left) and a code snippet for automated execution (to the right).

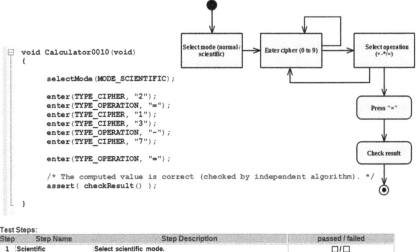

```
void Calculator0010(void)
{
    selectMode(MODE_SCIENTIFIC);

    enter(TYPE_CIPHER, "2");
    enter(TYPE_OPERATION, "=");
    enter(TYPE_CIPHER, "1");
    enter(TYPE_CIPHER, "3");
    enter(TYPE_OPERATION, "-");
    enter(TYPE_CIPHER, "7");

    enter(TYPE_OPERATION, "=");

    /* The computed value is correct (checked by independent algorithm). */
    assert( checkResult() );

}
```

Test Steps:

Step	Step Name	Step Description	passed / failed
1	Scientific	Select scientific mode.	□/□
2	Type cipher	Type "2".	□/□
3	Type operation	Type "=".	□/□
4	Type cipher	Type "1".	□/□
5	Type cipher	Type "3".	□/□
6	Type operation	Type "-".	□/□
7	Type cipher	Type "7".	□/□
6	equals	Type "=".	□/□
7	Check value	The computed value is correct (checked by independent algorithm).	□/□

Figure 3.6 Manual and automated test scripts for calculator.

3.2.4.3 Test Cases With or Without Test Data The activity diagram in Figure 3.6 does not show any details on the input data in the subdiagram "Enter cipher (0–9)" and on the expected result in "Check result." However, the test case generator needs this information to produce the manual and automated tests in Figure 3.6. Here, we have two possibilities. Either we model the input and output data directly in the subdiagrams or we also keep both the input data and expected results outside the model (e.g., in a data table). In the first case, we obtain a larger number of tests with concrete test data. In the second case, the number of generated tests is smaller, but the same test case will be executed several times with different sets of input/output data.

3.2.4.4 Artifact Generation in Practice In the 2014 MBT User Survey, we asked MBT practitioners about the artifacts they generate from the MBT model [4]. Several answers were possible. The results are clear: 84% reported generation of test scripts for automated test execution, but 57% also generate manual test cases (see Figure 3.8). The two approaches do not contradict each other. It is possible to generate tests both for manual and automated test execution from one MBT model.

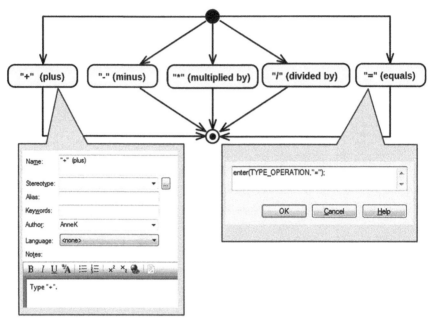

Figure 3.7 Subdiagram "Select operation (+−*/=)" with manual instructions and code snippet (activity diagram).

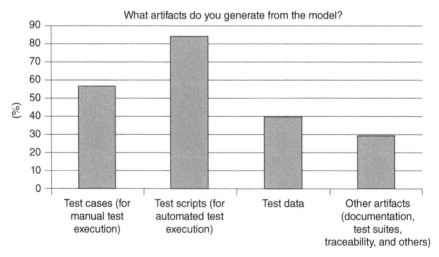

Figure 3.8 Generated artifacts reported by MBT practitioners (from 2014 MBT User Survey).

3.3　MBT AND SOFTWARE DEVELOPMENT LIFECYCLES

In the 2014 survey [4], we also asked the MBT users about their software development lifecycle. A slight majority of 56% reported phased software development lifecycles (V-Model, Waterfall, etc.) against 44% employing agile lifecycles (Scrum, XP, Kanban, etc.). Thus, MBT is equally apt for both categories of software development lifecycles, if the MBT process is adapted accordingly.

If the MBT approach fits the test objectives, that is, if we select the appropriate modeling language, the appropriate level of abstraction, and the appropriate tools, MBT provides the same benefits for both lifecycle categories. MBT models improve communication between testers and business analysts on requirements or user stories, as well as communication between testers and developers, for example, on test automation aspects with or without development iterations. They allow us to generate automated test scripts, which might be part of a continuous integration process. In both cases, we obtain early feedback, which is extremely beneficial for the overall quality of our product.

However, there is one major difference. Sequential software development lifecycles implement phases and roles. Thus, we have to clarify MBT-related tasks and roles and integrate MBT into the development phases. For example, it is important to plan the MBT modeling activities as part of an early development phase. Otherwise, you will lose the advantage of early requirement validation mentioned earlier. In addition, the project managers will require some progress metrics.

In agile development lifecycles, MBT is part of the iterations. Project managers obtain regular progress feedback at the end of the iterations. The MBT-related tasks are the same as in sequential software development lifecycles, but the approach is less driven by documented plans. Instead, agile teams rather organize themselves in a way that fits them best.

3.3.1　MBT for Different Test Levels and Test Types

Primarily, MBT is a black-box testing method. We test the system against the MBT models used for test generation. The focus clearly lies on functional testing, that is, testing the system against functional requirements. To a smaller extend, MBT also applies to nonfunctional testing such as robustness testing, security testing, performance testing, and usability testing. Recall Figure 1.5, where we presented the results of the 2014 MBT User Survey on test levels reported by MBT practitioners. Nearly all respondents use models for functional testing, whereas performance, usability, and security testing play a subordinate role with less than 20% each.

This mainstream focus of MBT on functional black-box system testing has a reason: MBT models generally represent the expected behavior of the system under test in the context of its environment, at a given level of abstraction. You mainly use behavioral modeling to express the expected behavior of the system and/or its environment to be tested.

Functional testing is addressed by all testing phases in the software development lifecycle, irrespective of the process in use (sequential or agile): component, integration, system, and acceptance test levels. While MBT is used on all test levels, we observe a tendency to higher test levels (see Figure 1.3). Half of the respondents (50%) of our survey reported model-based integration testing and three-quarters (77%) reported conducting model-based system testing. With 31%, model-based component testing plays a less important role compared with model-based system testing.[3] In fact, the 2014 MBT User Survey allowed several answers for the test level. Only 5% of the respondents use MBT models exclusively for component testing. The remaining 26% deploy MBT on other test levels, too. We will not go into further detail regarding model-based component testing.[4] The ISTQB MBT syllabus mentions the existence of approaches based on code annotation techniques, but they are beyond the scope of this book.

In most cases, MBT targets the higher test levels with a functional testing perspective:

- *Integration testing*
    During integration testing, we try to identify defects in the interfaces and interactions between integrated components or systems. The MBT models used for test generation formalize the data flow between components and the expected behaviors related to interactions between components.

- *System testing*
    System testing is the process of testing an integrated system to verify that it meets specified requirements. Model-based system testing usually targets functional, but sometimes also nonfunctional requirements. Typical MBT models for system testing describe the system as seen from outside (e.g., the graphical user interface), the system environment (e.g., usage profiles), or the way the system is challenged by the tests.

- *System integration testing*
    System integration testing verifies that a system integrates well into any external or third-party environment defined in the system requirement (e.g., different web browsers). MBT models for system integration testing focus on interactions and data flow between the system under test and its environment.

- *Acceptance testing or user acceptance testing (UAT)*
    The ISTQB glossary defines acceptance testing as "formal testing with respect to user needs, requirements, and business processes, conducted to determine whether or not a system satisfies the acceptance criteria and to enable the users, customers or other authorized entities to determine whether or not to accept the system." During this phase, we ensure that critical business processes and requirements are implemented in a proper manner, as required by the customer. Here, graphical MBT models are very helpful, because they facilitate discussions with nontechnical stakeholders.

---

[3]Software developers rather speak of "unit testing" instead of "component testing," but we stick with the ISTQB terminology in this book.

[4]In the 2014 MBT User survey, we observed a tendency towards reuse of existing models from system design in model-based component testing. However, the number of answers to this question is too small to be statistically reliable.

To illustrate the manifold applications of MBT, we present two additional test types in more details: regression testing and end-to-end testing.

- *MBT for regression testing*

    In a system lifecycle, testing should not only target new features that have to be released, but also verify changes in the code or in the system infrastructure to ensure that previously working (and tested) features have not regressed. Regression testing ensures that unchanged areas of the software do not suffer from side effects of changes performed elsewhere of the changes.

    Regression testing is a very costly activity. As the system under test evolves, the number of functionalities increases, resulting in more and more features to test. Especially in iterative and incremental development lifecycles, we face an increasing number of regression test iterations required to ensure that no previously working functions have failed. As executing the tests manually again and again is not sustainable, test execution automation is crucial to ensure a good level of regression testing. Chapter 9 shows how MBT helps test execution automation by generating test scripts and managing the evolution of the test repository (test cases and test scripts).

    If automated regression testing is not possible, the MBT models help reducing the effort by limiting the number of manual tests. We can use specific test selection criteria to generate a "best set" of regression tests in a reproducible and documented way. Even with complete automation, we will probably reach the point where it is no longer possible to repeat all automated test cases over night. Thus, we have to choose. In Chapter 8 we see, how test selection criteria help us to define "good" regression test suites.

- *MBT for end-to-end testing*

    End-to-end testing is a key testing activity for large-scale systems (or systems of systems) composed of multiple applications and components. It is not a test phase, but part of system testing and acceptance testing. End-to-end testing ensures that the major business process flow works as expected.

    With boundaries between applications blurring, risks and dependencies are hidden. The systems chains become longer and more complex, resulting in undetected defects anywhere in the chain. The consequences of those defects can become business critical and are difficult to predict.

    Figure 3.9 illustrates the idea of end-to-end testing. Each business process involves the use of several applications. In the figure, the flow is linear. To perform the tests, we begin at the starting point of the business process and proceed to the end through a chain of applications and components. The corresponding MBT model describes the chain, the flow of data and interactions, and the expected results.

3.3.2 MBT and Requirements-Based Testing

Risk and requirements-based testing has been popularized by Bach in the 1990s [21]. The approach drives the way and intensity of testing based on requirements coverage,

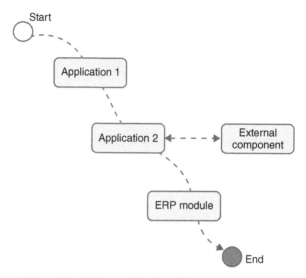

Figure 3.9 End-to-end testing of a system of systems.

their importance and their likelihood, or impact of failure. It is a key approach to optimize testing efforts with respect to its impact on the final quality of the system under
test. As Bach wrote, "the importance of managing the relationship between risk and a
shared understanding of what quality means for your product" should guide test analysts when designing the test repository. MBT supports risk and requirements-based
testing in at least two aspects:

1. When designing MBT models, we may adjust the level of description details
   depending on risks and requirements. For very mature features, the MBT model
   may represent only main success cases, whereas it should describe a larger set
   of success and error cases for new features.
2. When defining test selection criteria, we may adapt test generation strategies to
   risk and requirements coverage. For example, organizations may choose to start
   writing MBT models for those functionalities that have shown a higher leak-
   age of defects to production. In safety-critical domains, it is good practice to
   apply more stringent coverage criteria for test case selection for hazard-related
   features that for noncritical features.

3.3.3   MBT in Agile Software Development Lifecycles

Agility in software development is all about incorporating feedback about software
with turnaround times measured in hours or even minutes. Typically, this feedback is
provided by automated testing associated with continuous integration.

In test-driven development (TDD), developers start writing an automated test case that defines a desired improvement or new function.[5] By focusing on the test cases first, the developers think about the interfaces of functions or procedures before they start the implementation. Then, they produce the code to pass that test. Finally, they refactor the new code to acceptable standards.

TDD is usually deployed at component testing level. The approach automatically ensures that each new feature is tested. The tests are developed and maintained by the development team. They are usually managed in the same development environment as the source code of the system under test.

While component tests are the responsibility of the developers, we usually have dedicated testers for higher test phases. In agile processes, those testers should be part of the core development team, thus implementing the whole-team principle (see Ref. [22]). MBT helps agile testers applying the concept of TDD to business-level functional testing (i.e., system and acceptance testing). The buzzword to know in this context is "acceptance test-driven development" (ATDD). Using MBT models for business workflows and rules make it easier to generate and maintain high-level automated acceptance tests for large systems or systems of systems (such as end-to-end tests). Model-based ATDD enables us to generate new test based on intended business needs continuously.

In practice, agile testers write the MBT models iteratively and incrementally, just as developers do with code. They model only the features planned for the next delivery. The generated tests then match the customer needs for the current delivery. After each deployment, the tester either adds new model elements for new features or updates existing elements. Similar to code implementation, the MBT model requires regular refactoring to keep the model maintainable. From the updated model, the updated tests are generated automatically.

Let us be more specific and consider MBT and Scrum. Scrum is an agile process with specific roles and rules. The main idea of Scrum is to progress in a series of iterations called sprints. Each sprint is typically 2–4 weeks long. At the end of each sprint, the team delivers a working increment of the software (meaning "tested by the team and accepted by the customer"). Scrum is ideally suited for projects with rapidly changing or emerging requirements, which have become the normal case in software development.

Scrum defines three roles: the product owner, who represents the customer in all discussions, the Scrum master, who is a facilitator for the Scrum process, and the Scrum team (developers and testers). Figure 3.10 shows how MBT fits into the Scrum process. With Scrum, creating and maintaining the MBT models becomes part of the increments developed during a sprint. Customers communicate their requirements to the product owner. The product owner then discusses the features with the team.

---

[5]TDD is not limited to, but often combined with agile processes. Depending on the degree of independence of the test, it is the same person or a different person that writes the tests and implements the code.

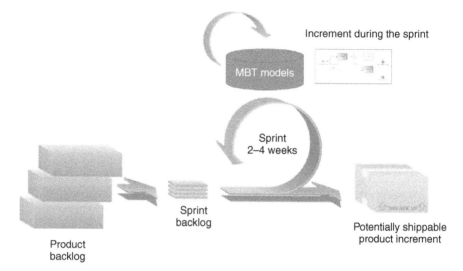

Figure 3.10   Model-based testing in the Scrum process.[6]

Based on this information, the agile testers create the model and use an MBT tool to generate functional acceptance and system tests.

In Scrum, we do not work with a requirements specification. Instead, we have so-called "user stories," which replace the requirements as test basis. Consequently, we link user stories to model elements to establish bidirectional traceability between those stories and the generated tests.

User stories captures the "who," "what," and "why" of a requirement in a concise way. A user story for an MBT tool would be "As a project manager, I want to generate a test suite covering only requirements with highest priority." The Scrum team has to find out during discussions, whether "highest priority" refers to the absolute scale or to the top-ten (which may all have medium priority on the absolute scale). This is one of the reasons, why MBT models fit so well in agile processes. They have a natural relationship with the business language used to describe the applications under test. This makes them understandable for product owner, business stakeholders, and technicians alike. In addition, they are sufficiently formal to be translated into executable tests used for system and acceptance testing.

The second advantage is automated test generation. Figure 3.11 shows the MBT artifacts in an agile development lifecycle. Each time the MBT model is updated, the tests are also updated automatically.

All artifacts in Figure 3.11 are developed iteratively and incrementally during the sprints.

---

[6]Picture adapted from reusable scrum presentation – Source Mountain Goat Software.

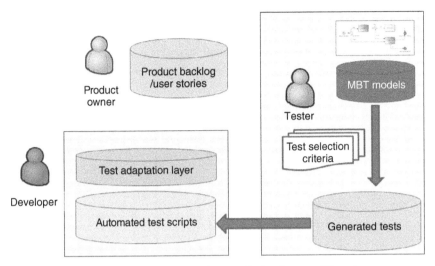

Figure 3.11 MBT artifacts in an agile development lifecycle.

To sum up, MBT embedded in an agile process helps supporting communication with the whole team and providing immediate feedback based on the graphical representation of high-level business tests. MBT introduces new practices in the agile team (testers are in charge of MBT models) and integrates the maintenance of the models as part of the iteration activities. If you want to learn more on test automation in the context of agile projects, please refer to Lisa Crispin and Janet Gregory's book [23].

3.4 HOW MBT SUPPORTS REQUIREMENT ENGINEERING

3.4.1 Requirements Validation Through MBT Modeling

Admittedly, we do a bit of brainwashing here, but early requirements validation is important. It is possible to spoil everything, if you do not benefit from this major advantage of MBT.

Start writing the MBT model as soon as possible. To write a model for test generation, you have to go in the details of business workflows and business rules. Most often, the requirements need clarification. They are unclear, inconsistent, or incomplete. When you start the modeling activity, you also start to question them. Graphical MBT models support this discussion. They make explicit the details, which helps you to discuss them with the stakeholders and to agree on what should be done. The updated MBT model documents the decision and serves to share this knowledge between all stakeholders (business analysts, system matter expert but also developers).

An example of unclear requirements

A woman asks her husband to go shopping. Wife: "Dear, please go to the grocery store to buy a carton of milk, and if they have eggs, buy six." Husband: "O.K., hun."

Twenty minutes later the husband comes back bringing six cartons of milk. Wife: "Dear, why on earth did you buy six cartons of milk?" Husband: "They had eggs."

It is up to you to decide, whether a model would have helped: see Figure 3.12.

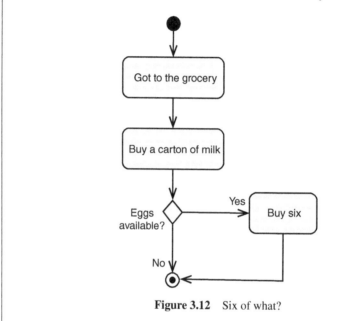

Figure 3.12   Six of what?

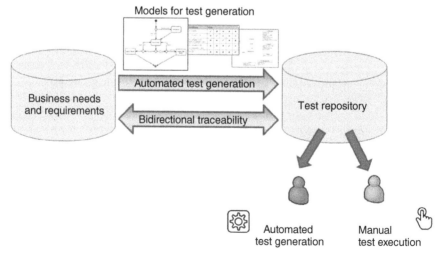

Figure 3.13   Relationship between requirements and test repositories.

3.4.2   Requirements Traceability

A good practice in MBT, supported by most of the tools on the market, involves linking model elements to the relevant requirements. From these links in MBT models, test generation tools ensure the automatic generation and maintenance of the traceability matrix between requirements and test cases (see Figure 3.13). We deal with this topic again in Section 6.3.

4

ASPECTS TO CONSIDER BEFORE YOU START WRITING AN MBT MODEL

This chapter covers the learning objectives of syllabus Section 2.1 "MBT Modeling."

There are probably as many different instances of model-based testing (MBT) approaches as companies applying this technique. The way we write and process our model strongly depends on the global approach, the system under test, the test objectives and the technical realization, that is, the tool chain.

The modeling activity is the most crucial part of MBT. This is where you spend most of your time. It is also the activity with largest impact on process quality. A bad MBT model leads to bad test cases. A good MBT model not only leads to good test cases, but also to good requirements, because it provides a comprehensive and understandable overview on the system under test, its environment, or the tests themselves. Therefore, writing the MBT model requires special care, starting with some preliminary considerations.

4.1 PRELIMINARY CONSIDERATIONS ON MBT MODELING

4.1.1 What Exactly Do I Want to Test?

First, we have to determine our test objectives and, thus, the scope of our MBT model. The question to ask is "What exactly do I want to test?" The answer strongly depends on the test level (component, integration, system testing, and/or

Model-Based Testing Essentials – Guide to the ISTQB® Certified Model-Based Tester Foundation Level, First Edition. Anne Kramer and Bruno Legeard.

acceptance testing). We also have different tests for verification and validation. During verification, we check whether the system under test was implemented as specified. We compare the system behavior with documented requirements. During validation, we check whether the system really corresponds to what the end-user requires. System validation focuses on business workflows, usability, and interoperability with other products.

Moreover, we distinguish between functional and nonfunctional quality characteristics of the system under test. Even if MBT is usually associated with functional tests, we encounter some test selection criteria in Section 8.1, which are particularly helpful for load and stress testing. Finally, the nature of the system under test and of the development process may change the way we deploy MBT. The MBT model for an automotive control unit differs from an MBT model for a large-scale information system in the insurance domain.

Once the general scope is set, we should become more precise. "What specific quality aspects of the system under test do I want to verity/to validate?" Is it the workflows for specific use cases or the reaction of the system on incoming events? Is it the system decomposition into subsystems or the data exchange through an interface? Is it the timing of a communication protocol or the overall performance of a web-based multiuser application?

If it is a bit of everything, write several models. It is a common misunderstanding that one model necessarily covers all the tests. MBT models can become quite complex, too. Since they are usually interpreted by a tool, they have to be very precise both in content and in format. Otherwise, the test generator will run into errors. Complex MBT models require more effort to keep them coherent than simpler MBT models do. In addition, they directly lead into test case explosion. However, avoid redundancies. Build up a model library and/or keep the implementation details in the test adaptation layer.

Therefore, the ISTQB MBT syllabus clearly recommends leaving out whatever is irrelevant for the given test objective [13].

Too theoretical? Imagine a fuel dispenser integrating a credit card reader. To verify the graphical user interface of the credit card reader module, we write an MBT model similar to the example in Figure 4.1. Later, we wish to check the integration of the credit card reader module with the fuel pump. In order to test the entire fuel distribution workflow, we still have to pay in the end. However, it is no longer necessary to check the PIN entry process in detail. Therefore, the model should not contain these details either (see Figure 4.2). If pushed even further, we could summarize the entire PIN entry process into a single step called "authenticate using a valid credit card."

Thus, we have two models describing the same functionality, but with different degrees of detailing (what we call "level of abstraction").

4.1.2   Which Modeling Language Is Best?

Next, we have to decide, which modeling language to use. We deal with this question in detail in Chapter 5. In short, the semantics of the modeling language you select has to match the specific aspects your test focuses on. For example, the two simple

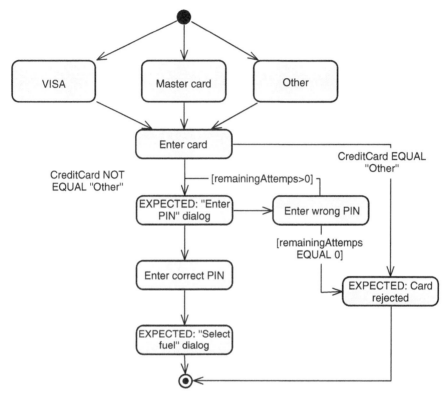

Figure 4.1 MBT model for a fuel dispenser's credit card authentication process (activity diagram).

graphical modeling languages presented in Section 2.3 of this book both describe behavioral aspects. The first focuses on actions and process flows, while the second focuses on states and events, which causes a state transition (and possibly an action). They fit well, unless you required a higher degree of formalism or additional model elements to describe the tests down to the last detail or to match the technical constraint of your MBT tools. However, if your test focuses on structural aspects such as input and output data, you have to select another modeling language.

Some modeling languages also provide domain-specific model elements; for example, the "Testing and Test Control Notation Version 3" (short: TTCN-3) for telecommunication. We briefly present some of them in Section 5.4, but this is MBT on an advanced level.

4.1.3 What Is the Appropriate Level of Abstraction?

One of the major advantages of models in general is that they allow for abstraction.

First, an MBT model focuses on the test objectives, leaving all other facets out. Remember: either models concentrate on specific aspects neglecting the rest

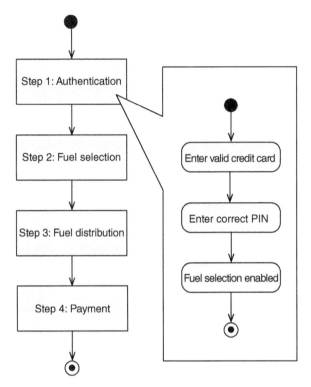

Figure 4.2   Testing a fuel dispenser with credit card payment (activity diagram).

or combine aspects to form a condensed overview (see Section 2.2.1). If we have several aspects to test, we write several MBT models. Following this "divide and conquer" strategy, we reduce the overall complexity of the task. Second, the level of detail an MBT model contains may vary from very abstract information providing a general overview on the test scenarios to extremely detailed descriptions or even code snippets. Third, it is possible to increase the level of abstraction even for MBT models intended for completely automated test case generation and execution.

The buzzword in this context is "keyword-driven testing." Instead of putting detailed instructions for manual test execution or even code snippets for automated test execution into the MBT model, we just use keywords (also called "action words"). Each keyword represents a set of instructions or a part of the automated test script. The advantages of using keywords are manifold. The stakeholders you discuss the MBT model with (e.g., during reviews), do not have to read and understand those implementation details. They automatically focus on what is important, that is, test design. Moreover, you do not have to modify the MBT model each time the interfaces of the system under test change. Instead, you just modify the test adaption layer, that is, the piece of code that links the keywords to your test automation libraries. Last, but not least, the same MBT model may serve for several product

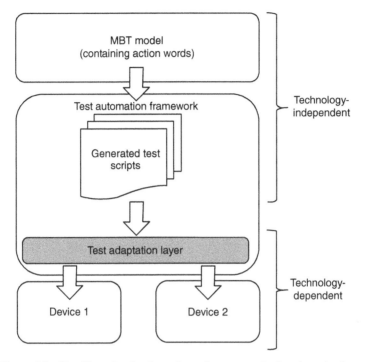

Figure 4.3   Handling of technology-dependent aspects in the adaptation layer.

variants or configurations, since the differences are handled in the test adaptation layer (see Figure 4.3).

With increasing level of abstraction of the MBT model, the effort spent on the detailed test description moves from the modeling activity to the implementation of the test adaptation layer. MBT models with high abstraction level are ideal to discuss the test design with nontechnical stakeholders, but they usually do not contain sufficient details to generate automated test scripts. MBT models with low abstraction level do not provide the same bird's perspective on test design as MBT models with high abstraction level. Thus, it depends on your objectives, which level of abstraction is best.

Do not expect to be like Kafka

One night in September 1912, Franz Kafka (1883–1924) sat down and wrote "The Judgment," a manuscript of 30 pages, in one sitting from start to end. It took him 8 h, from 10 o'clock at night to 6 o'clock in the morning. Afterward, he himself stated "Only in this way can writing be done" [24].

Do not expect to be like Kafka! My experience with modeling is completely different. You always struggle in the beginning, trying to find what we call the

> *appropriate level of granularity. Writing a model is an iterative process. Even for modeling experts, it takes time and patience. Especially in the beginning, you have to find the appropriate abstraction levels and a good hierarchical structure for your model. It is like writing a story. As an expert, you can type with ten fingers, but you still have to elaborate the plot; and only few of us are like Kafka.*
>
> *(Anne Kramer)*

In practice, finding the appropriate level of abstraction is an iterative process. You start to write the MBT model. Suddenly, you lack space for more elements. Therefore, you create a subdiagram. Figure 4.4 shows the result. It corresponds to the first draft of an MBT model describing the test of a direct flight with baggage.

The example in Figure 4.4 illustrates several problems. First, it is not clear why the way from home to the airport is condensed in a subdiagram, whereas the detailed steps for baggage preparation are visible on the topmost level. Second, some test steps are too detailed. It is completely irrelevant how we obtain baggage of appropriate weight and volume, because we never check the result. In addition, we modeled the conversation with the flight attendant, but not with the cab driver or the airport personal. Third, the name of the subdiagram does not correspond to its content. Forth and last,

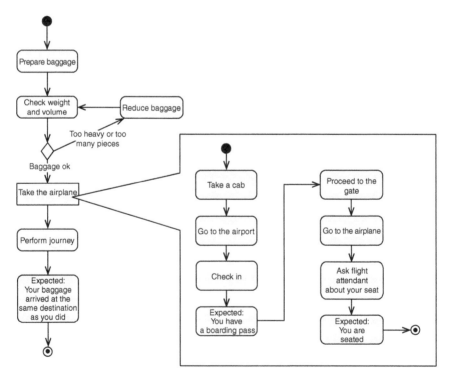

Figure 4.4   Example of an MBT model with optimization potential (activity diagram).

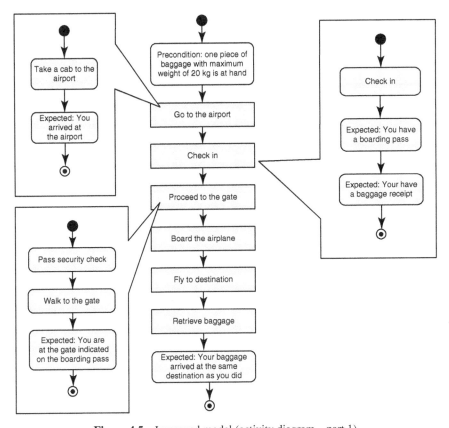

Figure 4.5 Improved model (activity diagram – part 1).

the expected result "You are seated" checks a detail, compared with "Your baggage arrived at the same destination as you did." Obviously, the related requirements are not on the same level.

Two hours later, the model looks as shown in Figures 4.5 and 4.6. Now, all (sub)diagrams have similar structure and a homogenous level of detail. The degree of abstraction decreases from top to down. The expected result "Your baggage arrived at the same destination as you did" is still located on topmost level, because it checks a user requirement and not a system requirement. A precise precondition has replaced the detailed steps for baggage preparation. Finally, we added expected results whenever adequate.

4.2 SUBJECT AND FOCUS OF YOUR MBT MODEL

4.2.1 MBT Models Combine Several Subjects

It makes a big difference whether you write a model for requirements elicitation or system design or an MBT model. In the first case, we write the model to specify

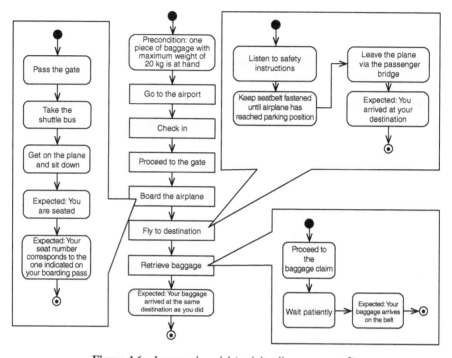

Figure 4.6   Improved model (activity diagram – part 2).

(or document) the plan for implementation. In the second case, we write the model to specify and generate the planned *tests*. Depending on the test objectives, an MBT model includes aspects of the system, its environment, the test itself, or of any combination of those three subjects.

Pure system MBT models describe the interface and the expected behavior of the system under test. We may use this kind of MBT model to verify whether the system has been implemented as intended, but not for validation purposes. In Section 11.3, we present a case study of MBT for security components. The MBT model presented there is a pure model of the system dedicated to automated test generation and developed specifically for test purposes.

Another example is presented in Figure 4.7. It shows a state diagram for a cruise control system. In that case, we compare the actual reactions of the system under test on incoming events with the planned behavior described in the model. Thus, Figure 4.7 describes a reactive system.

Figure 4.8 shows another diagram of the same MBT model, this time describing the interface of the cruise control system.

Pure environment MBT models, also called "usage models," describe how the environment interacts with the system. Usage models take into account that different users of the system under test may have different preferences regarding the functionality they use. In other words, the probability that a user chooses a particular option may depend on the user type. Figure 4.9 shows two different usage profiles, one for an

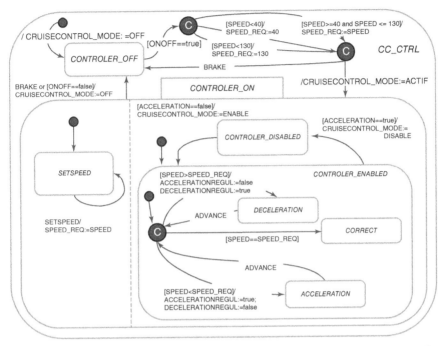

Figure 4.7 A system model of a cruise control system written in a state transition modeling language.

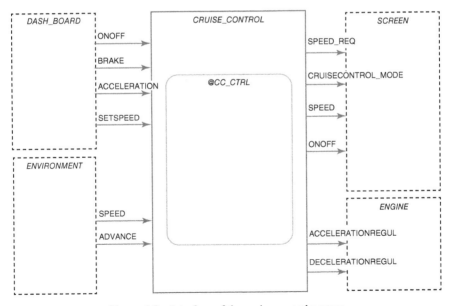

Figure 4.8 Interface of the cruise control system.

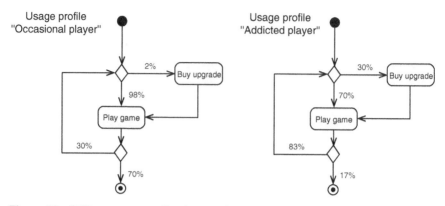

Figure 4.9   Different usage profiles for occasional and addicted players (activity diagram).

occasional player of online games and the other for an addicted player. As you can see, the addicted player has a higher tendency to buy upgrades and to continue playing.

Of course, this example is a bit oversimplified. The idea of taking usage profiles into account becomes more convincing if you think of the different people working in a medical center, all working with one patient data management system, but following different workflows. The physician will not enter patient data if he can avoid it, but often write some text regarding the patient's diagnosis and treatment. For the assistant, it is the other way round. The two usage profiles are reflected by probabilities in the model.

The usage information in the model helps us to select good test cases. For the occasional player in Figure 4.9, it should not be too risky to test the "Buy upgrade" function with limited effort. In addition, it is probably sufficient to test only one loop for "Play game." For the addicted player, we should definitely have one very long test case with many games and quite a lot of upgrades. The model also tells us where we should concentrate on during load testing.

Pure test MBT models concentrate on the actions, the tester or the test framework have to perform to provoke a specific situation, on the checks to perform, on possible input data, expected results and, finally, on the rules for returning a verdict. We write this kind of MBT model with the test cases we wish to generate in mind. The MBT model discussed in Section 4.1.3 (part 1 in Figure 4.5 and part 2 in Figure 4.6) is a graphical description of the test procedure. Depending on the chosen level of abstraction, a test model may also contain concrete test data or details for test automation.

Now, I understand!

In my experience, people used to model-based system design sometimes struggle with the concept of pure test models. They are so used to models describing the system that they cannot imagine models having another subject. I still remember

> *a workshop, where we demonstrated our way of performing MBT. Suddenly, one of the participants exclaimed: "Now I understand! Your model really describes the tests."*
>
>   *Exactly! We just forgot to make this clear from the beginning ...*
>
> *(Anne Kramer)*

The distinction between the three subjects "system," "test," and "environment" is somehow artificial. In practice, it is difficult to classify rigorously an MBT model into one of those categories, because it usually combines two or even all three subjects. Remember: an MBT model consists of several diagrams, each of them having a particular focus. For example, it is possible to combine a state diagram describing the system behavior with a sequence diagram[1] describing the way, the test framework triggers the system. Obviously, the state diagram's subject is the system, whereas the second diagram defines a specific test scenario. Moreover, we can also combine different subjects into one diagram.

MBT is all about *testing* a *system* in an *environment*. By nature, the MBT modeling activities brings those three subjects together.

4.2.2   MBT Models Focus on Structure and/or Behavior

Once a photographer has chosen the frame around his subject, he adjusts the focus. The focus determines the part of the frame that attracts our attention.[2] The rest of the photography being out of focus, our brain tends to consider it as unimportant. In MBT, the situation is comparable. The model focus determines those aspects we direct our attention to. It can be either the static structure or the dynamic behavior of the model's subject, that is, of the system, its environment, and/or the test.

The easiest structural model is a block diagram in which the components or functions are represented by rectangles connected by lines that show the relationships. In practice, we usually encounter UML class, package or component diagrams. They play an important role in software architecture. Class diagrams describe the internal structure of object-oriented software, package diagrams its decomposition into components, and component diagrams the interfaces between those components. In MBT, class diagrams may, for example, serve to provide an abstraction of the test data, whereas component diagrams may be used to describe the interfaces between the test framework and the system under test.

---

[1] UML sequence diagrams are closely related to message sequence charts (MSCs). Both are modeling languages that serve to describe sequences of interactions between processes or objects (e.g., the exchange of commands between client and server). Sequence diagrams in MBT may, for example, describe tests (we send commands and expect commands in return), or define a sequence of transitions in an associated state diagram (as described in the text).

[2] If you are a photographer, please bear with us. We deliberately neglected the depth of field. Therefore, the analogy is far from being perfect, but it should be sufficient to serve as memory hook.

Behavioral models focus on dynamic aspects. The majority of MBT models use behavioral model elements, mainly due to two reasons:

1. Most MBT test case generators require behavioral models as input for automated test case generation.
2. The application scope of behavioral models is much larger. They can be used on all test levels and for many different test objectives.

Remember the two simplified modeling languages presented in Section 2.3. They both serve to write behavioral models, either to describe activities, business processes, and workflows (Section 2.3.1) or to describe the response of reactive systems in a state diagram (Section 2.3.2). Usage models are always behavioral, since they describe typical actions performed by the user.

Similar to the model subject, MBT models usually combine behavioral diagrams for test case generation with structural diagrams for test data or interface specification. For example, Figures 4.7 and 4.8 are behavioral and structural diagrams, but both are parts of a single MBT model.

In literature, you will also find the term "data model." Data-oriented models focus on data, as the name suggests. Those who know DeMarco's notation for data flow diagrams [25] will immediately think of behavioral data models. In MBT, however, the term "data model" usually refers to structural data models describing input and output data. For example, a classification tree (such as in Figure 5.4) is a data-oriented MBT model that can be used for selecting combination of test data values.

4.3 THE INFLUENCE OF TEST OBJECTIVES ON MBT MODELS

From the previous sections, it should have become clear that there are no two MBT models alike. They differ in subject, focus, level of abstraction, modeling language and diagram layout. Subject and focus strongly depend on what you want to test, that is, the test objectives and the nature of the system under test. The appropriate level of abstraction depends on what you want to achieve with the model. The modeling language depends again on the targeted subject and focus of the MBT model, as well as on tool-specific constraints. Finally, the layout of an MBT model is definitely tool-specific.

To illustrate the dependency of the model's subject and focus on the test objectives, let us assume we want to verify the motor control of a car's wipers. The (simplified) motor control switch has three positions: Off, Normal, and Fast. We want to check the motor behavior as function of the control switch position.

Obviously, our MBT model has to be a behavioral model similar to that in Figure 4.10. When the engine starts, the system checks the previously stored value for the frequency, which is expressed in revolutions per minute (rpm). Depending on the value, the wipers go into state Off, Normal, or Fast. The decision allows for some deviations in the rpm value, but immediately sets the correct value in the action (indicated after the slash). Any change in the position of the control switch triggers a

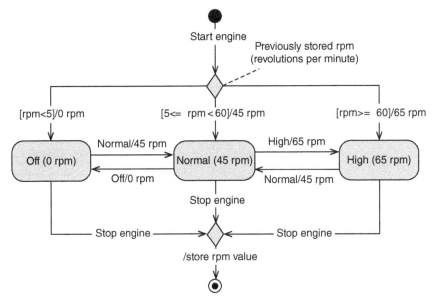

Figure 4.10   State diagram for car wipers (behavioral MBT model with subject "system").

change of the wiper's state. In addition, the motor control changes the rpm to a new value. Finally, when the engine stops, the rpm value is stored.

The model in Figure 4.10 describes the system behavior only. It contains neither test-related information, nor aspects from the environment. Still, it is an MBT model. The tests generated from this model help us to prove that the motor control reacts correctly on the control switch trigger, which was our declared test objective.

In practice, test objectives may change. What, if the test manager just came in and told us about an additional test objective? We shall test fault scenarios, too and, by the way, generate the test procedure specification from the model. Therefore, we have to add test-related activities such as injecting a faulty CAN message. Thus, we rather need an activity diagram, and the subject of the MBT model moves from a pure system model to a mixture of system and test.

Figure 4.11 shows an example. Note that the model in the figure is only one out of many possible realizations. We decided to verify the change from "High" to "Off," from any position to "Normal" and from "Off" to "High."

Before sending a message on the CAN bus, it might be a good idea to check the availability and correctness of this interface. Here, the structural model from system design serves well for comparison of the implementation with the initial, model-based plan.

Later in the project, our test objectives may change to environmental aspects. Do the wipers work well in a realistic environment? What about cloudbursts or drizzling rain? In the first case, the wipers will remain activated at 65 rpm for a longer time. In the second case, the driver will switch very often from "Off" to "Normal" and back again (and possibly decide to buy a more expensive car with interval position next

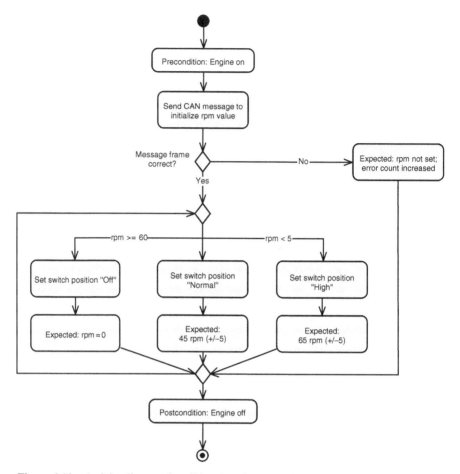

Figure 4.11 Activity diagram describing the wipers test (behavioral with mixed subjects).

time). Obviously, usage models are the best option if we want to make sure that our product suits the user need well under those extreme conditions.

For additional examples, please refer to Chapter 11 at the end of this book where we present several case studies.

Exercise 4 *Probably, you know the famous tile-matching puzzle game "Tetris" or one of its variants. In the video (or computer) game, geometric objects of different sizes fall down and the game player tries to tile them in a way that there are no gaps. To tile the objects, the player may move them to the left or to the right and possibly rotate clockwise or counterclockwise in angles of 90°.*

Each time a row is completely full, it is cleared, that is, it disappears. After a certain number of cleared rows, the game goes to the next level. The geometric objects fall down following a clock pulse. With increasing level, this pulse accelerates, that is, the objects fall down following a faster beat.

Let us assume, we want to test this kind of video game. More precisely, we have two test objectives:

1. *Verify that the game switches to the next level after 10 cleared rows and that the clock pulse accelerates for each level. Verify also that the level remains unchanged if the number of cleared rows is insufficient.*
2. *Verify that the geometric objects move correctly. This includes the directions "down" (which happens automatically following the clock pulse), left and right, as well as rotations in both directions.*

On one hand, we have the simple graphical modeling language for workflows defined in Section 2.3.1. On the other hand, we have the simple modeling language for state diagrams defined in Section 2.3.2.

Which of those two modeling languages is appropriate for which test objective, and why?

Exercise 5 *Now, it is your turn to write an MBT model for the famous tile-matching game. This exercise focuses on the first test objective:*

— *Verify that the game switches to the next level after ten cleared rows and that the clock pulse accelerates for each level. (Let us assume that the initial clock pulse is 0.5 s and that the pulse accelerates 10% per level.)*
— *Verify that the level remain unchanged if the number of cleared rows is insufficient.*
— *Verify that the game is over if the number of incomplete rows exceed the limit.*

Use the simple modeling language for workflows defined in Section 2.3.1. If you are stuck, have a look at the solution of the previous exercise in Appendix A. You will find some hints, there.

Exercise 6 *To get more practice, write a second MBT model for the famous tile-matching game. This exercise focuses on the second test objective:*

— *Verify that the geometric objects move correctly to the left and to the right as a reaction on user input (arrow keys "left" and "right"). If the object touches the border to the left or to the right, it shall not be possible to continue moving into this direction.*
— *Verify that the geometric objects rotate correctly (90° counterclockwise/ clockwise) as a reaction on user input (arrow keys "up" and "down"). If the object touches the border to the left or to the right, it shall not be possible to rotate it. (For sake of simplicity, we neglect the fact that the radius required for rotation depends on the object's shape.)*
— *Verify that the geometric objects move down automatically following the clock pulse.*

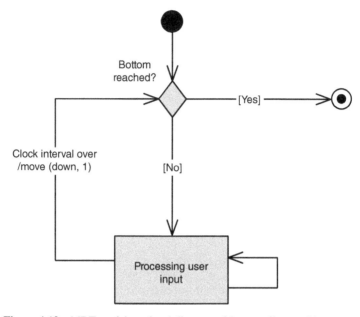

Figure 4.12   MBT model top-level diagram of famous tile-matching game.

To facilitate the modeling tasks, we already provide the top-level diagram: see Figure 4.12.

Write the subdiagram "Processing user input" using the simple modeling language for state diagrams defined in Section 2.3.2. If you are stuck, have a look at the solution of Exercice 5. You will find some hints, there.

Exercise 7   *Before you start with this exercise, please do Exercises 5 and 6 first. Take the MBT model in the sample solution of Exercise 5 (Figure A.4).*

1. *Does the MBT model describe the system, its environment or the test (model subject)?*
2. *Does it describe structural or behavioral aspects (model focus)?*
3. *Does the MBT model in the sample solution of Exercise 6 have different subject and focus?*

5

MODELING LANGUAGES – THE AGONY OF CHOICE

This chapter covers the learning objectives of syllabus Section 2.2 "Languages for MBT Models."

In Section 2.2.2, we discussed that languages are defined by their syntax and their semantics. In this regard, they are similar to natural language. However, unlike natural language, a modeling language is a theoretical construct. It follows some abstract syntax, which explains the concepts of the modeling language itself. The best-known abstract syntax for modeling languages is the Unified Modeling Language (UML) meta-model. In fact, the concepts of UML are themselves described using models.

All modeling languages have an abstract syntax. In the simplest case, it is just some textual description. Grammar rules describe the concrete syntax, while semantics rules describe the semantics of a modeling language. A grammar rule for our simple modeling languages in Section 2.3 is that arrows connect rectangles. Another one is that diagrams start with a start node and end with an end node.

The semantic rules may be static or dynamic. An example of a static rule is that rounded rectangles represent actions in the simple graphical modeling language for workflows and states in the simple graphical modeling language for state diagrams. As you can see, the syntax is identical for both languages (rounded rectangles represent the element), but their semantics is different.

An example of a dynamic rule is that parallel actions in activity diagrams shall wait for each other at the second horizontal bar (see also Figure 2.6 in Section 2.3.1).

Model-Based Testing Essentials – Guide to the ISTQB® Certified Model-Based Tester Foundation Level, First Edition. Anne Kramer and Bruno Legeard.
© 2016 John Wiley & Sons, Inc. Published 2016 by John Wiley & Sons, Inc.

5.1 MAIN CATEGORIES OF MODELING LANGUAGES

In this section, we provide an overview of the main categories of modeling languages.[1] The ISTQB MBT syllabus distinguishes modeling languages by their modeling concepts, formalism, and presentation formats.

5.1.1 Modeling Concepts

The modeling concepts are strongly tied to the reduction property of models. Remember: either models concentrate on specific aspects neglecting the rest or they combine aspects to form a condensed overview. Those aspects can be the structure and interfaces of the system, its behavior, or data aspects. The MBT model may also describe the behavior and/or constraint of the system's environment and even purely test-related aspects.

5.1.1.1 Structural MBT Models Structural MBT models are helpful to verify the system architecture, in particular the system component decomposition and the interfaces between those components. They do not describe any dynamic aspects. Consequently, we cannot use any of the two simple graphical modeling languages defined in Section 2.3, since they are not designed to describe static aspects. Instead, we may

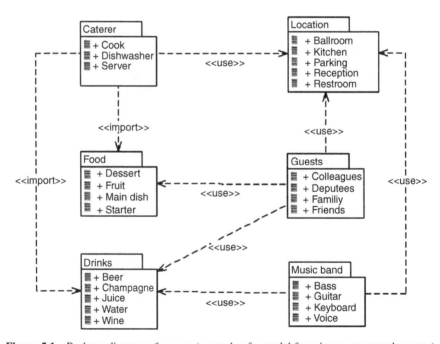

Figure 5.1 Package diagram of a party (example of a model focusing on structural aspects).

---

[1]Please keep in mind that this book is not a textbook on modeling languages, which are a science in its own. We will just present some key concepts according to the ISTQB MBT syllabus and do not go into details.

use UML package diagrams to condense several software classes into packages and describe the relation between these packages.

Exercise 8   *Figure 5.1 shows an example of a package diagram. Even without knowing in detail how to read it, you will certainly be able to imagine the party. How does it look like? Who is invited? Who will get what to drink and to eat?*

5.1.1.2   Behavioral MBT Models   The majority of MBT models are behavioral models. They are used to test business scenarios, workflows, or lifecycles, meaning all active actions of the system under test. We already went through several examples of behavioral models in this book.

Exercise 9   *In Figure 5.2, we are back at the party, looking at the states the music band is in. What does the diagram show? When does the band stop playing music?*

Figure 5.2 describes the behavior of one of the components from Figure 5.1; the music band. If you did the exercise, you discovered beer being the only motivation of the music band. They will never play unless their glass of beer is empty, and once there is no more beer, they will stop. It is written using the simple graphical modeling languages for state diagrams defined in Section 2.3.2. Figure 5.3 describes the same behavior of the music band, but in the simple graphical modeling language for activity diagrams. If you are very attentive, you can detect slight differences. The diagram in

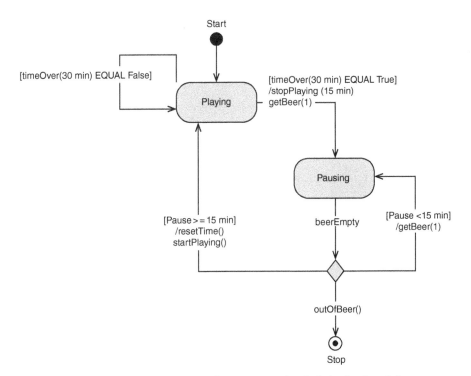

Figure 5.2   Music band state diagram (example of a behavioral model).

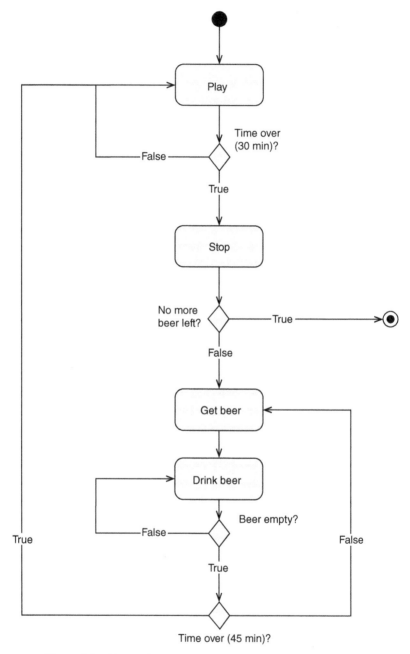

Figure 5.3   The music band states translated to an activity diagram.

Figure 5.3 takes into account that the musicians drink the beer, which does not show up in Figure 5.2. This is a good example, why it is so important to have a separate model for various testing purposes. The tester will write a different model than the developer, possibly even using a different modeling language and will, thus, discover different bugs.

5.1.1.3   MBT Data Models   According to the ISTQB MBT syllabus, MBT data models are models that describe the passive objects of the system under test (as opposed to the active components described in behavioral models).

Figure 5.4 shows such a data model. It is the classification tree of a washing machine. The branches of the tree visualize the different parameters we want to test. The leaves represent the values those parameters may take. The grid shows which combination of values is selected for one test case (= one row).

5.1.2   Formalism

The degree of formalism of modeling languages varies. The simple modeling languages presented in this book are less formal than UML. One of the UML rules systematically disregarded in this book is the merge after decisions. In the simple modeling language for activity diagrams, we use the merge diamond only if it improves readability. Consider the left diagram in Figure 5.5. Following UML, this is the correct notation. However, the right diagram contains fewer elements and still describes the same behavior. Consequently, it is easier to read for humans, as well as for test case generator. Figure 5.6 shows the counter-example. Here, we need the decision element to loop back on it. The right diagram is not only wrong with respect to the UML standard, it also has several disadvantages. First, we have redundant edges. Second, its logic is difficult to understand. Third, it is impossible to reach all nodes and edges with one single path. In the first case, we opt for the right, in the second case for the left diagram.

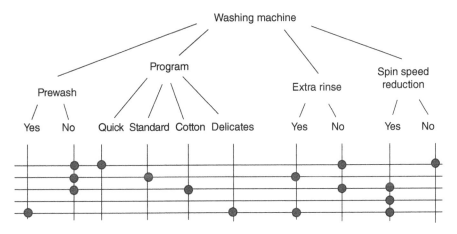

Figure 5.4   Classification tree of a washing machine.

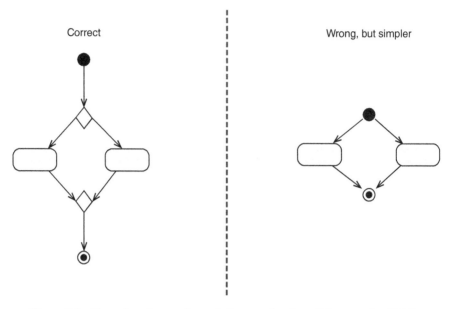

Figure 5.5   Examples of respecting and disrespecting the split/merge rule of UML.

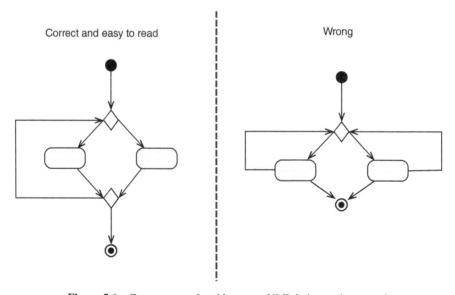

Figure 5.6   Counterexample with correct UML being easier to read.

Modeling languages with a low degree of formalization are often easier to understand, especially for nontechnical stakeholders. However, they have the disadvantage of being less rigid and, thus, less apt for tool-based processing. Obviously, you need a minimum of formal syntax as input for a test case generator. This syntax can be structured text or structured tables we derive our test cases from. In addition, we must have some kind of semantics, ranging from operational semantics to fully formalized semantics. Operational semantics mainly describe rules for an interpreter, while axiomatic semantics are formalized mathematical constructs.

What about UML and BPMN, two of the most popular modeling languages today? Are they formal enough for automated test generation? The level of formalism in UML and BPMN is a controversial subject. Problems in UML semantics have been identified since the beginning of the notation (see, e.g., Ref. [26]), and some ambiguities have gradually been resolved version after version. Indeed, this weakness of UML is directly connected with its major benefits: it is a general-purpose graphical notation targeting communication between people. BPMN is also a graphical notation for business process models and suffers from the same difficulty at this level. Tools that generate tests from UML or BPMN models have to cope with this difficulty. Usually, they work with a subset of UML or BPMN and define their own semantics. You have to keep this in mind when you introduce a model-based testing approach in your company or your team. As we discuss in Chapter 10, support of methodology and modeling good practices with guidelines and trainings is an important part of successful MBT deployment.

5.1.3 Presentation Formats

The most visible difference between modeling languages is their presentation format. Both graphical and textual modeling notations have their adepts. Somehow, people seem to develop a predilection for one or the other representation. It is true: both approaches have their advantages. Graphical diagrams are best for keeping the overview and for communication with stakeholders. Textual notations are best for tool-supported analysis and data exchange on tool level [27].

Textual modeling languages for MBT look pretty much like code. Writing textual models requires similar skills as programming does. The major difference is that a programming language claims to be universal, whereas textual modeling languages for MBT are more restricted and specialized for test generation. Therefore, textual models are efficient to both write and maintain [13], especially by experienced model-based testers.

To satisfy both communities, some modeling languages propose both a textual and a graphical representation. We present examples of those presentation formats in the next section.

In the end, it is the technical realization that decides on the model's form. Obviously, MBT tooling plays an important role. The same model would still look different in a different tool.

5.2 UML AND BPMN

BPMN and UML are probably the most popular graphical modeling languages, and tool support is rather good. Both are standards from the Object Management Group (OMG) and provide powerful modeling constructs.

5.2.1 The Unified Modeling Language (UML)

UML is a general-purpose modeling language used by IT professionals. It has everything under one roof, addressing the various modeling aspects of the software development lifecycle with 14 different diagrams (see Figure 5.7) to describe structural and behavioral aspects of the model subject (system, environment, or test).

All those diagram types use graphical presentation formats, but they differ a lot regarding the modeling concept.[2] Therefore, it is not surprising that the 14 UML diagrams cover all modeling concepts mentioned in Section 5.1.1.

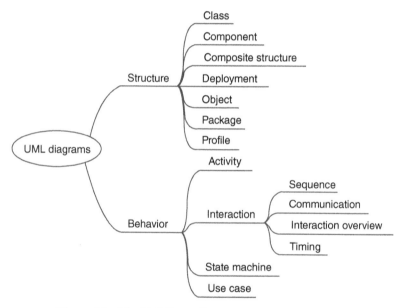

Figure 5.7 The 14 different diagram types of UML 2.2 [28].

5.2.2 The Business Process Modeling Notation (BPMN)

The nearly unlimited possibilities provided by UML are both a blessing and a curse. The specifications are rather difficult to read. You have diagrams for everything, but it is not always obvious to decide which one to take.

---

[2]To be precise, we should distinguish between modeling languages (defined by their abstract and concrete syntax and its semantics) on one hand and the (graphical, textual, or hybrid) notation on the other hand. However, by doing so we would dive into model theory, which is beyond the scope of this book. In this chapter, we just present some examples to illustrate different categories of modeling languages.

The Business Process Modeling Notation (BPMN™) is another graphical notation for behavioral models published by the OMG. OMG puts it as follows: "Where BPMN has a focus on business processes, the UML has a focus on software design and therefore the two are not competing notations but are different views on systems" [29].

Thus, BPMN is more specific. Both business analysts and IT professionals use it to describe business processes. Therefore, MBT models using BPMN are relatively easy to share with stakeholders in the project.

5.2.3   Some Examples of MBT Models Written in UML and BPMN

5.2.3.1   UML Component Diagrams for Structural Aspects   As mentioned before, UML package diagrams describe the system architecture, that is, its components and possibly hierarchies between them. If you want to describe the interface between components, UML component diagrams are a better choice, even if they are quite formal and more difficult to read than package diagrams. Figure 5.8 shows a very simple example that illustrates the basic elements of a UML component diagram. Rectangles represent components, and the line with the symbol represents the connector. The connector is composed of two parts. The left line together with the half circle represents a service required by component 1 (the daughter), while the full circle together with the right line represents the same service provided by component 2 (the father).

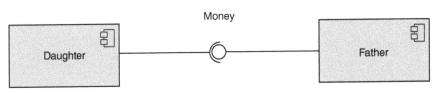

Figure 5.8   Example of a structural model describing interfaces (UML component diagram).

5.2.3.2   UML Class Diagrams for Data Aspects   Figure 5.9 shows an example of a data model. It is an excerpt of a database model we initially wrote during system design. We specified the data types and, in the case of the patient's gender, also the data values.

Later, we used the same model to check whether the implementation of the database tables really corresponded to the initially planned design.

5.2.3.3   BPMN Process Models for Behavioral Aspects   Figure 5.10 shows a business process model in BPMN. It illustrates a recruitment process and may be directly used to drive test generation for acceptance testing of the corresponding application. The syntax and semantics of BPMN are similar to UML activity diagrams. Rounded rectangles represent activities that can be considered as a set of actions that belong together. The plus sign ([+]) indicates subprocesses. Start and end nodes look only slightly different from their UML equivalent, but they are easily recognizable. Arrows indicate the flow.

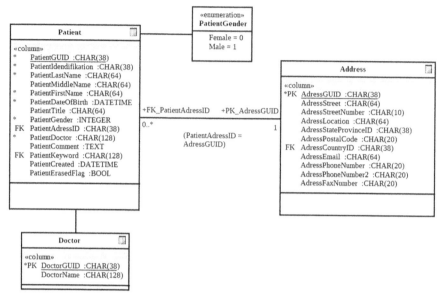

Figure 5.9   Example of a data model (class diagram).

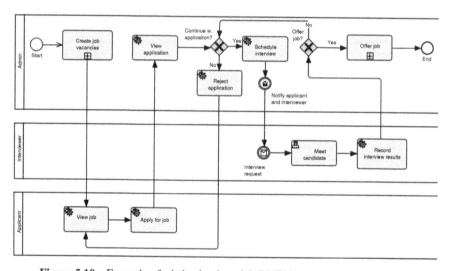

Figure 5.10   Example of a behavioral model (BMPN business process model).

The main particularity of BPMN is the so-called gateways, indicated by diamonds with symbols. Using those gateways, it is possible to distinguish between exclusive decisions (officially called "fork" and indicated by the "×"), parallel flows (indicated by "+"), and other gateways. In addition, BPMN provides a larger variety of particular elements, which are helpful to describe business processes. The best example is the e-mail symbol also used in Figure 5.10. Can you imagine a modern business process without e-mails?

Finally, we have the possibility to distinguish between different swim lanes. Swim lanes divide the diagram in vertical or horizontal areas and indicate areas of different responsibilities. In Figure 5.10, we have one lane per actor, but we could also imagine a lane per business organization.[3]

5.3 OTHER GRAPHICAL MODELING LANGUAGES USED FOR MBT

Even if UML comprises an impressive set of modeling languages (particularly for behavioral modeling which is most used for MBT), a few other languages have entered the MBT arena, too. In this section, we present the following four:

- Markov chain
- event-flow graph (EFG)
- cause–effect graph
- data flow (MATLAB Simulink).

Please notice that learning these languages is not part of the ISTQB Model-Based Tester certification exam. We added this section to the book to help you to position some languages you may have heard of when investigating different MBT approaches.

For each language, we provide a short presentation, an example, and illustrate its usage in the MBT context.

5.3.1 Markov Chain for Usage Models

Markov chains owe their name to the mathematician Andrey Markov, who originally defined them. They formalize random processes where transitions from one state to another are based on probabilities. In this section, we only consider the discrete case. A Markov chain may be specified by a square array between states where the elements define probabilities for the transitions (see Table 5.1), or graphically by a diagram similar to that in Figure 5.11.

The small example shows (imaginary) weather probabilities at the French Riviera in May (area of Nice). The probabilities for the next day depend on the weather of the current day. If the sun shines today, you have a probability of 87% that it will be

TABLE 5.1 Markov Chain – Square Array Representation

	Sunny	Cloudy	Rainy
Sunny	0.87	0.10	0.03
Cloudy	0.6	0.3	0.1
Rainy	0.51	0.38	0.11

---

[3] Again, this is not a textbook on modeling languages. We present only a few language elements to explain the figures. If you want to learn more about BPMN, please refer to a textbook or a tutorial.

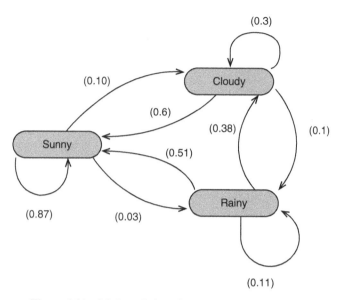

Figure 5.11   Markov chain – diagrammatic representation.

sunny tomorrow, too. In 10% of the cases, tomorrow will be cloudy and there is a tiny probability of 3% that it will rain.

In Markov chains, the probability distribution of the next state depends only on the current state. In other words, we limit the forecast to tomorrow. Markov chains do not describe dependencies for pairs of transitions.

In the MBT context, Markov chains serve to formalize the usage of the system under test. We encountered the notion of usage profiles already in Section 4.2.1, when we presented the three subjects (system, test, and environment) of an MBT model. Usage models are pure environment models. They are easy to recognize, because they describe actions of the environment with probabilities. In that sense, Figure 5.11 is a Markov chain, but not a usage model.

Figure 5.12 shows an example usage model based on Markov chains. The model represents possible usage scenarios of a coffee machine. In most cases, the user brews coffee, but each third time, he or she has to refill the water reservoir. In 70% of the cases, the user opts for a simple coffee (1 pod), in the majority of the remaining cases for a double coffee (2 pods) and in some rare cases (2%) for cleaning the machine.

From this usage model, you may generate test cases applying random test generation strategies (see Section 8.1.4). For example, we could select the most likely usage scenarios to test the system.

You may notice that something is missing in this model, that is, the expected result. Markov chains are pure environment models. By definition, pure environment models do not contain information on the reaction of the system under test or any other test aspects. If they do, they are no longer pure environment models.

If used for MBT, you have three possibilities. Either you compute the test oracle after test generation (which can be labor intensive), or you are satisfied with very

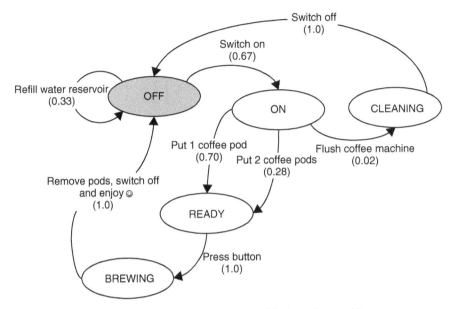

Figure 5.12 Markov chain usage model of a coffee machine.

generic results (the application crashes or does not crash), or you complete your model with some aspects of the system itself in order to be able to generate the expected results.

5.3.2   Event-Flow Graph for GUI Testing

EFGs are directed graphs where the vertices (circles) represent events and the arrows represent sequencing of events. EFGs are useful to model and test graphical user interfaces (GUIs). They allow us to describe the possible order of button presses and other user interactions, or the navigation between different screens.

Figure 5.13 shows the EFG of the print functionality of a well-known text editor.

From the "Start" screen (1), the GUI switches to a different view, if the tab "File" is selected. Pressing the menu item "Print" opens a third view. Then, we have the choice. Either we press the [Print] button directly or we may select a different printer (5) and/or change the printer settings (6). In the first case, a small progress window pops up and the GUI returns to the "Start" screen. In the two other cases, the GUI returns to the "Print" view. We may also switch back from the "Print" view to "Start," but it is not possible to return to the "File" tab (at least not in our version of the application).

The GUI model in Figure 5.13 is very simple. For example, we neglected the cancel button when printing starts (and many other possible settings). In most cases, the combinatorics of all possible interactions in a GUI component leads to a huge EFG. It is impossible to create and manage such graphs manually. In practice, we obtain those graphs using specialized GUI testing tools, which perform reverse engineering of GUIs for testing purpose [30].

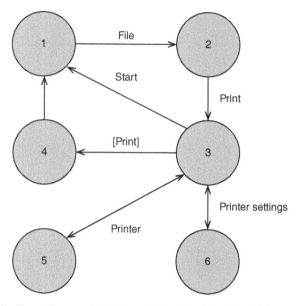

Figure 5.13 Event-flow graph for the print functionality of a well-known text editor.

Based on the extracted EFG, various test generation strategies may be applied to produce test cases that find each GUI element and exercise each event at least once in the test run. However, similar to Markov chain usage models, EFGs do not provide us with detailed expected results. Typically, you may just verify that a navigation link is not broken or that the application does not crash. This is due to the automatic extraction of the model directly from the GUI of the system under test. Another issue is the lack of meaningful input data values (e.g., for text boxes), which are difficult to generate automatically.

5.3.3 Cause–Effect Graph for Data Modeling

As its name indicates, cause–effect graphs map a set of causes to a set of effects. A cause is a *"distinct input condition or an equivalence class of input conditions"* and an effect is an *"output condition or a system transformation"* [31]. In a cause–effect graph, you may combine inputs with logical operators (and, or, not) using intermediate nodes. You can also annotate the graph with constraints to denote impossible cause/effect combinations.

Imagine that a bank has defined eligibility rules to apply for a loan. A loan is granted if:

- its duration is between 12 and 48 months,
- its amount is below $25,000 and

- if the applicant uses it to purchase either
  - ○ domestic appliance or
  - ○ consumer electronics.

Figure 5.14 shows an example of cause–effect graph representing the previous requirements. The nodes $c1$–$c4$ are causes and $e1$ is an effect. The node $i1$ is an intermediate node for the loan applicant's eligibility. The two symbols are logical connectors, respectively "or" ($c1$ or $c2$) and "and" ($i1$ and $c3$ and $c4$).

In MBT, cause–effect graphs have two major application areas. You may transform them to decision tables and integrate those tables into the MBT model (see the example in the beginning of this book on Figure 2.3 in Section 2.2.3). Furthermore, test generation algorithms may automatically generate test cases from the graph covering different combinations of causes and effects.

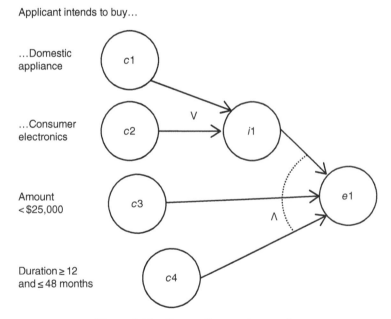

Figure 5.14   Cause–effect graph example.

5.3.4   MATLAB Simulink for Embedded Systems

MATLAB Simulink is a graphical notation integrated into the MATLAB toolbox and based on reusable standard components such as continuous and discrete blocks, math operations on signals, data acquisition blocks. You may also use industry-specific dedicated components, for example, targeting electric power systems or real-time automotive controllers.

MATLAB Simulink is proprietary. Therefore, we do not show an example, but you may find an example for an automatic climate control system in a car on the vendor's website.[4] The example also embeds a state machine for the "temperature control chart" using a proprietary notation called Stateflow.

MATLAB Simulink models are used for system design, simulation, and code generation. They may also serve for test generation, ensuring the coverage of model elements such as blocks, input data values, or in the case of Stateflow modeling, the coverage of the states, and transitions in the model. The integrated simulator allows you to test the model itself or to execute the generated test cases on the model to verify the system under test in a simulated environment.

5.4   TEXTUAL MODELING LANGUAGES USED FOR MBT

In MBT, textual modeling languages mainly serve to represent the expected behavior of the system under test. These languages for MBT are usually tailored adaptations of existing languages, which are either:

- programming languages similar to object-oriented programming languages such as Java or C#;
- formal modeling languages such as Object Constraint Languages (OCL) – in the UML context;
- textual test specification languages such as TTCN-3 or Test Description Language (TDL) from ETSI.[5]

The adaptation/extension of programming languages for MBT often integrates some construct to specify preconditions, postconditions, or invariants. Figure 5.15 shows an example of programming code for MBT in C#. This very simple textual MBT model specifies an accumulator with two behaviors: the action of incrementing the accumulator with a positive integer, and the action of reading the current value of the accumulator and then setting it back to zero. Other examples can be found in Ref. [32].

Such MBT models are programs, which is more convenient for developers than for tester. They may be used for automated test scripts generation, but can also be used for online model-based testing (see Chapter 3).

You will find a detailed example of OCL code used for MBT in the third case study (Section 11.3). Textual languages used for MBT are often combined with diagrammatic modeling elements. This is the case in the case study example, where the OCL code formalizes the behavior of operations defined in a class diagram.

An example of a dedicated test language is TTCN-3 [33]. Originally, this test specification language was designed for telecom system testing, but today it is also deployed in other domains such as automotive embedded systems or medical devices.

---

[4]Please refer to: http://uk.mathworks.com/examples/simulink/803-simulating-automatic-climate-control-systems – Last accessed July 2015.
[5]ETSI – European Telecommunications Standards Institute.

```
using System;
using System.Collections.Generic;
...

namespace Example
{
    static class AccModelProgram
    {
        static int var_acc;

        [Rule(Action ="IncAcc(x)")]
        static void IncAccRule(int x)
        {
            Condition.Istrue(x > 0);
            var_acc += x;
        }

        [Rule(Action = "ResetAcc()/result")]
        static int ResetAccRule()
        {
            Condition.IsTrue(var_acc > 0);
            int p_Val = var_acc;
            var_acc = 0;
            return p_Val;
        }
    }
}
```

Figure 5.15   An example of programming code for MBT in C#.

Figure 5.16 shows a small example of TTCN-3 code. It is possible to present TTCN-3 in tabular, graphical, and textual form. TTCN-3 tooling supports a model-driven testing approach, for example, the extraction of models from the TTCN-3 code (typically using message sequence charts).

A common characteristic of textual modeling languages for MBT is that they require programming skills (at least at first level). They are quite flexible and may be used in various test contexts and application domains.

5.5   HOW TO SELECT THE APPROPRIATE MODELING LANGUAGE

Between all those graphical and textual modeling languages, we have the agony of choice. The question that arises immediately is "Which modeling language shall I take?" and the obvious answer to this is "It depends!"; mainly on the test objectives, but also on the target system for your software product, on the MBT tooling, on your experience and on other aspects. For example, you may decide to use the same modeling language for requirements elicitation and for model-based testing in order

```
module helloworld {
    type port MyPort message {
        inout charstring;
    }
    type component MyComponent {
        port MyPort PortOne;
    }
    altstep a_altstepCatchErrors() runs on MyComponent {
        []any port.receive { setverdict(fail, "Unknown message
                            Received");}
        []any timer.timeout { setverdict(fail, "Timeout error");}
    }
    testcase MyHelloTestCase(in charstring p_string) runs on
            MyComponent system MyComponent{
        connect(self:PortOne, self:PortOne);
        activate(a_altstepCatchErrors());
        PortOne.send(p_string);
        alt{
            []PortOne.receive(p_string){ setverdict(pass, "Correct
                                        Message Received");}
        }
    }
    control {
        execute(MyHelloTestCase("Hello world"));
    }
}
```

Figure 5.16   Example of TTCN-3 code.

to share both the models and the modeling experience between those phases of your software lifecycle.

Standard modeling languages are much preferable to any proprietary language, since they bring together a common body of knowledge shared by software engineers, documented by textbooks and supported by a large set of tools, either commercial or open source.

To select the "best fit," it is necessary do know what you want and where you are limited in your choice. The result catalogue of criteria will probably contain contradicting requirements. Therefore, it is necessary to evaluate those criteria and to prioritize them. Table 5.2 illustrates how domain-specific requirements result in very specific requirements the modeling language has to fulfill. Table 5.3 shows some examples of possible choice as a function of the system under test, the test focus and objective.

TABLE 5.2   Examples of Domain-Specific Aspects Requiring Support by the Modeling Language

Domain	Specific Requirements	Modeling Language Selection Criteria
Medical	Audit-safe test documentation	– Possibility to link requirements to model elements – Possibility to annotate models with additional comments (e.g., hazards)
Embedded	Interface to Hardware-in-the-loop test framework	– Possibility to add keywords or code snippets to model elements
Banking/ payment	Certification of nonfunctional security requirements	– Possibility to model security properties – Possibility to establish traceability not only to requirements, but also to threads, documents, system interfaces, and subsystems
Enterprise IT	End-to-end testing on large-scale IT systems	– Possibility to model business processes and subprocesses – Possibility to express variants in business scenarios
Automotive	Test of embedded controllers	– Possibility to reuse design models – Possibility to simulate the system environment
Video game	Test the interaction between the system and users	– Possibility to model the sequence of events

TABLE 5.3   Examples of Test-Specific Aspects Influencing the Selection of the Modeling Language

System under Test	Test Focus	Test Objective	Possible Modeling Language
Microcontroller	Behavior	Test the reaction of the controller on incoming commands	State diagrams
IT application	Behavior	End-to-end workflow tests	Activity diagrams or business process models
IT application	Data	Business rules	Decision tables
Real-time systems	Behavior	Response times and synchronization	Timed models
Software product line	Structure	Product variants	Feature models
Web application	Behavior	Functional and robustness testing	State diagrams
Mobile application	Behavior	GUI testing	Event-flow graphs

Obviously, both tables are not exhaustive. There is no simple decision table you can take to choose your best modeling language from. In addition, there are many other aspects to take into account. The following checklist should help you to think about them, too.

1. Domain
   - ☐ Does your domain rely on model-based practices?
     For example, in the automotive domain, model-driven engineering is well established. The embedded systems domain works with model-in-the-loop systems. For IT systems, you may use activity diagrams or business process models, which are quite popular in this area. In the telecommunications domain you possibly use ETSI's TTCN-3 conformance test suites. Align your MBT process on these practices.
   - ☐ Do you work with Domain-Specific Languages (DSL)?
     Most DSLs are textual notations. Take advantage of the fact that you are familiar with them.

2. Company
   - ☐ Do you already have specific modeling expertise (and possibly tools for it)?
     Check, if there are major arguments against using the existing knowledge and infrastructure. If not, go ahead and use it.
   - ☐ Do other departments of your company work with MBT?
     Do not re-invent the wheel. Talk to them (and adapt and improve what they are doing).
   - ☐ Does your established test automation framework require particular input?
     Check, how you can provide this input through models.
   - ☐ Do you apply test-first or test-driven approaches?
     Use a notation that allows a top-down modeling approach.
   - ☐ Are there other company-specific processes to take into account?
     Warning! This is a trap. If you do not check this case, something is going horribly wrong.
     Check the X-management processes, starting with requirements management and configuration management. Just make sure you do not forget something basic in your product development lifecycle.

3. Project
   - ☐ Are your testers sufficiently qualified to write program-like models?
     If not, do not automate everything at once and use graphical notations for your MBT models.
   - ☐ Will you discuss your models with nontechnical persons (usually the product users)?
     Use activity diagrams or business process models.
   - ☐ Do you still have the choice regarding the MBT tooling?
     If yes, perform a thorough evaluation (see Chapter 10) to select an appropriate tool. If not, you should nevertheless evaluate the tool's possibilities and limitations to identify possible risks and find out the best way to use it.

☐ Has the team made bad experiences with a particular notation (or tool) and developed an aversion?

Do not underestimate this aspect! Try to find out, what went wrong. Whatever notation you select, you may fail just because of this point.

This checklist should help you to analyze where you stand in your domain, your company, and your project. One possible result is that you never really had the choice because you have to comply with preexisting processes or with the characteristics of the MBT tooling you choose.

UML – No, thanks!

My personal experience is that the idea of using UML tends to frighten potential MBT adopters. If done correctly, UML is very formal. The standard is hard to read, but even with a good textbook, UML stays impressive due to its large scope and the corresponding number of elements. In addition, it uses technical terms like use cases or state machines. This leads to reactions like the following statement, I once heard from a customer: "I am not sure everybody here is familiar with UML."

Let us be clear. It is not necessary to know UML for MBT. Take advantage of the simple graphical modeling language for workflows defined in Section 2.3.1. It is sufficiently easy to be understood by everybody. I experienced this myself when I explained to my mother what model-based testing is. To illustrate the term "model," I showed her the following example (she was a bit unnerved by the cats at that time): see Figure 5.17.

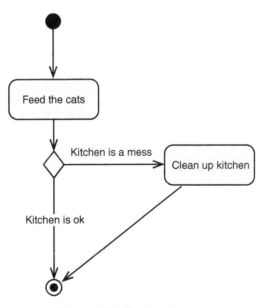

Figure 5.17 Feeding the cats.

All I told her was that diamonds represent decisions. She had a short glimpse at the figure and surprised me with her comment: "There should be another decision in the beginning: 'no cats.'"

By the way, if called differently, use case diagrams pass quite well. The resistance does not stem from the stickman and the bubbles, but from the term "use case." Just call them "business scenarios" or something equivalent.

(Anne Kramer)

6

GOOD MBT MODELING PRACTICES

This chapter covers the learning objectives of syllabus Section 2.3 "Good Practices for MBT Modeling Activities."

6.1 QUALITY CHARACTERISTICS FOR MBT MODELS

In model-based testing (MBT), obviously, errors in the models propagate into all generated artifacts. Figure 6.1 illustrates this effect. Did you find the mistake?

None of the five variants of the complex meal will be good. They are either completely salted or tasteless, just because we confounded "Yes" and "No" after the decision.

Therefore, it is important to verify your MBT models early, regularly, and thoroughly. We have to check, whether the model is formally correct, whether its content is valid, and whether it is suitable for the given test objective. Those three quality characteristics are also called syntactic, semantic, and pragmatic quality.

6.1.1 Syntactic Model Quality

Even without using strict Unified Modeling Language (UML), our MBT model has to obey to some modeling language. In addition, we discuss in Section 6.4, how important modeling guidelines are. Both the modeling language and our modeling guidelines define formal rules the MBT model has to follow. If it does not, we cannot

Model-Based Testing Essentials–Guide to the ISTQB® Certified Model-Based Tester Foundation Level,
First Edition. Anne Kramer and Bruno Legeard.
© 2016 John Wiley & Sons, Inc. Published 2016 by John Wiley & Sons, Inc.

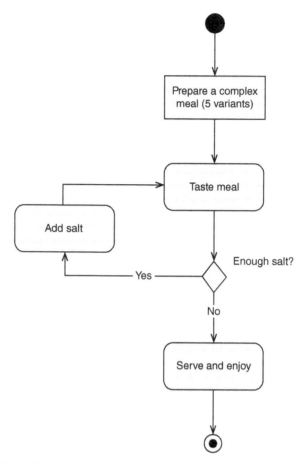

Figure 6.1   MBT model with obvious "bug" (semantic error in an activity diagram).

be sure everybody understands it in the same way. In particular, the test case generator will run into errors, if we disregard syntactic rules the test case generator relies on.

Figure 6.2 shows a simple example of a syntactic error. Each path in the diagram should terminate in an end state, which is not the case here. There is no way out of the dead end. A test case generator will not be able to cover this action and, thus, produce an error.

Dedicated model checkers and some modeling tools are able to detect problems with the model syntax. In addition, most MBT tools verify the model syntax with respect to their own expectations.

6.1.2   Semantic Model Quality

The example of the salted meals we discussed earlier in Figure 6.1 illustrates a problem with semantic model quality. The content of the model is simply incorrect. While

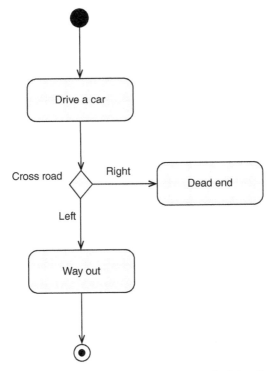

Figure 6.2 Model with a simple syntactic error (activity diagram).

the error in Figure 6.1 is quite easy to detect, it can be much more challenging to find errors in complex models. Therefore, we advise you to keep your MBT models as simple as possible.

To check the semantic quality of an MBT model, it strongly helps to try the generated test cases. If your automated testing framework executes the tests without running into errors or if your manual tester does not complain about the rubbish you ask him to do, the model is probably not that bad.

Of course, this check can only be an indicator. No tool is able to perform a complete check of the model content. To find semantic errors in your MBT model, you have to review it, for example, in a walkthrough meeting with the business analyst or with the customer. Show your model to all stakeholders. You will discover that it is much easier to discuss the figure than to convince them to read hundreds of pages.

6.1.3 Pragmatic Model Quality

We write our MBT model to achieve specific test objectives. If the model does not match these test objectives, it is simply not good. First, we should verify whether the chosen modeling language fits the test objectives. Second, our MBT model and our test case generator should fit together. It is useless to write activity diagrams if the test case generator only understands state diagrams. Third, the model should contain all information required to generate the desired output completely. A model with instructions for manual testers will be of no use for the test automation engineer expecting keyword-driven test cases.

It is very important to detect suitability problems as soon as possible, because they usually touch basic decisions such as the choice of the modeling language. Obviously, reviews will equally detect flaws in the pragmatic quality of your MBT model, but the best solution is to avoid them from the beginning. The review should only detect missing information, for example, missing variants in business rules or guard conditions, but no fundamental mismatch between the test objectives and the model-based test design.

6.1.4   Statics versus Dynamic Verification of Models

Reviewing complex MBT models takes time, but the effort you invest pays off with interest. They are the only way to judge how understandable the MBT model is for human beings. Other aspects to check are as follows:

- Is the MBT model comprehensive with respect to the test objectives?
- Do we need additional explanations of the diagrams and is this information available somewhere?
- How easy will it be to maintain the model?
- Will we be able to reuse parts of it?

Reviews and tool-based model analysis are static verification methods. If we wish to "execute" the model without executing the generated test cases, we need a simulation engine. Model simulators explore the various paths through the model and possibly execute actions related to the traversed model elements. Simulators may also simulate the behavior of the system or environment represented by the MBT model. Unlike static model checkers, simulators are able to detect errors in the logic of behavioral models such as unreachable paths.

Figure 6.3 shows an example of a state diagram with an error in the logic. The syntax of the model is correct. However, if you have a closer look at the actions on the transitions, you will discover that it is impossible to reach the state "Off." Each time the system resets, the error counter "errCount" is set to 0 and there is no way to fulfill the guard condition "errCount > 5." Simulators are able to detect this kind of deadlock.

If you generate test cases from a previous version of your MBT model, it is also possible to compare the new generation of generated test cases to the old one. Some test cases will be identical while others have changed. When analyzing those changes, you may identify "broken" tests. Just follow the path defined by the older test case and check the reason, where (and why) the new test cases takes a different direction. This is a kind of regression test on your MBT model.

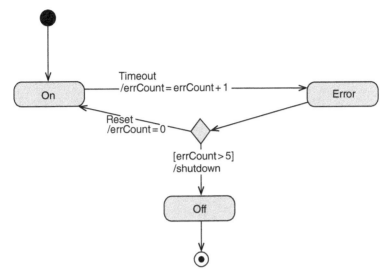

Figure 6.3 Behavioral model with deadlock (state diagram).

6.2 TYPICAL MISTAKES AND PITFALLS IN MBT MODEL DESIGN

There are two main pitfalls in MBT model design newcomers tend to step in: putting too many or too few details in the MBT model and trying to write one model that covers everything. Both stem from the wish to achieve too much with one single MBT model.

Managing the right level of abstraction is a key issue in MBT. We already discussed this question in Section 4.1.3. If you put too few details, you will not obtain the tests you need. If you put too many details – details that are not useful for your test objectives – you will rapidly lose the overview.

Mindset

Alain is an experienced and skilled developer. Now, he is part of a validation team for middleware testing. Alain took the whole job: from test analysis and design to test implementation and automation. After a while in his new job, he discovered model-based testing with some colleagues, and immediately said: this is exactly what I want to do. No more manual test script writing. Then, he started MBT modeling. The specifications of the test object as well as the test objectives were clear. Mastering the MBT modeling language (in a textual programming style) was easy for him. He moves fast, writing a large piece of code in a short time. But, when he tried to generate the test cases, it didn't work. Too much details, too complex the MBT model, not at the right abstraction: the test generator failed to produce the expected results.

Then he understands. "Wow, I have to change my mindset ... This is not the same way to model that I know." No sooner said than done – and it works.
Yes, model-based testing requires sometimes that you change your mindset.
(*Bruno Legeard*)

It is very important to understand that the all-in-one MBT model cannot exist. Even for one system under test, it may be necessary to write different models with different focus to address the whole set of test objectives. Divide and conquer is often a good strategy to keep models as simple as possible.

Figure 6.4 illustrates this statement. It shows four hierarchical levels of an MBT model describing a calendar application. The first level corresponds to the overall workflow. The second level describes the detailed activities. The third level is even more detailed. On the forth and lowest level, we have the equivalence classes of a single control, in this particular case, the spin control used to select the month.

This is exactly the kind of model that leads straight into test case explosion, because we try to combine two test objectives. On one hand, we want to test the workflow with all its variations. On the other hand, we take all possible values on the lowest level into account. Both tests have their reason to exist, but we should write separate models for it, each of them having the appropriate level of detail for

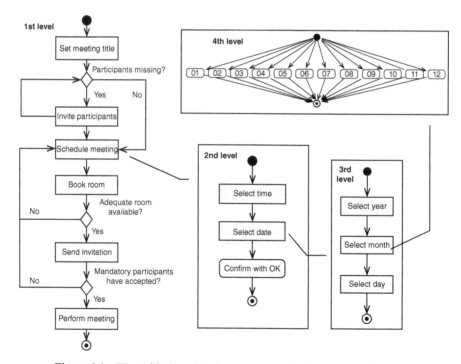

Figure 6.4 Hierarchical model of a calendar application (activity diagram).

the targeted test objectives. In case of doubt, it is preferable to write several smaller, but focused models, because

- smaller models are easier to understand and to maintain;
- we may select the appropriate modeling language that fits the test objective best;
- we reduce the risk of test case explosion.

An MBT model is "good" with respect to pragmatic model quality, if it contains neither too many nor too few information, but has precisely the level of abstraction required for the given purpose.

6.3 LINKING REQUIREMENTS AND PROCESS-RELATED INFORMATION TO THE MBT MODEL

As discussed in Section 3.1, MBT not only supports test analysis and design, but also test planning and control, as well as test implementation and execution activities. In particular, it is possible to link requirements and other process-related information to the MBT model.

6.3.1 Requirements Traceability

The automation of bidirectional traceability between requirements and test cases is a key benefit of MBT. Bidirectional traceability enables you to trace the relationship between two outputs of the software development process in both directions. Starting points of the MBT process are, as usual, functional requirements, use cases, user stories, descriptions of business processes, and all other sources that provide a functional description of the application under test. Altogether, they form a repository of requirements we wish to test. To be effective, each individual requirement should have a unique identifier we may refer to in our test cases.

In manual test case design, establishing traceability between requirements and test cases is laborious and error prone. In MBT, it is good practice to link the model elements to the relevant requirements.

There are many ways to link requirements with MBT model elements depending on the modeling language and the MBT tool. Figure 6.5 illustrates three possible variants used in the context of the two graphical modeling languages defined in the ISTQB MBT syllabus (see Section 2.3). The workflow requirement is associated with the entire diagram; the two other requirements are linked to specific model elements.

Establishing traceability is a powerful way to support test design and test management activities. We may plan test implementation and execution based on requirement priorities. High-priority requirements should be tested more exhaustively and, if possible, first. If a requirement changes, the traceability tells us, which test cases we should change or at least repeat for regression testing. However, it requires considerable effort to establish and maintain the links. Without tooling, we tend to write the

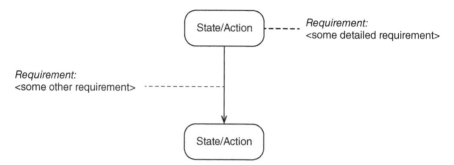

Requirement:
<workflow requirement>

Figure 6.5   Three possibilities to link requirements to model elements.

traceability matrix last, simply in the hope it will not change any more. This is where tools come in.

Linking requirements to model elements has two major advantages. First, it is much easier to manage the traceability in the figures. The total number of links between model elements and requirements is smaller than the number of links between requirements and test cases. Most commercially available test case generators are able to propagate this information into all related test cases and even to generate the traceability matrix. The automatism makes it easier to maintain the traceability matrix. If a link changes, it suffices to regenerate the test cases to update the traceability matrix.

Second, the direct relation between model elements and requirements helps us to keep the overview, because the model represents several test cases. It becomes easier to verify, whether a requirement is completely covered by the test or not. Even if the test process prescribes the review of the generated test cases, it is the model we discuss to clarify dependencies.

6.3.2   Other Information Contained in MBT Models

The simple graphical modeling languages presented in Section 2.3 provides us with a minimum set of basic models elements to describe the expected behavior to be tested. However, MBT models may contain additional information, which are usually not visible in the diagram, but accessible in a parameter view of the modeling tool. If we wish to use a tool to generate executable test cases from out MBT model, we should obviously store detailed information on test execution in the model. The test case generator will then collect this information on its path through the MBT model and assemble it to test cases.

The exact format of the information depends on what we wish to generate:

- risk and priorities related to model elements, if you want to apply some test strategies such as risk-based testing;

- actions to take and results to expect for manual test execution, if the generated output is a test procedure specification for manual test execution;
- code snippets, if the generated output is a test script for automated test execution;
- keywords, if the generated test cases are integrated into a keyword-driven testing framework.

In the previous section, we saw that linking requirements to model element supports test management. In safety-critical domain, it is common practice to distinguish between "normal" requirements and "safety requirements," sometimes also called "hazards." Linking hazards to model elements allows us to identify the tests with highest priority. Obviously, the same argument holds for linking risks to model elements, with risks relating to various origins, for example, uncertain feasibility of functional or nonfunctional requirements, project milestones, and budget. Alternatively, we can annotate priorities directly in the MBT model.

Finally, it is possible to put any other helpful test management information in the MBT model. Examples are estimated execution times for actions or entire sequences, required test equipment, special rules for testing product variants, or simply the test case aim and its pre- and postconditions.

6.3.3 Test Management Using MBT Models

6.3.3.1 Managing Project Planning and Risks It is very important to start the MBT modeling activity early to validate the requirements as soon as possible. This requires a top-down approach, starting from general business processes or workflows and going into detail, for example, regarding the exact user interface, once those details are known. On each level of abstraction, we are able to check the direction we take both in implementation and in testing. Thus, MBT is definitely mitigating project risks. In a keyword-driven approach, we do not even have to know the exact interface to test automation. We just put keywords in the MBT model and leave it to the test automation engineers to implement the related code as soon as possible.

The early test design also provides a basis for effort estimation regarding test script implementation and test execution, but there is no simple rule like "complex MBT models will require more time that simpler ones." In paper-based test design, we will try to keep our tests as short and independent as possible, because we are simply not able to manage dependencies that are more complex. As a result, the test covers fewer requirement combinations than desirable. In MBT, test case selection criteria help us to find the "best set" of test cases for a given test objective. Thus, even complex MBT model might result in fewer test cases than in the paper-based approach.

6.3.3.2 Managing Project Constraints If you remember the IBM Rational Unified Process (RUP), you will also recognize Figure 6.6. It shows the effort distribution during the development lifecycle for four of the nine disciplines defined in the RUP. Due to the iterative development, testing consists of a sequence of small humps with some larger effort close to product release. In addition, we observe a small implementation hump for bug fixing close to the end.

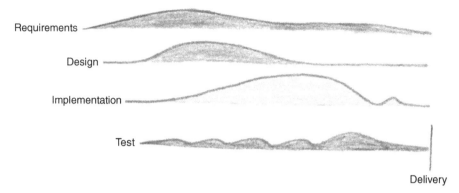

Figure 6.6 Effort distribution for selected disciplines according to Ref. [34].

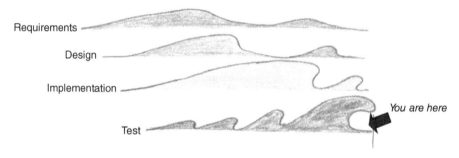

Figure 6.7 RUP in practice.

In practice, software development is far less smooth. It feels more like Figure 6.7. Usually, the delivery date is the only constant you can rely on. In the end, there is never enough time for testing and we risk drowning.

In the beginning, we had a wonderful plan. We selected the best set of test cases with the firm intention to execute all of them. However, as the German field marshal Helmut Graf von Moltke stated, "No plan survives contact with the enemy." [35]. In testing, our enemy is time and, consequently, the initial plan will not survive. We have to prioritize the test cases and some of them will never come to execution, although they exist. This is the most crucial test management task. Again, models prove to be helpful. Without the "big picture" they provide, it is extremely difficult to keep the overview.

As discussed in the previous sections, MBT models visualize dependencies to requirements or risks and may contain other test management information. In some situations, project constraints even motivate changes in the MBT model as illustrated in Figure 6.8. The model to the left shows the initial version, clearly intended to check all requirements. When time is running short, we should consider the requirement's priorities. Req2 being less important than Req1, we may skip the second part.

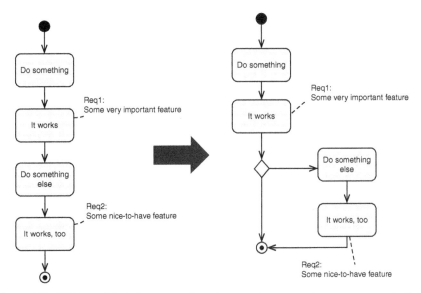

Figure 6.8 MBT model before and after changes due to project constraints (activity diagrams).

However, we should not delete it completely from the model. Hope dies last. Time might come when we will have time to test Req2. To the right side of Figure 6.8, we have the solution. We drew a "shortcut" from the first verification point directly to the end node. Now, we have a short path that covers the first requirement and a longer one covering both.

6.4   THE SIGNIFICANCE OF MODELING GUIDELINES FOR MBT

Imagine you are new to the test team. You learned UML at university. Therefore, you feel prepared for modeling tests. Then, a colleague shows you this book. You look at the models and ... are no longer sure what to think. "That's not UML!" No, it is not. We use mainly the graphical modeling language for workflows defined in Section 2.3.1, which is a simplified version of UML activity diagrams.

This is the reasons, why we need modeling guidelines. They tell us how to read and write MBT models in a particular project. Modeling guidelines are essential to foster common understanding of the models in your team and among all stakeholders involved, for example, in reviews. In addition, they provide guidance for model authors, telling them the syntax and semantics to use. Finally, they are the ideal place to anchor good modeling practices. In Section 11.2.4.3, you will find some examples of topics covered by typical modeling guidelines.

Modeling guidelines are always specific to your project, your system under test, and your process context. In particular, they strongly depend on the tools

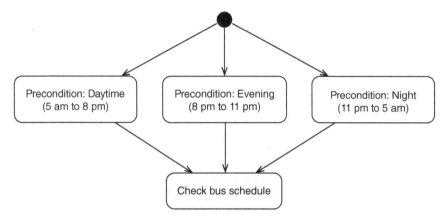

Figure 6.9 Special naming convention for preconditions (example using an activity diagram).

you use. If the test case generator expects the test procedure specification in a particular attribute of the model element, model authors should know about this. MBT modeling guidelines often overwrite the semantics proposed by the modeling tool, because they define project-specific meanings for predefined model elements. Figure 6.9 shows an example, where naming conventions are used to distinguish preconditions from normal actions.

Do not underestimate the importance of modeling guidelines. Similar to coding guidelines, they ensure a minimum level of homogeneity in MBT model design. It becomes easier to read, reuse, and adapt models from other authors and from other projects, because those models obey the same rules. In addition, you avoid the human tendency to reformat and partly rewrite parts of the model (or code), when they take it over from a colleague. Last, but not least, modeling guidelines teach good practices and help you to avoid the typical mistakes and pitfalls mentioned earlier.

6.5 THE QUESTION OF REUSING MODELS FROM OTHER DEVELOPMENT ACTIVITIES

6.5.1 Single Source versus Principle of Independence

True, reusing models from development was the initial idea of MBT. Unfortunately, it only works in some particular cases and, then, mainly for software verification. Nobody would expect that a software specification document is identical to the test specification. In MBT, however, this is often less clear to people. "We already have models to describe our system design. Why can we not just take them and generate our test cases from it?" Obviously, such an approach reduces effort and, thus, costs. That is what we call the "manager's dream." Carried to the extreme, we could use code generators and test case generators to automate both sides. However, these tests

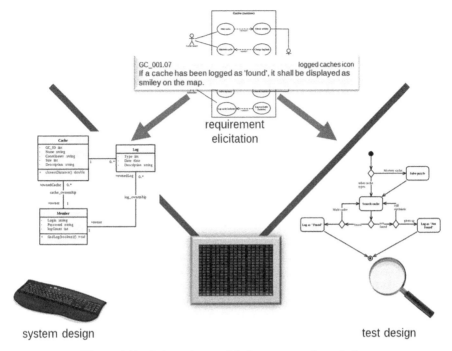

Figure 6.10   Independent models for system and test design.

are of little benefit as they mainly check the generators. In this single source approach, we just compare something to itself. Errors in the initial system design model lead to wrong code, which successfully passes the tests, because we expect the wrong behavior.

The *ne plus ultra* regarding independence is two model authors, say a software architect and a test analyst, that start from the same basis (usually the system requirements) and work separately (see Figure 6.10). The software architect develops dedicated models for system design (architecture, components, features, etc.), whereas the test analyst develops the MBT models for test design. Both models are optimized for their purpose, which is the best way to proceed.

Back at school

To understand the advantages and disadvantages of reusing existing system design or requirement models, imagine yourself back at school. You had two possibilities to do the homework. Either you found someone to copy from or you did it yourself. Copying took less time, but there was the risk of copying a wrong solution. Doing it yourself was safer, but also more laborious. Finally, if you forgot to do the homework, or if you were the pupil everybody copied from, you did not have an option.

> *In model-based testing, we have the same situation. If we work with one model (be it for system design or test purpose), we never have any discrepancies and the perceived development effort is considerably lower than with two independent models. If we derive one model from the other, the models will share the same errors and we cannot use one model to check the other one. Still, there are situations where an approach with one model fits better. We present an example in Section 11.2, where we do not even have documented requirements for our system under test.*

6.5.2   Limitations

Apart from the single-source problem, reusing models from requirement analysis or system design has other limitations. First, the modeling concept of the system design model has to fit the test objectives. Probably, the static system design model in Figure 6.10 will not be of much help to test the system behavior. A state diagram would serve better, but even then, we check the implementation only against its design (see box "Verification versus validation").

> **Verification versus validation**
>
> *During verification, we check whether the system under test works as specified. Is the implementation conforming to design? System validation goes one step further and checks, whether the system works as expected by the end users. Have we developed the right system to reach our goals?*

Second, system design models are usually not so precise regarding error situations. They do not describe in detail what may go wrong, for example, with user input. MBT models do! For the developer, it is sufficient to know that for a person's age only integer values are valid and that, otherwise, the software has to display an error message. The tester will try to enter a noninteger number (3.1428), a character ("A") and possibly even a special character ("$") just to check that the error messages always come up.[1] Thus, even if you start with a copy from the system design model, you will end up with a larger version of your initial system design model, containing many test-specific actions or transitions. In addition, you will have to keep both copies aligned. Any change in the system design model will probably affect the MBT model, creating additional maintenance effort.

Third, system design models do not necessarily respect your MBT modeling guidelines. Humans may cope with those differences, but test case generators do not. Therefore, you will have to edit it anyway.

Fourth, you cannot start modeling the tests unless the system design model is stable. This means that you give up a major advantage of MBT, that is, early validation of the system requirements.

---

[1] The example is inspired by ISO/IEC 29119-2 Appendix 2.

6.5.3 Side Effects

Reusing models from system design may lead to growing model complexity and, as a result, to test case explosion. To understand this, let us consider the example of the electric shutters introduced in Section 2.2.4. The state diagram in Figure 2.5 gave us an idea of the different tests we may perform to check whether the shutters behave as expected. The test cases derived from this diagram check the use case "Use electric shutters" in Figure 2.4. Figure 6.11 shows another diagram describing the "Repair electric shutters" use case in more detail. The trap lies in the "Verify shutter" step. It is tempting to say that the service technician does nothing else than the user. Why not reusing the diagram for "Use electric shutters" in Figure 2.4? As we will see, this is not a good idea.

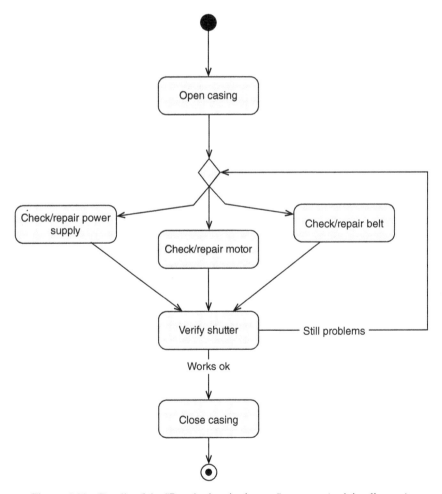

Figure 6.11 Details of the "Repair electric shutters" use case (activity diagram).

First, we should not mix things up. Imagine you just changed the belt. Do you really want to test again that the shutters, once down, stay there if you press DOWN a second time? Probably not. The verification after repair is much simpler. You check that the shutters go up at UP and down at DOWN, nothing else. If we reuse the diagram of Figure 2.5 we somehow have to exclude the other paths, but this is often more difficult than describing the (simpler) check again.

Second, reusing very detailed subdiagrams leads straight into test case explosion. Each path through the diagram in Figure 6.11 is multiplied by the number of paths through the diagram in Figure 2.5. Therefore, do not put everything into one model. Do not step into this very common pitfall!

6.5.4   Good Candidates for Reuse

The best candidates for reuse are requirements models such as business process models or activity diagrams related to use cases. Those models are very helpful for system validation. Developing such models is good practice in business analysis and requirements engineering [36]. They provide a unique source of knowledge on the system under test and generally provide a useful starting point for your MBT modeling activities. However, keep in mind that it is only a starting point. You have to adapt these models to fit your test objectives and to respect the constraints of the MBT tool you are using.

Another example is protocol conformance testing. Here, the focus lies on providing evidence that the software meets the standard. Anything not specified is beyond scope. Thus, there is no need to add test-specific elements to the model.

6.5.5   Reuse in Practice

In the 2014 MBT User survey, nearly 60% of the participants stated that they use models also in other development phases, for example, for requirements elicitation or system design. Next, we asked those participants, how different their MBT models are from those other models.

Figure 6.12 shows the results. In 56% of the cases, the reused model had been largely or totally modified for testing purpose. Twenty-nine percent of the respondents performed slight modifications, but only 15% of them reuse existing models without any modification.

If we take all survey participants into account (including those without any model from other development phases to reuse), only 25% work with MBT models with are close to or identical to the reused models (see Figure 6.13).

6.6   TOOL SUPPORT FOR MBT MODELING ACTIVITIES

To write test cases, we need an editor. In MBT, editing test cases is synonymous to writing models. The simplest drawing tools are pencil and paper or, in modern times,

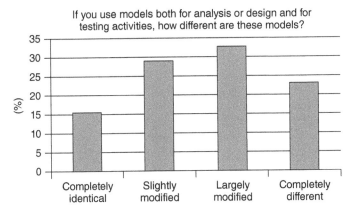

Figure 6.12 Difference between analysis or design models and MBT models (from 2014 MBT User Survey).

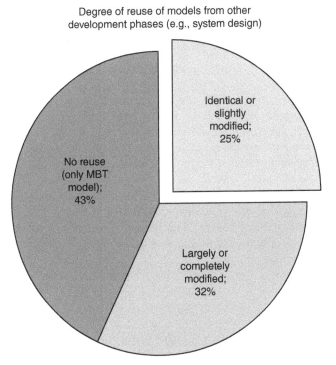

Figure 6.13 Reuse of models from analysis and design (from 2014 MBT User Survey).

flowchart editors for graphical models and text editors or scripting tools for textual models. However, those "simple" tools are generic and do not support MBT-specific activities. Therefore, they are only of limited use (mainly for documenting the test idea).

Usually, the test case editor is either a stand-alone modeling tool (possibly a UML tool) or a model editor integrated into the MBT tool. UML tools support the modeling activity by providing predefined model elements with attributes that conform to the UML standard. This makes it easier to write MBT models with correct syntax. If the attributes in the property window of a transition in a state diagram are labeled "trigger" and "guard," the person who writes the MBT model will most probably not confound them.

Most UML tools offer features to check the syntax and (to a smaller extend) the semantic of a model. Depending on the tool, the model checking capacities range from detecting unconnected model elements to a complete check of the syntax.

UML-based MBT tools use a subset of UML for test generation purposes. The degree of integration of the model editor into the MBT tool varies from weak to strong. In a weak integration, the tester writes the MBT model in a UML tool, but using only the UML subset supported by the MBT tool. Then, he transfers the model from the model editor to the MBT tool through export/import of some exchange file. Usually, the file exchange is based on the Extensible Markup Language (XML) Metadata Interchange format (short: XMI), an OMG standard for exchanging metadata information based on XML. In a slightly stronger integration, the information is transferred via an API.

Strong integration embeds MBT features into the UML modeling environment or vice versa. This makes it possible to provide integrated support between both the modeling and test generation activities of the MBT process.

Model checking is only one possible way to verify model quality. Being a static check, it detects mainly errors in the model's syntax, or discrepancies with respect to predefined semantic rules. To verify the semantics, dynamic checks are better. Using a model simulator, you are able to execute different paths through the model. In some sense, any test case generator is a model simulator.

To establish traceability between requirements and MBT model elements, the MBT tool has to provide the means to import requirements catalogs from third party requirements management tools.

Last, but not least, a good MBT model editor provides support for change management.

6.7 ITERATIVE MBT MODEL DEVELOPMENT

In practice, model-based test design is an iterative process. We start with a first draft and refine it to the extent of our knowledge increases. However, the lack of knowledge is not the only reason for changes. Models also have bugs. In the worst case, they do not adequately match the test objectives. Therefore, it is highly recommended to perform regular checks of the model.

Since MBT models can also become very complex, we have to face the truth. It may not be sufficient to review the model occasionally. We also have to keep an eye on the generated output, or rather four, since "four eyes are better than two." The ISTQB MBT syllabus recommends establishing a truly iterative model development process, with small model increments and regular peer reviews, but also reviews with other stakeholders. The former detect flaws in the MBT model leading to better test cases, the latter reveal incomplete or inconsistent product requirements, resulting in a better product. In other words, we avoid errors when it is still not very costly and time-consuming to fix them – and this far ahead test execution. Thus, the overall efficiency and effectiveness of the test process improves.

Each time, the MBT model changes, you should also update the generated tests to make sure the change does not have unexpected side effects such as illogical test sequences or simply generation errors due to syntactic errors in the MBT model. Similar to model simulation, the test case generator will detect dead ends or traverse transitions, you did not see in the diagram, because one arrow hides another one.

All those changes require a well-established configuration management applying to all artifacts, that is, requirements, diagrams, generated test cases, but also test selection criteria, tool settings, and other relevant information.

A medical advice

Do you wonder why your elbow hurts more although you are spending fewer hours playing tennis or squash? You probably have a "mouse elbow."

The "mouse elbow" is very similar to the famous tennis elbow. Many people working with a computer suffer from it and I can tell from personal experience that writing MBT models all day may be the cause. During modeling, you continuously move the mouse, then type some text on the keyboard, then grasp the mouse again. This causes repetitive strain, resulting in pain.

If you suffer from this "Repetitive Strain Injury," search the internet for "mouse elbow" and have a look at the recommended stretching exercises. They help!

(Anne Kramer)

6.8   OTHER RECOMMENDATIONS

In the previous sections, we presented universal good practices for MBT. In this section, we wish to share some more concrete recommendations, the kind of good

practices you will find in typical modeling guidelines. They stem from general software engineering best practices, our own experience, the predecessor of the ISTQB
MBT syllabus,[2] and an MBT methodology guide of the European Telecommunications Standards Institute ([37]).

- Use self-explanatory names for all model elements.
- Do not place too much information in one figure. The diagram should fit in one
  page (A4 or Letter). In your modeling guidelines, limit the number of elements
  in one diagram. Anyway, you are limited by the "one page" constraint.
- Pay attention to the layout of your model. Elements should not overlap and lines
  should not cross each other unless this has a particular meaning. If it has, do not
  forget to define it in the modeling guidelines.
- Structure your model hierarchically, but keep the depth limited. Models with
  many hierarchical levels can be quite confusing. After drilling down to the lowest level, you already forgot where you came from. The current recommendation
  is to limit to the number of levels to approximately five levels. However, very
  complex systems may require more hierarchical levels.
- Limit the number of element types you use. The activity diagrams in this book
  contain only seven different element types: start and end node, actions, activities
  (= sub-diagrams), splits/merges of decisions ($\Diamond$), flows (arrows), and requirements (= linked text).
- If applicable, limit the number of parameters in functions or methods. ETSI
  considers five parameters as upper limit and a maximum of two parameters per
  function as ideal.
- Comment your diagrams to make them easier to understand. However, textual
  descriptions should also stay as simple as possible. In a diagram, the layout
  constraints limit the amount of text. For textual descriptions outside the model,
  ETSI recommends an upper limit of 100 lines with a maximum of five branches
  and three loops. Personally, we think these limits are even lower in the graphical
  representation. Three loops in one diagram are already a lot.
- Keep the logical operations simple. ETSI recommends a limit of five operands,
  but this may be too much or too few in your particular context. As a general
  rule, the model should remain a picture and not become code.
- Keep the reading direction in mind. People read models like text. In Western
  culture, this is usually from left-to-right and top-to-down. Therefore, the start
  node should be at the top and the end node at the bottom of the diagram.

---

[2]The ISTQB MBT syllabus is based on an anterior initiative of the International Software Quality Institute
(iSQI). The author team of the iSQI Certified Model-Based Tester syllabus (published in May 2013) then
joined the ISTQB Model-Based Tester working group to elaborate the current version.

- It is also a good idea to place the main workflow to the left and optional variations to the right.
- Avoid test case explosion from the beginning. Each MBT tool implements different mechanisms to avoid this effect. Anchor those mechanisms in the modeling guidelines to ensure, everybody knows about them.

Keep in mind that these good practices are just recommendations and not God-given. For very complex systems, it can be hard to adhere to all of them.

7

HOW MBT RELATES TO TEST DESIGN TECHNIQUES?

This chapter covers the learning objective of syllabus Section 3.1.4 "Relation to CTFL test design techniques."

As mentioned in the beginning, model-based testing (MBT) does not replace classic black-box test design techniques, but extends them. In this book, we do not repeat the content of the ISTQB Certified Tester – Foundation Level syllabus [6]. Still, we provide a brief overview on the most commonly used techniques and illustrate how they show up in MBT models. These techniques are as follows:

- equivalence partitioning and boundary value analysis
- decision tables
- state transition testing
- use case testing.

7.1 EQUIVALENCE PARTITIONING AND BOUNDARY VALUE ANALYSIS

There are various techniques to determine test data required for efficient testing that could fill a book on its own (see e.g., Ref. [38]). Equivalence partitioning and

Model-Based Testing Essentials–Guide to the ISTQB® Certified Model-Based Tester Foundation Level, First Edition. Anne Kramer and Bruno Legeard.
© 2016 John Wiley & Sons, Inc. Published 2016 by John Wiley & Sons, Inc.

boundary value analysis are just two of them. The following example illustrates those two fundamental (and essential) techniques:

In Germany, the minimum age limit for buying cigarettes is 18. To test this restriction, we should send at least two persons to the store: a teenager and an adult (according to German law). Technically, we divide the data range for the customer's age (input data) into two equivalence partitions: one with "age < 18" and "age ≥ 18." Similarly, there are two equivalence partitions for the output data: "cigarettes sold" and "cigarettes refused." The minimum we should do is to select one representative of each equivalence partition for our tests. However, experience shows that errors occur close to boundaries. Therefore, we should not send arbitrary teenagers and adults, but two persons close to the age limit (e.g., 17.5 and 18.5 years old). This is basically the concept of the "boundary value analysis."

Now, let us consider the slightly more complex example of a German movie theater. Again, we have an age limitation. Children less than 12 years old pay a reduced tariff 1, whereas everybody of age 12 years and more pays the more expensive tariff 2. In addition, access to some films is restricted depending on the age of the spectator.

The left-hand side of Figure 7.1 shows the high-level diagram of the corresponding MBT model. Depending on the movie's rating and the spectator's age, access is allowed or denied. Of course, the spectator does not have to pay a ticket if he is too young for the movie. The right-hand side shows the subdiagrams "Set spectator's age"

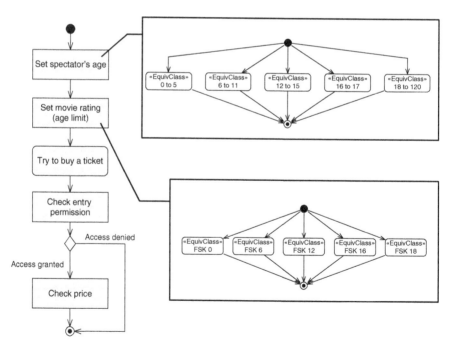

Figure 7.1 Taking age restrictions for movies into account (equivalence partitions in an activity diagram; we assume that 120 years is a reasonable upper limit for the spectators age).

and "Set film rating (age limit)." Here, we see the five categories for the spectator's age corresponding to the German classification system FSK.[1] Each movie is classified into one of the following categories: FSK 0, FKS 6, FSK 12, FSK 16, and FSK 18. The numbers correspond to the age limits. They determine the five equivalent partitions for the spectator's age. Fortunately, the limit between tariff 1 and 2 coincides with the age limit between FSK 6 and FSK 12, so we do not have to introduce another equivalence partition.

To test the access control, we should at least combine each film category with each equivalence partition for the spectator's age. The model in Figure 7.1 visualizes these combinations. In the figure, we marked the equivalence partitions with a flag ≪EquivClass≫. This does not correspond to a UML rule, nor any other modeling language. We just did this for better understanding!

The model still leaves some degree of freedom concerning the concrete age of the spectator. The equivalent partitions only determine the allowed data ranges for test data. It is not obvious whether the test for equivalent class "12 to 15" is executed with an age equal to 12, 13, 14, or 15. This concrete value has to be part of additional test data set outside the model.

Obviously, if the model does not contain concrete data values, the derived test cases will not contain them either. Following the ISTQB glossary, we call those test cases "abstract test cases" [1]. If we want to generate "concrete test cases," that is, test cases with all test data already set, we have to include this information in the model. Figure 7.2 shows the same model, but with concrete values. Besides, the figure also illustrates the modeling of boundary values for the spectator's age.

An anecdote from personal experience

As I am deeply convinced of the approach's advantages, I use model-based testing techniques since 2006. However, some time ago, I had to adapt an existing test specification of several hundred pages. There were only a few changes and two new features to test. Thus, for the first time after several years I heard myself saying: "This is one of the rare cases where models will not be useful."

When it came to the point to write the tests for the two new features I realized something strange. I really had problems writing a test case "from scratch." Of course, I tried to find the best sequence that covers everything with just a few steps. I ended up ... drawing a model! Just a small one without many details, but it helped me to find the shortest sequence that fulfilled the coverage criteria I wanted to have.

Apparently, you get so used to this way of thinking that you can no longer switch back your mind. You get addicted to models.

(Anne Kramer)

---

[1]FSK stands for " Freiwillige Selbstkontrolle der Filmwirtschaft" (in English: Voluntary Self-Regulation of the Film Industry).

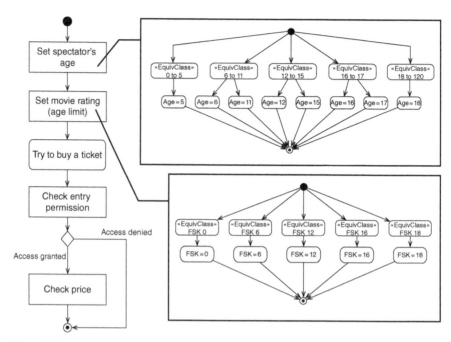

Figure 7.2 MBT model containing concrete data values (boundary values in an activity diagram).

7.2 DECISION TABLES

Figure 7.3 shows a so-called decision table for buying a ticket in our movie theater example. This time, we focus on the ticket price, considering additional data, but neglecting the access restriction.

In the upper part, we see the different rules that influence the ticket price. In the middle part, we find the consequences of the rules, called "actions." For example, if the spectator is under 12 he gets the ticket for the reduced price "tariff 1." If the film is in 3D, it is charged €3.00 more. The lower part is usually not part of a decision table. It just illustrates how the expected result relates to the rules and actions.

This kind of decision table may very well serve as input for MBT. Figure 7.4 shows a simple MBT model combining a behavioral workflow diagram with a decision table. The decision table formalizes price list and options for the "Buy ticket" action. The MBT tool then processes both the diagram and the decision table, generating test cases for the different business scenarios described in the diagram (in our example just one) and the various cases defined in the table. In Chapter 11, we present a case study that relates to this topic.

Exercise 10 *Take a minute and look at the model in Figure 7.4 keeping the conditions defined in Figure 7.3 in mind. Do you find the four test cases that check a rather weird combination?*

Condition	Alternative	Rules											
Spectator is under 12	Moviegoer is 12 or more	Y	Y	Y	Y	Y	Y	N	N	N	N	N	N
Weekend	Not weekend	Y	N	Y	N	Y	N	Y	N	Y	N	Y	N
3D film version	2D film version	Y	Y	Y	Y	N	N	Y	Y	Y	Y	N	N
3D glasses required	No glasses required	Y	Y	N	N	N	N	Y	Y	N	N	N	N
	Actions												
	Charge tariff 1 (€5.50)	x	x	x	x	x	x						
	Charge tariff 2 (€7.00)							x	x	x	x	x	x
	Charge for weekend (€3.00)	x		x		x		x		x		x	
	Charge for 3D (€3.00)	x	x	x	x			x	x	x	x		
	Charge for glasses (€1.00)	x	x					x	x				
	Expected result												
	Price (in €)	12.50	9.50	11.50	8.50	8.50	5.50	14.00	11.00	13.00	10.00	10.00	7.00

Figure 7.3 Decision table for movie ticket price.

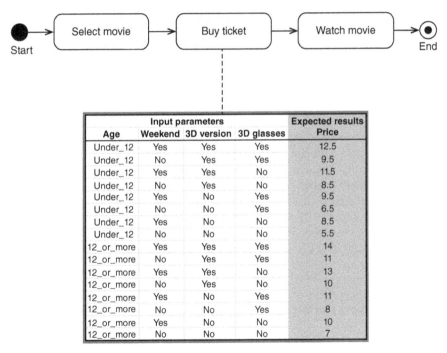

Figure 7.4 MBT model combining a behavioral diagram with a decision table for movie ticket price (If you start wondering about the content, please do the exercise first).

7.3 STATE TRANSITION TESTING

As illustrated by several previous examples in this book (Figure 2.9 or 4.10), state diagrams are commonly used for MBT. The modeling language is particularly adapted to represent the lifecycle of the system under test. Figure 7.5 shows a state diagram

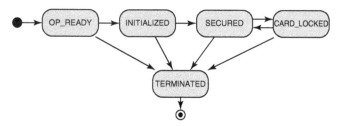

Figure 7.5 Smart card lifecycle according to the GlobalPlatform™ card specification (state diagram).

describing a smart card's lifecycle states as defined in the GlobalPlatform™ card specification 2.2.1.

During production, the smart card successively passes through the states OP_READY, INITIALIZED, and SECURED. The state SECURED indicates that the card contains all required keys and security elements and is ready for use. In the state CARD_LOCKED, the card only allows the selection of applications with specific privileges. The transition between SECURED and CARD_LOCKED is reversible. TERMINATED corresponds to the card's end of life. SECURED, CARD_LOCKED, and TERMINATED are states of the so-called "postissuance phase."

Obviously, MBT is a first class support for state transition testing, which is defined in the ISTQB glossary as a "black box test design technique in which test cases are designed to execute valid and invalid state transitions" [1]. Thus, we have to test the different transitions in Figure 7.5. Without tool support, we have to exploit those state diagrams manually. However, we are rapidly limited by the complexity of the task. If the diagram includes many substates and guard conditions, we get lost easily. MBT tools implement algorithms that allow us to derive tests from much more precise and complete state diagrams. Test generation becomes more efficient.

In Chapter 8, we introduce typical test selection criteria such as state coverage or transition coverage that you may apply on such MBT models to generate your test cases.

7.4 USE CASE TESTING

Use case testing is a "black-box test design technique in which test cases are designed to execute scenarios of use cases" [1]. The corresponding use case diagrams are rather informal. Figure 7.6 provides an overview on the use cases for an automated teller machine (ATM). It shows the two main actors (the ATM operator and the customer) and a selection of use cases. In practice, use case diagram may be more complex, containing additional model elements describing dependencies or specializations and nonhuman actors (e.g., the bank system). For security testing, the technique may also serve to describe attacks in so-called "misuse cases."

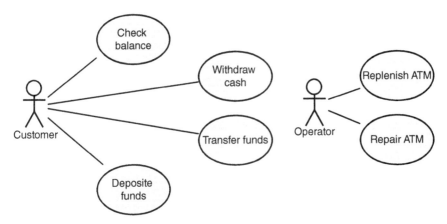

Figure 7.6 Use cases for an automated teller machine (ATM).

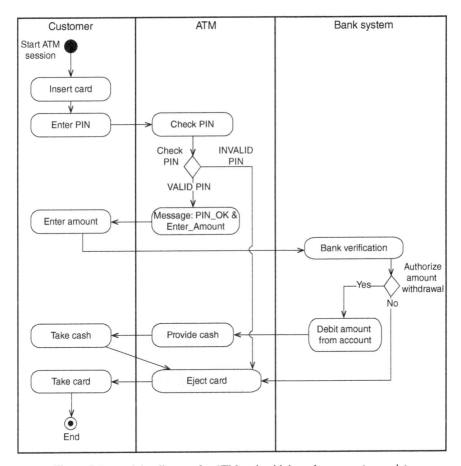

Figure 7.7 Activity diagram for ATM cash withdrawal use case (example).

The use case diagram itself is usually not sufficient to provide the full information required. Therefore, we add informal text to each use case and/or provide details through additional diagrams (e.g., activity diagrams or business process models). In an MBT approach, we may reuse those existing diagrams and derive the required test cases from it. If reuse is not possible, we may translate the informal textual description into an MBT model.

Figure 7.7 shows a (simplified) example of an activity diagram for the use case "Withdraw cash." This kind of activity diagram is a good starting point for MBT modeling activities. You may import it in your MBT tool and, then, adapt it according to your test objectives.

A good test completion criterion for use case testing is that each use case should be covered, meaning the coverage of all activity diagrams or business process models related to these use cases.

8

DERIVING TESTS FROM AN MBT MODEL

This chapter covers the learning objectives of syllabus Chapter 3 "Selection Criteria for Test Case Generation" except Section 3.1.4 "Relation to CTFL Test Design Techniques," which has been introduced in Chapter 7.

8.1 TAXONOMY OF SELECTION CRITERIA

We have seen in Chapter 3 that we need both a model-based testing (MBT) model and test selection criteria to drive test generation with respect to our test objectives. The MBT model provides an abstraction of "what" shall be tested, whereas the test selection criteria provide the "how-to" or rather the "to which extent" shall be tested.

The number of different test selection criteria applied in MBT is quite high. Several authors established taxonomies of selection criteria in literature (see Refs. [39–41]). From these previous publications, the ISTQB MBT syllabus authors selected six families of test selection criteria, corresponding to the most commonly used criteria in industrial application:

- requirements coverage
- structural model coverage
- data coverage

Model-Based Testing Essentials–Guide to the ISTQB® Certified Model-Based Tester Foundation Level, First Edition. Anne Kramer and Bruno Legeard.

- random test selection
- scenario- or pattern-based test selection
- project-driven test selection.

For further reading, for example, on current research on fault-based test case selection based on model mutation,[1] please refer to Ref. [41] and other, more recent publications.

8.1.1 Requirements Coverage

Requirements coverage is a very popular selection criterion for tests conducted against a requirements specification. We reach full requirements coverage, if each requirement in the selected set of requirements is checked by at least one test case.

Technically, we link the requirement to model elements and let the test case generator select all paths covering those model elements. Figure 8.1 shows an MBT model for a TV system, which allows the user to

- watch TV,
- pause the emission for a break,

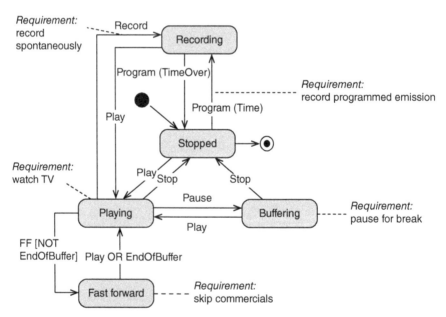

Figure 8.1 Requirements in an MBT model for a sophisticated TV (state diagram; Note: we deliberately neglected the state "Programmed" between "Stopped" and "Recording" to improve readability).

---

[1] A model mutant is a copy of the initial model, but with altered operator or data value.

- skip TV commercials (provided that there was a pause before),
- record programmed emissions, and to
- spontaneously record emissions.

Any set of test cases reaching all states and transitions linked to those five requirements fulfill 100% requirements coverage. This can be one long test case or a set of several shorter ones.

The requirements coverage criterion seems to be quite easy, but at closer look, some questions arise. First, we can only apply this test selection criterion, if documented requirements of our system under test exist. In the case of nonexistent or badly specified requirement, the MBT model itself will complete the documentation. In the example, the requirements do not specify whether it is possible to start recording during a pause or not. The tester discovered this undocumented requirement after several conversations with the developer.

Second, it strongly depends on the granularity and the detailing of the requirements how many different test cases are necessary to cover the requirements *content* completely. Again, take the example in Figure 8.1. Do we have to test all possible combinations, which would correspond to full path coverage? The answer is "no," simply because "yes" will ruin your company.

Thus, requirements coverage alone might not be sufficient to achieve the project test objectives. Therefore, we usually combine it with other criteria, for example, structural model coverage or data coverage.

8.1.2 MBT Model Element Coverage

MBT model element coverage, also called structural model coverage (or just "model coverage"), is a generic term for a variety of coverage criteria based on the structure of the model. The idea is always the same. We identify some coverage item and try to reach 100% coverage for this item. Possible coverage items are graphical elements such as actions or states and flows or transitions in graphical models, as well as statements or conditions in textual models.

In graph theory, we speak about nodes and edges. Actions and decisions (including those in the subdiagrams) are the nodes in our simple modeling language for workflows (see Section 2.3.1). Flows (the arrows) correspond to edges. People working with state diagrams prefer the terms "state coverage" and "transition coverage," whereas people working with business process diagrams talk about "tasks and gateways" instead of "actions and decisions." However, the principle remains the same.

Well-known examples applied to graph-based models are node coverage, edge coverage, and full path coverage. If we link the requirements to model elements, requirements coverage also becomes a specific type of structural model coverage. To understand the differences, have a look at Figure 8.2. Note that for the sake of readability, we do not mention the decision nodes 2 and 5 explicitly, even if they are also on the path.

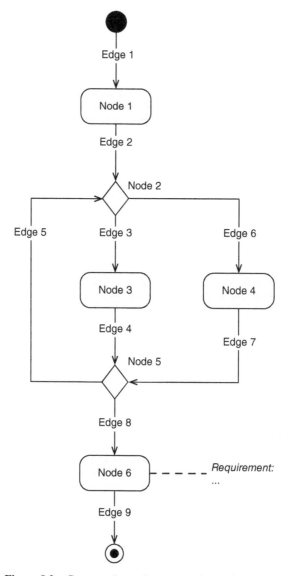

Figure 8.2 Coverage items for structural model coverage.

The sequence:

- "Start => Node 1 => Node 3 => Node 6 => End"

reaches the only node linked to a requirement. It fulfills (at least formally) 100% requirements coverage, but only 83% node coverage, because it misses one of the six nodes (not counting start and end nodes). To obtain 100% node coverage, we could select the following two paths:

- "Start => Node 1 => Node 3 => Node 6 => End" and
- "Start => Node 1 => Node 4 => Node 6 => End"

These two paths reach all edges but one (Edge 5), which corresponds to $8/9 = 89\%$ edge coverage. Therefore, the best sequence is definitely:

- "Start => Node 1 => Node 3 => Node 4 => Node 6 => End".

corresponding to 100% edge coverage. Edge coverage always includes node coverage, because all edges point to a node. Thus, edge coverage (or transition coverage in state diagrams) is the stronger criterion of those two.

The strongest criterion, however, is full path coverage. Full path coverage includes all possible combinations, starting with:

- "Start => Node 1 => Node 3 => Node 6 => End";
- "Start => Node 1 => Node 4 => Node 6 => End";
- "Start => Node 1 => Node 3 => Node 4 => Node 6 => End";
- "Start => Node 1 => Node 4 => Node 3 => Node 6 => End";
- "Start => Node 1 => Node 3 => Node 3 => Node 6 => End";
- "Start => Node 1 => Node 4 => Node 4 => Node 6 => End";
- "Start => Node 1 => Node 3 => Node 3 => Node 4 => Node 6 => End";
- "Start => Node 1 => Node 3 => Node 4 => Node 4 => Node 6 => End";
- "Start => Node 1 => Node 3 => Node 3 => Node 3 => Node 6 => End";
- and so on.

It is impossible to reach full path coverage for diagrams with loops. You have to stop the test case generation process either by limiting the number of loops or the complete path length.

Exercise 11   *Figure 8.3 shows a diagram having exactly the same structure as in Figure 8.2, but with some content. Please take some time and think about the question which test cases are required to check the **content** of the requirement in Figure 8.3 completely.*

8.1.3   Data Coverage

Data coverage merely focuses on input and output data. To understand the data coverage criterion, we should go back to the movie theater example in Section 7.1 and, more precisely, to Figure 7.2. The basic idea is to split the data space into equivalence partitions. From each equivalence partition, we select one representative with

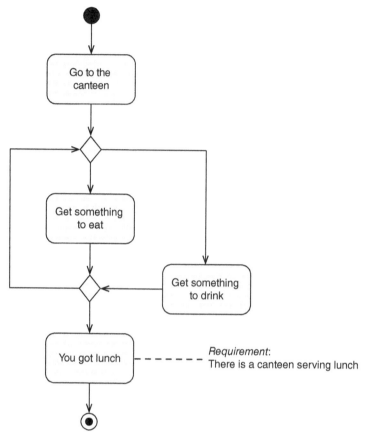

Figure 8.3 Example diagram for structural model coverage (activity diagram).

the "hope that the elements of this class are 'equivalent' in terms of their ability to detect failures" [39]. Usually, we combine equivalence partitioning with a boundary value analysis, because bugs tend to occur close to these boundaries [6]. This is exactly how we obtained the values for the cinema spectator's age in Figure 8.4.

In this example, we modeled the data. Thus, data coverage is obtained through structural model coverage. If we reach each node, we also cover each data value.

The situation becomes more complicated, if the MBT model does not contain the test data. In that case, we just have one node "Set age" (shown in Figure 8.5) instead of the entire subdiagram in Figure 8.4.

Obviously, we cannot reach data coverage without covering the node, but it is not a sufficient criterion. The way to obtain 100% data coverage strongly depends on tool support. Without a tool, you have to use your brain.

A first coverage level is that each parameter value occurs at minimum once in our test cases. If we wish to push coverage further on, we may go to pairwise or even to

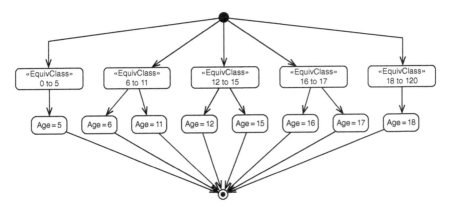

Figure 8.4   Equivalence partitioning and boundary value analysis for the spectator's age.

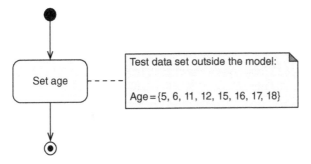

Figure 8.5   Data items set outside the model.

n-wise coverage. Pairwise coverage means, that any pair of any two-parameter values occurs at least once in our set of test cases [42]. The "*n*" in *n*-wise stands for an integer number, but you will probably never go that far. This is one of the roads leading to test case explosion.

8.1.4   Random

This selection criterion is comparable to a random walk through the model. Whenever we have to decide, which way to go, we roll the dice. In the easiest case, all alternatives are equally probable. Thus, if the die shows an even number we go to the left, otherwise to the right. If the first alternative is five times more probable than the second is, we only go right if the die shows a six (see Figure 8.6). The resulting path determines the selected test case.

If the edges have different probabilities, we speak about stochastic selection, which is the correct academic term. However, to keep it simple, we will stick to the term "random" unless it is important to point out the difference.

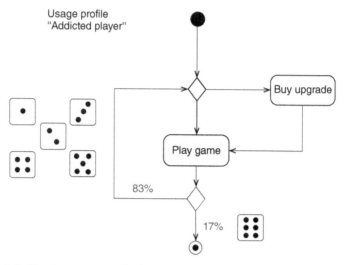

Figure 8.6   Random test case selection (usage profile mapped on an activity diagram).

Random test case selection is commonly used for generating test cases from usage models. Usage models describe the behavior of different user groups by indicating different probabilities of each alternative. We already saw an example of a usage model in Figure 5.12.

Another application scenario for the random selection criterion is load testing. Here, we challenge the system under test with an "increasing numbers of parallel users and/or numbers of transactions, to determine what load can be handled by the component or system" [1]. One possibility of performing load testing involves executing a large number of test cases in parallel. Ideally, these test cases differ from each other. If supported by the test case generator, random test case selection is an easy way to obtain a large number of different test cases just by pressing a button. All you have to do is to specify the probabilities and the number of generated test cases you wish to generate.

8.1.5   Scenario- or Pattern-based

As the name indicates, this criterion bases test case selection on given scenarios or patterns. Examples of scenarios are the main path of a use case, corresponding to the most frequently used functionality or an error scenario of the same use case. The latter is called "fault-based scenario."

In literature, scenario-based test case selection is usually associated with two models: one describing the system behavior and a separate one specifying one or several test case(s).

Figure 8.7 shows an example of scenario-based test case selection. To the left, we have the description of the system, that is, the state diagram of a soccer game. After

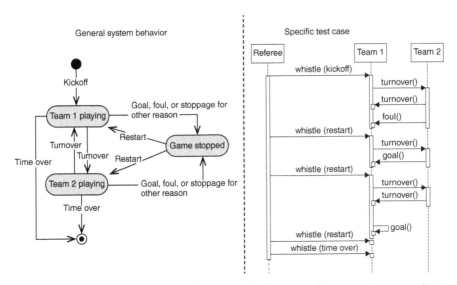

Figure 8.7 Example of scenario-based test case selection (state diagram and sequence chart).

kickoff, team 1 is playing. If they lose the ball, team 2 is playing. A goal, a foul, or other events cause the game to stop. Afterwards, one of the two teams restarts playing. When time is over, the game stops completely.

To the right, we have the description of one particular game. It defines one possible path to take through the state diagram. Thus, it corresponds to our test case specification. Broadly, you just tell your test generator which way to go.

Exercise 12   *Just to get a bit more practice in reading diagrams of all kind: what is the final score of the soccer game in Figure 8.7 and who wins it?*

Another technical realization of scenario-based test case selection relies on path names. You define the paths you want to test (your scenario) and identify them somehow in the model. Of course, the corresponding annotation in the model must follow some well-defined tool-specific format, if a test case generator shall interpret it.

Patterns are less restrictive. In pattern-based test case selection, you partially indicate which way to go and you let the test generator unfold the pattern on the MBT model. Thus, with one pattern, you may produce several or many test cases.

Figure 8.8 is an example of a test pattern written in a textual notation. It relates to the model in the left part of Figure 8.7.

```
Do_many(4..8)[turnover then possibly goal]
Stop_when team_1(goal) = 2 * team_2(goal)
```

Figure 8.8 Example of a test pattern.

The language uses four constructs:

- "Do_many($n \cdots m$) [test_action]"
  indicates that test_action is applied n to m times;
- "test_action1 then test_action2"
  prescribes a sequence of actions (test_action1 is performed before test_action2);
- "possibly"
  states that a test_action can be performed or not;
- "Stop_when condition"
  indicates the stopping condition for the test pattern.

The test pattern in Figure 8.8 tells us that there may be several turnovers (4–8 times), each time possibly resulting in a goal. When applied to the state diagram in Figure 8.7, this pattern will produce 72 test cases. "Do_many($4 \cdots 8$) [turnover then possibly goal]" corresponds to all combinations of 4–8 turnovers, each turnover with zero or one goal. The combinatorics is restricted by the expression "Stop_when team_1(goal) = 2*team_2(goal)". The test case stops as soon as team_1 has scored twice as many goals as team_2 (e.g., 4:2).

To understand the pattern better, let us consider the case of four turnovers. If we neglect the possibility of own goals and count each restart as turnover, we obtain 7 test cases respecting the stopping condition (see Table 8.1).

As you may see, test patterns are a powerful test selection criterion. A short expression of two lines provide many tests with respect to a given test objective. Still, the pattern limits test case explosion. We do not consider test cases for less than four or more than eight turnovers, and restrict the selection to those tests that fulfill the stopping criterion.

It is possible to reduce the number of test cases even further, if we consider the cells in Table 8.1 as equivalence partitions. In that case, it would be sufficient to select one test case per cell, reducing the total number of tests to 13.

Pattern-based test selection requires tool support. To be honest, we also used a tool to generate the overview in Table 8.1. Different tools implement different mechanism for pattern-based test selection.

TABLE 8.1   Number of Generated Test Cases with Pattern-based Test Selection

Number of Turnovers	Number of Test Cases for Given Score		
	0:0	2:1	4:2
4	1	6	–
5	1	5	–
6	1	11	3
7	1	8	3
8	1	18	13
Total	5	48	*19*

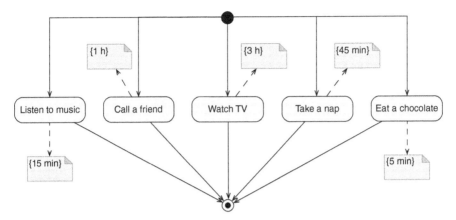

Figure 8.9   Example model including information on the duration (activity diagram).

Exercise 13   Provide an example of a generated test case for 6 turnovers and a final score of 4:2, applying the test pattern in Figure 8.8 to the model in Figure 8.7 (left part). Count the restart after a goal as turnover and do not take own goals into account.

The resulting test case should have two columns: one for the step description and one for the expected result. Let the tester check the intermediate score after each goal.

8.1.6   Project-driven

This last group covers all selection criteria related to test management or project management aspects. In Figure 6.8, we saw an example of the requirement priority influencing the test case selection.

In fact, we are free to put any additional information into the model that may help selecting our "best" set of test cases. For example, Figure 8.9 contains information on the time required during test execution. If the test lab is available for half an hour, only three of the six test cases will fit into this time slot. In this case, the test case selection criterion is the test case duration, but it could also be costs related to test execution (at least €0.89 for a good chocolate) or the availability of test equipment (TV, MP3 player, a friend).

Some words on tool support

Different MBT test case generators support different selection criteria. Once you get used to a specific tool, the way it works seems to be the only possible way. Some test case generators produce only the test cases fulfilling the selection criteria. Others first generate all possible paths and let you filter them afterward. Some tool vendors speak about state transition coverage, others about edge coverage. Some tools explicitly support project-driven selection criteria, others less.

Keep this in mind when discussing the pros and cons of particular tool with others.

DERIVING TESTS FROM AN MBT MODEL

8.2 TEST CASE SELECTION IN PRACTICE

It is a common misunderstanding that we only have to take the "good" test selection criterion to obtain the "best set" of test cases. In practice, things are more complicated. On one hand, we usually have to combine several criteria to achieve our test objectives (and also to avoid test case explosion). On the other hand, we will probably want to add some particular tests for very specific situations.

The Microsoft calculator MBT model in Figure 3.6 is a good candidate to illustrate test case explosion. Figure 8.10 shows the model again, this time including all subdiagrams. The model in itself is not wrong, but it leads to a huge number of tests, not all of them being helpful. It is definitely a good idea to test whether the sequence:

- "Select scientific mode => Type '5' => Type '*' => Press '=' => Check value"

produces a correct result (which is, by the way, 25 and not 5, as you might have expected). However, it is NOT necessary to test this sequence with all possible numbers ranging from 0 to 9999999999. Moreover, it is not the most important scenario to test. Thus, in this particular case, full path coverage is definitely not the test selection criterion to take.

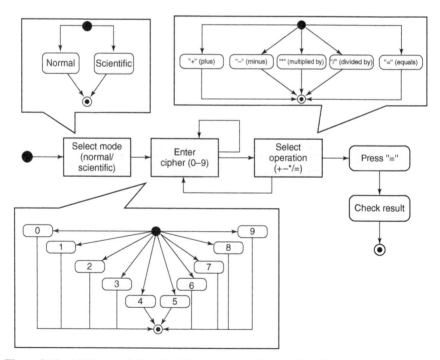

Figure 8.10 MBT model for the Microsoft calculator with all subdiagrams (activity diagram).

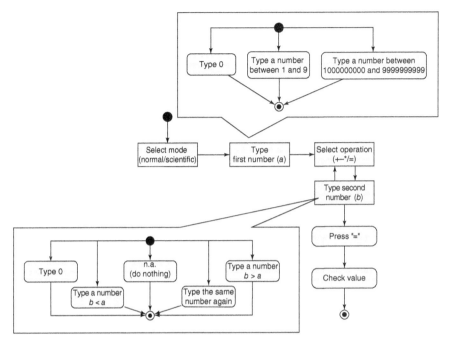

Figure 8.11   MBT model for the Microsoft calculator avoiding test case explosion (activity diagram).

Unfortunately, this is exactly the kind of model you inherit from system design, which also explains, why people sometimes feel frustrated about model-tested testing. The model in Figure 8.10 represents the way we work with the system, not the way we should test it.

To write a good MBT model, we first have to be clear about the test objective. In the calculator example, we want to test the following situations:

- operations "$a+b$," "$a*b$," and "a/b" using arbitrary positive numbers;
- operation "$a-b$" using positive numbers with $a > b$, $b > a$ and $a = b$;
- operation "$a+b$," "$a-b$," "$a*b$," and "a/b" with $b = 0$;
- sequence of operations "a <operator> b <operator> c";
- sequence of operations "a <operator> <operator>."

Usually, it is possible to cope with test case explosion by changing the model. Figure 8.11 shows a slightly modified MBT model for the Microsoft calculator. We no longer test all combinations of ciphers, but focus on the equivalence classes "zero," "one digit," and "large number." Thus, we no longer have to loop several times to obtain a large number.

In the node "Type second number (b)," we force the specific cases required for testing negative results and the particular handling of the case "$b = 0$." There is also the possibility of skipping the second number, represented by the action "n.a. (do nothing)." Finally, we have one loop back to "Select operation $(+-*/=)$" to obtain a sequence of operations.

From our test objectives, it is sufficient to go back once from the subdiagram "Type second number (b)" to "Select operation $(+-*/=)$". This considerably reduces the number of possible combinations. We still get $2*3*5*5*5*5=3,750$ test cases, but at minimum, these test cases add value, which was not the case before. We may also decide to test the calculator exhaustively in the scientific mode and to select only one test case for the normal mode, thus reducing the number of test cases to $1,875 + 1$.

For automated test cases, we are now approaching a manageable order of magnitude. For manual test execution, we should apply one of the test selection criteria described in the previous section to reduce the number of test cases further. One possible solution involves removing the loop. We then obtain $2*3*5 = 30$ test cases covering three out of five test objectives. In addition, we can then apply scenario-based test case selection for the two remaining sequences:

- "a <operator> b <operator> c";
- "a <operator> <operator>."

Another alternative is to keep the test data outside the model, for example, in a data table and to work with data-related test selection criteria [13]. If you have worked with data tables in the past, this is definitely a good idea, because you will profit from your experience and combine it with the advantages of MBT. If you are not familiar with those data-driven techniques, we recommend to model the data as shown in Section 8.1.3 and to apply structural model coverage criteria.

The precise way to avoid test case explosion also depends on the tool, because different tool providers have implemented different mechanisms to cope with the problem. For example, you do not have so many problems with loops, if the generation algorithm of the tool by definition never traverses the same path twice. The result, however, is the same. If I want to enter a three-digit number, I cannot model this data entry by looping three times on a step "Enter one digit." Instead, I have to condense it into a single step "Enter a number with three digits." You should understand the mechanisms of your test case generator and keep them in mind from the beginning.

8.3   EXAMPLES OF COVERAGE CRITERIA

For further illustration, as well as for you to get more practice, we consider some additional examples of coverage-based test case selection criteria, applied on MBT model written in various modeling languages.

8.3.1   Business Process Models and Activity Diagrams

Activity diagrams being very close to business process models from a model structure point of view, this section applies to both modeling languages. The only differences

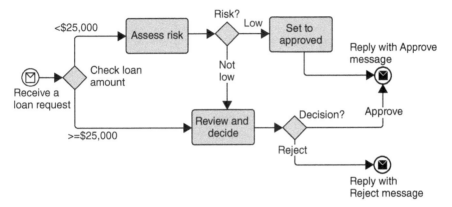

Figure 8.12   Business process model describing the loan decision process of a bank.

TABLE 8.2   Examples of Test Selection Criteria Applied on Business Process Models or Activity Diagrams

Test Selection Criterion	Description	Exemplary Test Cases (Figure 8.12)
Activity/task coverage	Structural model coverage criterion; To reach 100% activity coverage, each activity in the diagram (the rectangles) must be covered by at least one test case	• Start => Assess Risk => Set to Approved => End (Approve) • Start => Review => End (Reject)
Decision/gateway coverage	Structural model coverage criterion; To reach 100% decision coverage, each outcome of a decision (e.g., TRUE or FALSE) has to be covered by at least one test case	• Start => Assess Risk => Set to Approved => End (Approve) • Start => Assess Risk => Review => End (Approve) • Start => Review => End (Reject)
Path coverage	Structural model coverage criterion; To reach 100% path coverage, all possible paths through the model have to be tested; may be with or without loops	• Start => Assess Risk => Set to Approved => End (Approve) • Start => Assess Risk => Review => End (Approve) • Start => Assess Risk => Review => End (Reject) • Start => Review => End (Approve) • Start => Review => End (Reject)

are the terms (activities/decisions in activity diagrams and tasks/gateways in business process models).

Figure 8.12 shows a business process model describing, how the bank decides on a loan request. If the amount is lower than $25,000, and if the associated risk is low, the bank grants the loan easily. Otherwise, they first perform a review and then decide afterward. Table 8.2 shows possible test selection criteria applied on the example in Figure 8.12.

In the small example of Figure 8.12, full path coverage is manageable, but as soon as you have loops in your business process model, this is no longer the case. Then you should apply some reduced version of path coverage, limiting the number of paths to "path coverage without loop" or "one-loop path coverage."

Exercise 14 *We changed the business process model in Figure 8.12 by introducing the case where the bank employee in charge of the review requests more data from the customer: see Figure 8.13.*

How many test cases can you generate from this updated model using full path coverage with 0 to 1 loop? How many test cases would you get with 2 loops?

Hint: For the number of loops, count the number of times the test cases passes through "Review and decide."

8.3.2 State Diagrams

Figure 8.14 represents a state diagram for a rechargeable battery. Two possible transitions bring the battery from state high to state low: T1 corresponds to the main

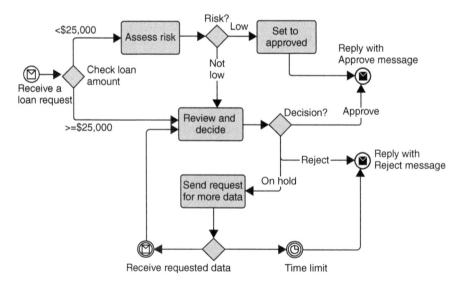

Figure 8.13 Updated business process model describing the bank's loan decision process.

scenario "frequent use," T2 to the error scenario "defective battery." To recharge the battery, we have again two possibilities: T3 is the main scenario where we connect a recharger to a socket-outlet and T4 is the alternative scenario using a charged power bank.

In Table 8.3, we give some possible test selection criteria applied on the example in Figure 8.14. For simplicity, we indicate the transition names Tn.

Exercise 15 *We derived four test cases from the MBT model in Figure 8.14:*

$T0 => T1 => T3 => T5 => T2 => T6$
$T0 => T2 => T4 => T5 => T2 => T6$
$T0 => T1 => T4 => T5 => T2 => T6$
$T0 => T2 => T3 => T5 => T2 => T6.$

Now, time is running short and we have to drop one or several test cases. How many test cases and which test cases can we drop and still have 100% transition coverage?

8.3.3   Data Domains (Structural Models)

Imagine that you have to test a car configurator application. Such "build & price" application is essentially a step-by-step process on a website, which allows you to configure the options of your future car. Depending on the chosen car model, you may select from multiple options: version, engine, color, interior trim, and so on. At the end, the application computes the price.

How can we test this application? Do we have the slightest idea on how many combinations we need for exhaustive testing of such a configurator? Probably not. This is where test selection criteria based on data domains are helpful. They provide heuristics to manage efficiently the selection of test data values:

- Equivalence partition coverage
  Full equivalence partition coverage is reached if we select at least one representative per equivalence partition.
- Boundary value coverage
  Boundary value coverage is useful to test numerical data ranges. Full boundary value coverage is reached if we select two representatives per equivalence partition: one close to the lower and one close to the upper boundary.
- Pairwise testing on defined domains
  Pairwise testing ensures that all possible discrete combinations of each pair of input parameters are produced.

In the context of the car configurator, a possible approach involves combining pairwise testing with equivalence partitioning.

TABLE 8.3 Examples of Test Selection Criteria Applied on State Diagrams

Test Selection Criterion	Description	Exemplary Test Cases (Figure 8.14)
State coverage	Structural model coverage criterion; To reach 100% state coverage, each state in the diagram (the rectangles) must be covered by at least one test case	• T0 => T1 => T3 => T5 => T2 => T6
Transition coverage	Structural model coverage criterion; To reach 100% transition coverage, each transition in the diagram (the arrows) has to be covered by at least one test case	• T0 => T1 => T3 => T5 => T2 =>T6 • T0 => T1 => T4 => T5 => T2 =>T6
Transition pair coverage	Structural model coverage criterion; To reach 100% transition pair coverage, each consecutive pair of transitions has to be tested (meaning each combination of T1/T2 and T3/T4; highlighted in italics in the right column)	• T0 => *T1* => *T3* => T5 => T2 => T6 • T0 => *T2* => *T4* => T5 => T2 => T6 • T0 => *T1* => *T4* => T5 => T2 => T6 • T0 => *T2* => *T3* => T5 => T2 => T6
Path coverage	Structural model coverage criterion; To reach 100% path coverage, all possible paths through the model have to be tested; for state diagrams, path coverage usually excludes loops due to the risk of test case explosion	• All of the above plus • T0 => T1 => T3 => T5 => T1 => T3 => T5 => T1 =>T6 • T0 => T1 => T3 => T5 => T1 => T3 => T5 => T2 =>T6 • T0 => T1 => T3 => T5 => T1 => T4 => T5 => T1 =>T6 • T0 => T2 => T3 => T5 => T1 => T3 => T5 => T1 =>T6 • and so on (an infinite number of loops)

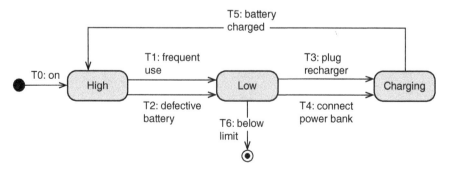

Figure 8.14 States of a rechargeable battery (state diagram).

Let us consider testing the configurator for Peugeot 208.[2] You have several steps to pass before you get the result (summary and price): (1) Choose version, (2) Choose engine, (3) Choose color, (4) Choose interior and, finally (5) Choose extra options. Figure 8.15 provides the data domains for this application.

For the Peugeot 208 (dating from 2015), we have the choice between four versions and seven different engines. For "color" and "interior" domains, we defined equivalence partitions: C1–C5 are sets of available colors having the same price within each partition. T1–T3 are similar equivalence partitions for the interior options.

Exhaustive coverage of all combinations of data values requires 1,260 test cases. However, in an industrial project where time allocated to testing is limited, you do not want to test (manually) such large number of test cases. Moreover, you have some constraints to handle: The version "Access A/C" offers only two possibilities for the engine (1.0 VTi 68 and 1.6 HDi 75) and the version "GT line" offers three possible engines (1.2 VTi 110, 1.6 HDi 100, and 1.6 HDi 120). Using pairwise test selection criteria and adequate tooling will provide you with 42 tests. Each pair of domain values is covered and the constraints regarding versions and engines are satisfied.

The left table in Figure 8.16 shows the result of a pairwise combination of the car's version and the possible engines. Due to the constraints mentioned above, we obtain only two lines each for the "Access A/C" and "GT line." The middle table combines the equivalence partitions for the color, the interior, and the extra options using a pairwise algorithm.

"All" we have to do now is to combine the rows of those two tables in a way that produces a minimum number of test cases. Figure 8.16 shows an excerpt of the 42 generated test cases. As you can see from the bold cells, the first five tests cover all allowed pairs between "Access A/C" and the possible engines, colors, interiors, and extra options.

Pairwise test selection requires tool support, and the number of generated test cases may depend on the generation algorithm, if applied on data domains with many dimension.

Version	Engine	Color	Interior	Options
Access A/C	1.0 VTi 68	C1	T1	Alarm
Active	1.2 VTi 82	C2	T2	Active City Break
Allure	1.2 eVTi 82	C3	T3	Exterior Pack
GT line	1.2 VTi 110	C4		
	1.6 HDi 75	C5		
	1.6 HDi 100			
	1.6 HDi 120			

Figure 8.15 Data domains of the car configurator.

[2]http://www.configurator.peugeot.co.uk/configure-your-peugeot/208/5-door/.

Version	Engine
Access A/C	1.0 VTi 68
Access A/C	1.6 HDi 75
Active	1.0 VTi 68
Active	1.2 VTi 82
Active	1.2 eVTi 82
Active	1.2 VTi 110
Active	1.6 HDi 75
Active	1.6 HDi 100
Active	1.6 HDi 120
Allure	1.0 VTi 68
Allure	1.2 VTi 82
Allure	1.2 eVTi 82
Allure	1.2 VTi 110
Allure	1.6 HDi 75
Allure	1.6 HDi 100
Allure	1.6 HDi 120
GT line	1.6 HDi 100
GT line	1.6 HDi 120

X

Color	Interior	Options
C1	T1	Alarm
C1	T2	Active City Break
C1	T3	Exterior Pack
C2	T1	Exterior Pack
C2	T2	Alarm
C2	T3	Active City Break
C3	T1	Active City Break
C3	T2	Exterior Pack
C3	T3	Alarm
C4	T1	Alarm
C4	T2	Active City Break
C4	T3	Exterior Pack
C5	T1	Alarm
C5	T2	Active City Break
C5	T3	Exterior Pack

=>

Version	Engine	Color	Interior	Options
Access A/C	**1.0 VTi 68**	**C1**	T1	Alarm
Access A/C	**1.6 HDi 75**	C2	T1	**Exterior Pack**
Access A/C	1.6 HDi 75	**C4**	**T1**	**Alarm**
Access A/C	1.6 HDi 75	**C5**	**T2**	**Active City Break**
Access A/C	1.6 HDi 75	**C3**	**T3**	Alarm
Active	1.0 VTi 68	C2	T3	Active City Break
GT line	1.6 HDi 120	C1	T2	Exterior Pack
GT line	1.6 HDi 120	C3	T2	Active City Break
Allure	1.0 VTi 68	C3	T2	Exterior Pack
GT line	1.6 HDi 120	C5	T3	Exterior Pack
Access A/C	1.6 HDi 75	C3	T3	Alarm
GT line	1.6 HDi 100	C2	T2	Alarm
Active	1.0 VTi 68	C4	T1	Alarm
Allure	1.0 VTi 68	C5	T2	Active City Break
...	...	...	...	...

Figure 8.16 Excerpt of the test cases generated for the car configurator with pairwise test selection.

Exercise 16 *The five tests indicated by the bold cells in Figure 8.16 (right table) cover all pairwise combinations of one value for the version with all other data dimensions.*

Do you find the second value for which pairwise combinations exists with all other data dimensions? Which one of the values is it?

8.3.4 Textual Models

Figure 8.17 shows an example of pseudocode describing the expected behavior of bank's loan process we already encountered before. It is a textual description of

```
1  Decide_on_loan(p_Request)
2
3  If  (p_Request.amount < LOAN::RANGE_MIN)
4          assessRequest(p_Request);
5          If(p_Request.risk = RISK::LOW) then
6              ---REQ_001: Grant loan without review
7                  expectedMessage(MESSAGE::APPROVE);
8          endif
9  endif
10
11 If  (p_Request.amount >=LOAN::RANGE_MIN or p_Request.risk = RISK::HIGH)
12         reviewRequest(p_Request);
13
14         If  (REVIEW::RESULT = APPROVED) then
15             ---REQ_002: Grant loan after review
16                 expectedMessage(MESSAGE::APPROVE);
17         else
18             ---REQ_003: Reject loan after review
19                 expectedMessage(MESSAGE::REJECT);
20         endif
21 endif
22
23 end_op
24
```

Figure 8.17   MBT pseudocode example.

Figure 8.12. If the amount in the loan request is below a fixed limit, the bank will assess the request regarding its risks. If the risk is low, the requester will receive an approval message. If the amount exceeds the limit or the risk is high, the bank reviews the request. If the review result is APPROVED, the requester will receive an approval message. Otherwise, he or she receives a reject message.

On such textual (pseudocode) behavioral model, test selection criteria are inspired from white-box testing of source code:

- statement coverage
- branch coverage
- decision coverage
- condition decision coverage
- multiple condition coverage.

Statement and branch coverage are coverage criteria based on the decomposition of the code into units. Decision, condition decision, and multiple condition coverage target the coverage of arithmetic expressions in decisions.

In Table 8.4, we give some possible test selection criteria for the example in Figure 8.17.

TABLE 8.4 **Examples of Test Selection Criteria Applied on Textual Models**

Test Selection Criterion	Description	Exemplary Test Cases (Figure 8.17)
Statement coverage	Statements are the smallest indivisible unit of execution in the (pseudo)code. In our example, each line corresponds to a statement, but some languages allow constructs with several statements per line Full statement coverage is reached if each statement in the textual model is reached at least once	• amount < RANGE_MIN; risk = LOW • amount >= RANGE_MIN; result = APPROVED • amount >= RANGE_MIN; result = Not APPROVED
Branch coverage	Branches are blocks of statements following a programming construct that allows alternative paths. The best known examples for such programming constructs are IF and CASE Full branch coverage is reached if each branch is covered at least once For an IF-statement, full branch coverage requires that the generated test cases cover the THEN branch and the ELSE branch	• amount < RANGE_MIN; risk = LOW • amount < RANGE_MIN; risk = HIGH; result = APPROVED • amount >= RANGE_MIN; result = Not APPROVED
Decision coverage	Decision coverage is similar to branch coverage. The different name results from the fact that this criterion aims at covering the possible values of a decision instead of covering the different block following the decision Full decision coverage is reached if each decision is covered at least once. For an IF-statement, full decision coverage requires that the generated test cases cover the THEN and the ELSE condition	• Same as branch coverage

(continued overleaf)

TABLE 8.4 (*continued*)

Test Selection Criterion	Description	Exemplary Test Cases (Figure 8.17)
Condition decision coverage	This criterion only applies in case of multiple conditions in a decision. A condition is an atomic Boolean expression. The decision is composed of conditions connected by AND, OR, or NOT To reach 100% condition decision coverage, each elementary condition has to be tested for TRUE and FALSE	• amount < RANGE_MIN; risk = LOW • amount < RANGE_MIN; risk = HIGH; result = APPROVED • amount < RANGE_MIN; risk = HIGH; result = Not APPROVED • amount >= RANGE_MIN; result = APPROVED
Multiple condition coverage	To reach 100% multiple condition coverage, all combinations of conditions inside each decision of the model have to be tested. This criterion leads in general to test case explosion	• amount < RANGE_MIN; risk = LOW • amount < RANGE_MIN; risk = HIGH; result = APPROVED • amount < RANGE_MIN; risk = HIGH; result = Not APPROVED • amount >= RANGE_MIN; result = APPROVED • amount >= RANGE_MIN; result = Not APPROVED

Exercise 17   *Have a look at the exemplary test cases in Table 8.4. Explain why the proposed set of test cases for statement coverage does not fulfill branch coverage. Find a different set of three test cases that **does** fulfill both statement and branch coverage.*

In some cases, statement and branch coverage are identical. How can you recognize this case from the IF statements in the textual model?

8.4   PROS AND CONS OF SPECIFIC TEST SELECTION CRITERIA

We presented several examples of test selection criteria and the question now is "Which one(s) shall I take?" The answer is similar to the one in Section 5.3 on modeling languages: "It depends!" again mainly on the test objectives, but also on the domain you work in, on the tooling, on your experience, and on other aspects.

Here are some arguments in favor and against the six families presented in this book.

8.4.1   Coverage-based Test Selection Criteria

Coverage-based test selection criteria include requirements coverage, model coverage, and data-related test selection criteria. All three families of criteria have the advantage of providing a quantitative evidence for the effectiveness of your tests. Assuming your model describes the system well, 100% coverage of a specific coverage item is an objective criterion. You may discuss whether it is sufficient to work with state coverage or whether you need full path coverage, but at least, you know where you stand.

Requirements coverage is a commonly used test selection criterion. If the requirements specification is part of a contract, it helps you to prove that the contract has been fulfilled. In safety-critical domains, you do not even have the choice due to regulatory constraints. However, the major difficulty with requirements coverage has already been discussed in Section 8.1.1. Unlike with model coverage, no tool is able to check full coverage of the requirement's content. Requirements coverage always needs thorough review.

Model coverage is a formal criterion based on the model structure. Therefore, a tool may check the coverage without problems. Model coverage has the advantage of being "visible" in the model. Tools can highlight uncovered paths and show us exactly, what we are missing.

By the way, we should distinguish between the planned coverage, which is usually 100% and the actually reached coverage, which might be lower. If we decide to skip some test cases due to lack of time, we are at least able to quantify the loss in coverage. To obtain full transition pair coverage in Figure 8.14, four test cases are required (see Table 8.3) If we execute only three of them, the actual transition pair coverage is 75%.

The major difficulty with model coverage is the question "What is sufficient?" and, if we put the bar too high, it results in test case explosion. There are only few situations where full path coverage is an option.

Data coverage strongly relates to classic test design techniques, such as equivalence partitioning and boundary value analysis. As such, it is a basic element of any structured testing activity. Virtually, you cannot write good tests without it.

In model-based testing, data coverage also strongly relates to model coverage. In Section 8.1.3, we saw two alternatives for managing equivalence partitions. We may either model the data directly in the model or keep it outside, for example, in a data table or in a structural model. In the first alternative, data coverage and model coverage are the same. In the second alternative, we have to use different technical solutions, but overall, obtaining data coverage is still the same task. Therefore, we also encounter the same difficulties. Due to combinatorics, the number of generated test cases rapidly increases up to an unmanageable amount.

8.4.2 Other Test Selection Criteria

All noncoverage test case selection criteria have a disadvantage in common. They are far less universal. Instead, their application domain is restricted to specific test objectives. Random test case selection is ideal to test usage profiles and to obtain many different test cases for load testing. Scenario- or pattern-based test case selection is the best choice if you want to impose your choice to the tool. This sounds slightly negative, but during regression testing, you may know better than the tool, where the risks originate. Finally, project-driven test case selection suits well for test management decisions by definition.

All those three families of test selection criteria are important. All have positive impact on efficiency and effectiveness of the tests, but none of them provides quantitative evidence of the test's effectiveness as coverage-based test selection criteria do.

Apart from this general consideration, we should also mention some more specific disadvantages you should keep in mind, when choosing your selection criteria. Both scenario- or pattern-based and project-driven test case selection require additional maintenance effort [13]. In the first case, we have to write and update the scenarios or patterns. In the second case, we have to put the additional, project-related information in the model. The maintenance effort depends on the selected information. Priorities will not change as often as the expected duration.

Random test case selection does not generate additional maintenance effort, but if the model contains loops, it may produce long test cases, thus taking more time during execution. In addition, those long paths may be unrealistic from a business process point of view. Figure 8.18 shows the states of an article during an auction. Random test case selection will produce test cases with the vendor changing and rechanging his mind several times in a row. In practice, no auctioneer will accept a similar behavior. Stochastic test case selection is better, since it considers probabilities. However, this requires that we annotate the probabilities in the model, which may, again, lead to additional maintenance effort.

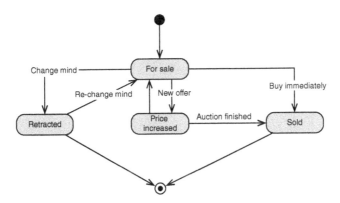

Figure 8.18 States on an article during an auction (state diagram).

8.5   SOME RECOMMENDATIONS REGARDING TEST CASE SELECTION

Rarely, one test selection criterion fits all your needs. In practice, either the set of generated test cases is insufficient to cover the given test objective or it is still too large to execute it in a realistic time. In addition, we may have several MBT models to describe different testing aspects and may apply different test selection criteria to each of them.

The ISTQB MBT syllabus distinguishes two approaches for combining criteria. The so-called "addition" corresponds to the logical OR. We unite the result of all criteria to obtain a complete test of test cases that matches our purpose best, as illustrated in the left part of Figure 8.19. The opposite case is the so-called "composition,"

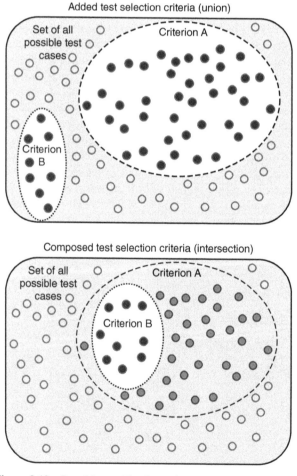

Figure 8.19   Possible combinations of test selection criteria [13].

where we superpose different criteria to narrow the test case selection (the right part in Figure 8.19). The composition corresponds to a logical AND of selection criteria.

Defining and documenting the test selection criteria is an essential task of test planning in MBT. It is good practice to combine the choice of test selection criteria with a risk-based approach to testing. You can define rules as a function of risk or priority, for example,

- path coverage for high priority and for safety-relevant requirements
- transition coverage for testing requirements with medium priority
- state coverage for testing requirements with low priority.

The test concept, as well as the reasons why we consider the chosen criteria as a good choice, has to be documented in a test plan, deviations from the plan in a test report.

Do not neglect this documentation! If you combine several selection criteria, it will be hard to remember the exact choice later. You should also document all tool-specific parameters you use for test case generation. The ultimate goal is reproducibility [13]. Thorough documentation enables you to generate the same set of test case later, under two assumptions:

- The model has not changed meanwhile.
  Changes in the model considerably influence test case selection. In Figure 8.18, it is possible to achieve 100% state coverage with one path. If we remove the "re-change mind" transition, we need at least two paths to cover all states.
- The test case generator is still the same.
  The precise test case selection strongly depends on the tool's generation algorithm. Thus, different tools will select different test cases, even if both the model and the test case selection criteria are identical.

Do not step into the trap of forcing your test case selection on the tool. Good tools will generate whatever you want, but your personal choice does not necessarily yield the best results. In Section 1.4.1, we compared tool-based test case selection to delegation. If your goal is "full transition coverage," it does not matter which paths the tool selects, as long as they meet the goal. You should spend most of your time on improving the MBT model itself, which is the master, and not on forcing the generation or selection of some particular test cases. As stated in the introduction, this requires a change in mindset [13].

With all those test selection criteria, you should be able to cut the number of generated test cases down to a manageable amount. If not, consider rewriting the model as explained in Section 8.2. At this point, we would like to recall a recommendation from Section 6.8: avoid test case explosion from the beginning. Adapt your modeling concept to the tool-specific mechanisms and anchor related rules in the modeling guidelines.

8.6   DEGREE OF AUTOMATION IN TEST GENERATION

Model-based testing is usually associated with test case generation. However, this "generation" is not necessarily tool-based, even if the use of tools is highly recommended. In a low-maturity approach to MBT, the model mainly serves to document the test idea. Tool support is limited to modeling tools. In the extreme, this may even be a pencil-and-paper solution. Test cases are derived manually from the model.

Manual test case generation is definitely better than no model at all, but without automated test case generation, most benefits regarding efficiency and effectiveness are beyond reach. The process to derive test case from the model is still as laborious and error-prone as before.

You may also have a fully automated generation. In this case, we generate the tests with "one click" and may use them as is without further postprocessing.

In practice, we usually find intermediate solutions where a tool is used, but manual steps are required in-between or at the end, for example, to combine test selection criteria.

9

EXECUTING MODEL-BASED TESTS

This chapter covers the learning objectives of syllabus Chapter 4 "MBT Test Implementation and Execution."

9.1 UNDERSTANDING THE CONCEPTS

9.1.1 How MBT Relates to Data- and Keyword-Driven Testing?

From mid-1980s, when the testing community seriously started to automate tests, there have been several approaches to test automation: capture and replay, linear scripting, and data-/keyword-driven scripting. All those approaches face a common challenge, that is, maintenance (see Ref. [43]), which they address more or less successfully:

- Capture and replay
  Capture/replay tools record user interactions with the system under test in a test script and let us replay them later. Pure capture and replay scripts are not adaptable. After each change of the interface, we have to record them again.

Model-Based Testing Essentials–Guide to the ISTQB® Certified Model-Based Tester Foundation Level,
First Edition. Anne Kramer and Bruno Legeard.
© 2016 John Wiley & Sons, Inc. Published 2016 by John Wiley & Sons, Inc.

- Linear scripting

  Nonstructured test scripts (e.g., Python[1] scripts) interact directly with the system under test. We have to change them, each time test data or test actions change. This represents considerable maintenance effort.

- Data-driven scripting

  In data-driven scripting, the scripts themselves are parameterized and the concrete test data values are recorded in a file or spreadsheet called data table. Parameterized scripts are easier to maintain, but implementation changes (e.g., in the interface) may still affect a larger number test scripts.

- Keyword-driven scripting

  In keyword-driven testing, scripts are structured programming constructs based on action words (the keywords). The use of keywords separates logical test aspects from data and implementation aspects. If the implementation of an interface changes, the test scripts with the keywords remain unchanged. We just have to modify the concrete implementation of the keyword in the adaptation layer. This approach minimizes source code redundancy and, thus, maintenance effort.

The improved maintainability of test scripts is a strong argument in favor of data- and keyword-driven test automation approaches.

Model-based testing (MBT) supports data- and keyword-driven test automation approaches and pushes the idea of separating logical aspects from data and implementation aspects further on. In an MBT approach, we no longer maintain individual test scripts, but perform changes directly in the MBT model and the test adaptation layer. Thus, maintenance of the test scripts takes place on a higher abstraction level, because the model provides a graphical and abstract representation of the test scripts. Using a test generator, the update of test scripts is an automated process. We simply regenerate the test cases whenever required and publish them again in the test automation framework.

In practice, the MBT model contains action words instead of detailed test actions (keyword-driven) and/or equivalence partitions and logical operators instead of concrete values for input data and expected results (data-driven). This brings us to the concept of abstract and concrete test cases.

9.1.2   Abstract and Concrete Test Cases in the MBT Context

According to the Advanced Level syllabus [42], abstract test cases[2] "provide guidelines for what should be tested, but allow the test analyst to vary the actual data or even the procedure that is followed when executing the test." Thus, it is not possible

---

[1] The programming language Python is quite popular in the testing community, probably because. Python test scripts are easy to read.

[2] The ISTQB glossary uses the terms "logical test case" rather than "abstract test case." Other synonyms recognized by ISTQB are "high-level test case" and "low-level test case." In this book, we stick to abstract/concrete test case, because those terms prevail in the MBT community.

to execute abstract test cases just following a test procedure specification. Instead, the tester uses his experience and knowledge of the system to interpret the high-level instructions during test execution.

Concrete test cases are more precise. Concrete test cases provide specific information and procedures needed by testers to execute the test case and to verify the results. In other words, concrete test cases *do* contain precise test actions and required test data values.

Abstract test cases have two major advantages. First, you can start writing them early, even if the requirements are not yet well defined. Once you have more information available, you can still turn them into concrete test cases. Second, they are flexible. They "may provide better coverage than concrete test cases because they will vary somewhat each time they are executed" [42]. However, they also have drawbacks. In particular, they are not reproducible. Of course, you can write the selected values down and repeat the test cases using the same values, but then you turned the abstract test case into a concrete one. Moreover, you need experienced testers to find "good" values.

Concrete test cases are completely reproducible. Any tester will perform the same actions using the same values and (most probably) obtain the same results. However, concrete tests may "require a significant amount of maintenance effort and tend to limit tester ingenuity during execution" [42].

In MBT, it is possible to derive both abstract and concrete test cases from an MBT model. To understand this, let us consider an example. Figure 9.1 shows the MBT model of a simplified consumer credit application. We encountered this application for the first time in Section 2.2.3, where we saw a decision table for it and a second time in Section 8.3.1 to illustrate test selection criteria. The application checks credit characteristics and customer eligibility to accept or reject a credit request. In this section, however, we slightly changed the bank's condition for accepting the loan request.

The two requirements referenced in Figure 9.1 are defined as follows:

- Credit_Characteristics: The credit is eligible if the credit duration ranges from 12 to 48 months and if the amount is below $5,000 and $25,000.
- Customer_Eligibility: An eligible customer should be between 21 and 77 years old, with a debt ratio less than 35%.

Even without any additional information, we are able to generate abstract test cases from the MBT model in Figure 9.1. Table 9.1 shows the nominal scenario. It corresponds to the path straight down from start to end (customer already registered, all conditions for credit acceptance fulfilled).

Abstract test cases define the test procedure as a sequence of high-level test actions for specific test conditions, but do not provide concrete data values for execution.[3] In our example, we do not have any concrete value regarding credit and customer

---

[3]Test conditions are the items you intend to verify with the test cases (in our example, the two requirements).

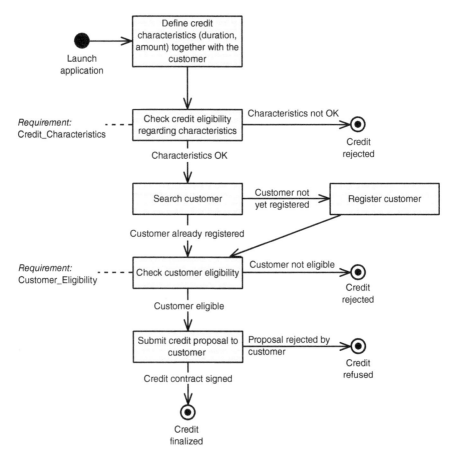

Figure 9.1   MBT model for a simplified consumer credit application (activity diagram).

characteristics and only little information on the detailed actions to perform. All we
know is that both credit and customer are eligible. Thus, the test case specifies the
equivalence partition, but the tester is free to choose any concrete value within the
ranges defined as valid in the requirements.

Table 9.2 shows a concrete test case for the same scenario (credit accepted for a
registered customer). We observe two main differences:

- The test actions for each step are more precise.
- The test steps 2, 4, and 5 contain concrete test data values.

Thus, the complete test procedure specification is more precise and test execution
becomes reproducible.

TABLE 9.1   Abstract Test Case – Consumer Credit Accepted for a Registered Customer

Step	Description	Expected Result
1	Launch application	
2	Define credit characteristics (duration, amount) together with the customer	
3	Check credit eligibility regarding characteristics	Characteristics OK
4	Search customer	Customer already registered
5	Check customer eligibility	Customer eligible
6	Submit credit proposal to customer	Credit contract signed
7	Credit finalized	

Requirement: Credit_Characteristics, Customer_Eligibility   passed □   failed □

TABLE 9.2   Concrete Test Case – Consumer Credit Accepted for a Registered Customer

Step	Description	Expected Result
1	Launch application "Consumer credit"	
2	Enter credit characteristics – case OK: Duration: 24 months Amount: $12,000	
3	Check credit eligibility regarding characteristics	Characteristics OK
4	Search customer – case eligible: First name: Paul Last name: Talinot	Customer already registered
5	Check customer eligibility – case eligible: Age: 35 Debt ratio: 28%	Customer eligible
6	Submit credit proposal to customer	Credit contract signed
7	Credit finalized	

Requirement: Credit_Characteristics, Customer_Eligibility   passed □   failed □

To generate such concrete test cases, we have to complete the MBT model and somehow add more details regarding test actions, test data, and expected result. How you add the information in the model strongly depends on the technical features of your MBT tool. You may provide external documents or store the information in the MBT model. Usually, the MBT model editor provides attributes to add descriptive text (test action), define parameters (test data), and to specify the expected outcome (expected result).

TABLE 9.3   Test Description for the Activity "Define Credit Characteristics"

Activity	Test Actions	Test Data	Expected Result
Define credit characteristics (duration, amount) together with the customer	Enter credit characteristics – case OK	Duration: 12–48 months Amount: $5,000–$25,000	Characteristics OK
	Enter credit characteristics – case KO	Duration: <12 months OR > 48 months Amount: <$5,000 OR >$25,000	Characteristics not OK

Abstract test cases with concrete data values

Even if the MBT model contains concrete data values as far as they are required to fulfill the test objectives, the generated test cases may still be "abstract" in the sense that they cannot be executed without additional data. This is a common situation in telecommunication. Assume that we want to test that the sending unit splits a longer SMS into smaller packages and that the receiving unit reconstructs the message correctly. In our MBT model, we specify the message text. Thus, the generated test cases definitely contain concrete data. Nevertheless, we need additional data to broadcast the message. These additional data are not important for the test objective, but technically required at test execution.

The example in Table 9.3 illustrates one possible implementation. For each activity in Figure 9.1, we define several test actions with test data and expected result. Table 9.3 shows two alternatives for the activity "Define credit characteristics (duration, amount) together with the customer." Please notice that we do not specify concrete values for credit duration and amount, but provide only data ranges. With appropriate tool support, the test generation algorithms may choose relevant values inside the interval or at interval boundaries and generate concrete test cases.

Other tools implement other mechanisms. In particular, it is also possible to model the two test actions in a subdiagram or to specify concrete data values instead of intervals.

The simple consumer credit example illustrates the recommended flow from abstract to concrete MBT test cases in real-life projects:

1. Write behavioral MBT models to describe business workflows; then generate abstract test cases and review them (and the MBT model) together with business analysts.

2. Refine the MBT models by adding detailed descriptions of test actions and test data to the workflow activities; then generate concrete test cases and execute them (or ask your testers to do it).

To cut a long story short, MBT models vary a lot with respect to the level of detail they contain. However, even if the MBT model embeds information for very precise and concrete test cases, it is usually possible to single out a high-level view, for example, for reviews by business analysts.

9.1.3 Different Kinds of Execution

Model-based test execution may be:

- manual or automated,
- offline or online.

Manual test execution means that a human tester executes each generated test case by interacting with the system under test, following the instructions provided by the generated test case and documenting the results. Automated test execution implies that the generated test is already an executable test script of some form. Automated test execution requires tool support, whereas manual test execution is possible without using a tool (even if the use of a test management tool is highly recommended).

If the test cases are generated first and executed afterward (either manually or automatically), we call it "offline" as opposed to "online" (or "on-the-fly") test execution. Offline MBT is not so different from classic test execution. It does not really matter, how we obtained the tests, as long as they are available and ready for execution.

Online MBT *is* different. It combines test generation and test execution into one simultaneous activity. Online MBT tools traverse the model and immediately perform the test action encountered on the path. The result of the test step may influence the remaining path taken through the model, if conditions are used.

In practice, online MBT is always employed in combination with automated test execution.

9.1.3.1 MBT for Manual Test Execution Contrary to a popular misconception that tends to relate MBT with automated test execution only, many companies use MBT in the context of manual test execution. In the 2014 MBT User survey, 57% of the respondents reported generation of manual test cases (see Figure 3.8).

The reason for the relatively high percentage of manual test execution is clear. Most expected benefits of MBT are already within reach even with manual test execution:

- MBT models help mastering the complexity of the test project and keeping the overview of what we want to test;
- The graphical representation facilitates communication between project stakeholders and helps validating requirements early in the development lifecycle;

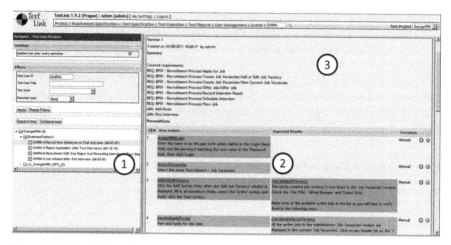

Figure 9.2   Model-based testing generated test case (in the open-source test management tool TestLink).

- Automated test generation facilitates the creation and the maintenance of your documented test repository;
- Other projects capitalize on MBT models as domain knowledge base and/or by reusing models of previous projects.

The major output of an MBT process for manual test execution is the test procedure specification, that is, the textual description of the concrete tests. MBT tools typically propose different export formats for this specification. You can either generate a standard text, work sheet, or HTML document. You may also export the tests into a test management tool.

If exported to a standard text document, the test cases look similar to Table 9.2. They are concrete enough to be executed by the testers. Usually, the generated document contains an additional column for the actual result. During test execution, the tester completes this column with the verdict (passed/failed) and other relevant information (e.g., defects or return values). In addition, the generated document usually contains a traceability matrix between requirements and generated tests and vice versa.

If a test management tool is used, the MBT test cases look similar to any other test case for manual execution written directly in this tool. Figure 9.2 shows a test case published in TestLink, an open-source test management tool.[4] The first frame shows the test case tree. The second frame shows the detailed description of the selected test case with test steps and expected results. Finally, the third frame lists the requirements covered by the test case.

---

[4]The figure originates from the case study presented in Section 11.1.

It is common to use different export formats for the same MBT model during a project. It all depends on the target and the potential user. For example, we may export the test cases in HTML for review purposes. Later, we may publish them in a test management tool to plan them in test runs, document the execution and possibly link defects. Test execution and defect management are not MBT-specific, but follow the fundamental test process defined by ISTQB.

Once published, you are no longer able to distinguish generated model-based test cases from manually designed test cases. Therefore, it is tempting to edit those tests directly in the text editor or in the test management tool. Never do this! Otherwise, you will lose most benefits of MBT. Whenever needed, we should update the MBT model and re-publish the test cases.

9.1.3.2 MBT for Automated Test Execution
Automated tests have well-known advantages over manual tests. They run faster, are less expensive to repeat, and work over night without asking for a bonus. Once written, we may execute them continuously. They are ideal for regression testing and support frequent software product releases.

Nevertheless, many automation efforts fail to provide the expected benefits [44]. One reason relates to project management. Test automation projects are small software development projects on their own. They require specific skills, methods, and attention. Another reason relates to scope. Test automation should not aim at automating all available tests. Instead, it should target the "right" tests. Running irrelevant tests more frequently will never help you to achieve your quality goals.

As Jennifer Lent nicely says, "You can't succeed at automated testing until you succeed at manual testing".[5] MBT being beneficial for manual test execution, it is also helpful for automated test execution. MBT models and test generation tools facilitate test automation more specifically:

- by structuring activities and artifacts of the test automation process
  MBT clearly separates test design from implementation of the test automation. This helps to separate the roles between the test analyst (in charge of the MBT model) and the test automation engineer (in charge of the adaptation layer) and to assign people with different skills.
- by optimizing change management in the test automation process
  Changes in the test design do not necessarily affect the test adaptation layer and vice versa. In fact, we have a single point of maintenance for the test cases (the MBT model) and a single point of maintenance for the test automation implementation (the adaptation layer).
- by focusing on the "right" tests to automate
  The MBT model provides us with a better overview. It is easier to identify critical or frequently used business scenarios. Thus, MBT helps to select test

---

[5]See   http://searchsoftwarequality.techtarget.com/opinion/Automated-testing-tools-Four-reasons-why-projects-fail – [last accessed June 2015].

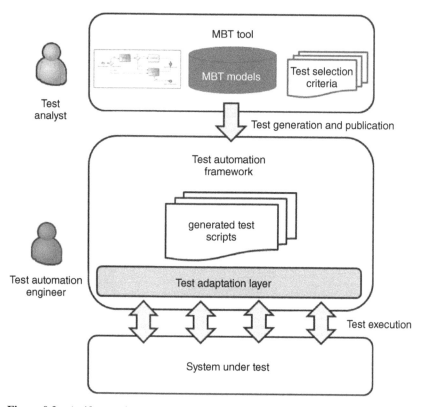

Figure 9.3   Artifacts, roles, and tool in the MBT process for automated test execution.

automation candidates (e.g., for regression testing). In addition, we have better control of requirements coverage.

Figure 9.3 shows the main artifacts, roles and tool of the MBT process for automated test execution. On one hand, we have the test analyst who writes the MBT model, applies the test selection criteria and generates the test scripts. Then, he publishes those test script in the test automation framework (see box for disambiguation between test automation framework and test management tool). The test automation engineer implements the test adaptation layer. Then, the test scripts are ready for automated execution.

Test management tool versus test automation framework

A test management tool supports all phases of the fundamental test process including test execution and reporting. Test management tools usually support manual test execution and integrate with test automation tools of the same vendor. The

> *integration of test automation tools from other vendors is often more difficult and requires customization.*
>
> *The test automation framework consists of the test automation tool, function libraries, test data, and other reusable objects. Typically, it also includes a test harness, that is, the capability to drive the automated test execution and to check and record test results (e.g., pass/fail/inconclusive). The test adaptation layer is part of the test automation framework.*
>
> *If test management and test automation tools are closely bound, we generate the test scripts from the model and publish them in the test management tool. The test management tool then calls upon the test automation tool to execute the scripts and automatically retrieves the results. If the tool integration is loose, it might be necessary to generate several artifacts in different formats: test cases for the test management tool and test scripts for the test automation framework.*

Depending on the nature of the system under test and on the targeted test level, there are three main approaches to test automation:

- At GUI level[6]

  Based on the test scripts, the test automation framework generates user interface events and observes the resulting changes in the user interface to check the expected results.
- At API (or service) level[7]

  If your system under test is accessible through a programming interface, the test automation framework may call this interface to run the test scripts.
- At code level

  Unit test frameworks perform test automation directly at code level to verify individual functions or procedures.

Those approaches do not exclude each other. For example, you may prefer to test the services of your application separately from its graphical user interface (GUI) to keep the tests more stable, but still test the GUI component itself.

The choice of the test automation framework depends on the levels mentioned earlier. For GUI test automation, you need a dedicated framework capable of managing user interface objects (menu bars, buttons, text fields, etc.). Access to those objects is highly technology-dependent. Thus, the test automation framework will depend on GUI implementation (e.g., as web application). Similar dependencies exist for API and code-level test automation, where the test automation framework depends on the programming language used to develop the system under test.

9.1.3.3 *Online MBT* Online (or "on-the-fly") MBT tools realize test generation and execution simultaneously. They traverse the MBT model step by step, generating

---

[6]GUI = graphical user interface.
[7]API = application programming interface.

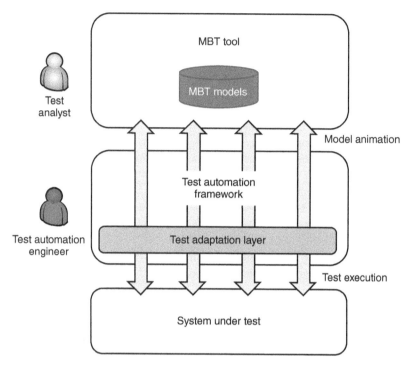

Figure 9.4   Online model-based testing.

the test step, then executing it via the test execution framework before generating the next step. If conditions are used, the execution result may influence the path taken through the model. Online MBT is fully automated.

Figure 9.4 shows a typical online MBT process. The main difference with offline MBT is the lack of test script publication. Instead, we speak of model animation (or model navigation; both terms are used). Model animation corresponds to a walk-through of the model with synchronous test execution.

Compared with offline MBT, online MBT has the advantage of being able to deal with nondeterministic dynamic behavior of the system under test. Moreover, it produces instant results (including feedback to modelers) for both test generation and execution [45]. It is possible to exercise very long tests, which allows you to dive deeply into the expected behavior of the system under test. For test generation, online MBT tools usually use a combination of random test selection criteria and some model-based coverage criteria. For example, you may choose to navigate through the model in a completely random manner and use a stop criteria based on the coverage of some model elements and/or time limit.

By applying random selection criteria, online MBT becomes a model-driven auto-mated exploratory testing technique able to test situations in the application, which are difficult to reach with scripted tests.

Reuse of offline MBT test   Online MBT execution based on
for online execution   random-like strategies

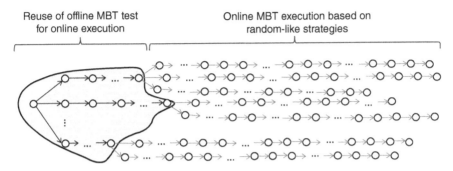

Figure 9.5   Combination of offline and online MBT.

Online and offline MBT can be complementary. Figure 9.5 illustrates the combination of both approaches. To the left, we have a set of test cases generated from an MBT model for offline execution. With an online MBT tool, we can take those test cases, execute them online, and continue their execution following a random walk strategy. Thus, we combine the advantages of both approaches. The first part of the test cases (initially generated for offline execution) may guarantee specific coverage, depending on the chosen test selection criterion (e.g., requirements coverage). The second part of the test cases randomly traverses the model, which is a form of explorative testing.

In this combined approach, both offline and online executions call upon the same test adaptation layer.

9.1.4   The Test Adaptation Layer

Depending on the degree of details in the MBT model, the generated test cases may require more or less adaptation before test execution. As discussed in Section 9.1.2, we cannot execute abstract test cases. They lack information. Somehow, we have to provide the missing information to the testers, irrespective of the type of execution.

In the case of manual test execution, we have to deliver concrete values instead of equivalence partitions of test data, but also concrete test actions and possibly some interface descriptions for product variants. For example, imagine the test of a smartphone app. It depends on the operating system of the smartphone how the tester installs and accesses the app. To qualify the manual tester for his task, we have to provide him with sufficiently detailed documentation on the interfaces.

In test automation, the test automation engineer translates the same information into the programming or scripting language of the test automation framework. There are three main approaches to bridge the gap between abstract test cases and test scripts for automated test execution (see Figure 9.6).

1. The adaptation approach corresponds to classic keyword-driven testing combined with MBT principles. The generated test cases mainly contain a list of keywords and the test adaptation layer provides their translation into executable test script code.

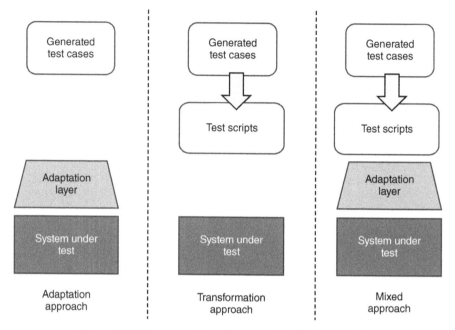

Figure 9.6   Three test adaptation approaches (from Ref. [46]).

2. In the transformation approach, we do not have the test adaptation layer. Instead, the MBT tool directly converts the generated test cases into automated test scripts, by combining the path with additional information provided in the MBT model.

3. As its name suggests, the mixed approach combines the two other approaches. The MBT tool converts the generated abstract test cases into (more) concrete test cases, but we still have an adaptation layer (e.g., to implement technology-dependent access to different variants of the system under test). The mixed approach is the most commonly used approach in practice.

9.2   ADAPTING TEST CASES FOR AUTOMATED EXECUTION

9.2.1   The Test Adaptation Layer Specification

For manual test execution, the detailed test description is usually part of the MBT model and we have some degree of freedom regarding the level of detail. Unlike an automated test framework, the manual tester has some tolerance regarding incomplete or fuzzy instructions. A human person will not stop working or "hang" because of a simple typo or an additional dialog box to confirm. This makes it easier to write the model, because it may be less precise. Still, it is important to fix the tolerance level. If the additional dialog box is completely inacceptable for usability reasons, the tester should know about that and let the test case fail.

For automated test execution, the situation is different. The generated test cases have to be extremely precise, but the details are not necessarily contained in the model. Usually, we have the test adaptation layer, which provides necessary code to execute the keywords contained in the generated test cases. If we put little details in the MBT model, the test adaptation layer becomes more complex and vice versa.

The test automation engineer (or any other qualified developer) implements the test adaptation layer based on the specification. Usually, this adaptation layer specification is part of the MBT model, for example, as textual description in an attribute of the model elements and may serve as work instruction for manual testers. Alternatively, we can also provide external documents, but keeping the information together in the model facilitates consistency between the generated abstract test cases and the implementation of the adaptation layer. If the model changes, we immediately see, whether the change affects the adaptation layer or not.

Stepwise approach to test automation

Experience shows that the development of the test adaptation layer tends to lag behind the test specification. It is possible to manage this problem with a stepwise approach to test automation. We start with an MBT model containing sufficiently details to generate concrete test cases for manual execution. In addition, we add keywords or function calls and, thus, complete the adaptation layer specification. Thus, we may execute our test cases manually until the code is available.

9.2.2 Turning Abstract Test Cases into Fully Automated Test Scripts

Figure 9.7 shows typical MBT artifacts for automated test execution. On one hand, we have the test scripts and the test adaptation layer specification. Generating the test scripts is the first step. Theoretically, it is possible to derive the test scripts manually, but tool support is highly recommended. The MBT tool simply translates the test cases into a format the test execution tool understands. Most MBT tools propose a variety of export formats for commonly used test automation tools. Typical export formats are Java, C++, Python, or proprietary scripting languages. The adaptation layer specification can be a text document or any other useful format, your MBT tool allows you to generate.

On the other hand, we have the "hand-coded" part, that is, the test adaptation layer code and possibly the mapping between abstract and concrete data. If combined with data-driven testing, the generated MBT scripts are parameterized. Thus, we have to provide the concrete data values and somehow link them to the test cases. Again, it depends on your specific MBT approach and on available tools, how test scripts and test data values are brought together technically. We have seen approaches where the MBT tool read the data from external spreadsheets and include them directly in the generated test scripts. In other approaches, the MBT model contains symbolic names for data values and the test automation framework inserts the concrete values.

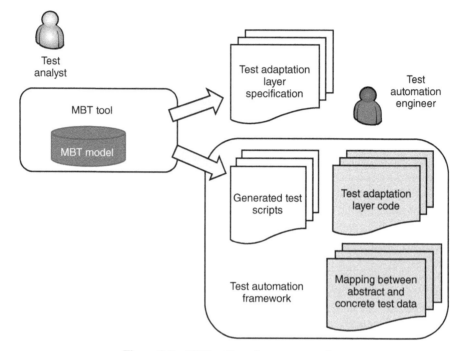

Figure 9.7   MBT artifacts for test automation.

In Table 9.4, we provide some examples to illustrate the different test adaptation activities required to adapt the generated test cases for automated test execution. For better understandability, we distinguished between keyword-driven, data-driven, and linear scripting MBT approaches. In practice, you will usually find combinations of those approaches.

In this section, we concentrated on automated test execution, but it is also possible to combine data- and keyword-driven approaches with MBT for manual test execution. In that case, we have to provide a test adaptation layer specification with all required concrete data and detailed instructions, but no adaptation layer source code.

9.2.3   Executing Several Test Scripts in a Row

If you are an experienced test automation engineer, you will know the scenario. One test case fails, leaving the system in an undefined state and you may throw away the rest of the results. To cope with this problem, each test script tries to establish a known state in the beginning and to clean up at the end (also called "setup" and "tier-down" code).

Usually, those setup and tier-down activities are concentrated in so-called pre- and postconditions. In the given scenario, postconditions are only of limited use, since the

TABLE 9.4 Test Adaptation in Different MBT Approaches

Generated test scripts	Required adaptation by test automation engineer
Keyword-driven MBT approach	
Contains sequences of keywords	Implement the keywords in the programming or scripting language of the test execution tool (each keyword corresponds to an interaction with the interface of the system at GUI or API level)
Example[8]	
GoToHome() (Specified as"Go back to main page")	public void GoToHome(final CreditApp receiverInstance) throws Exception { driver.findElement(By.name(CreditAppComponentAdapter. RETURN_BUTTON)) .click(); }
Data-driven MBT approach	
Contains parameters representing abstract data values	Map parameters on concrete data values (possibly stored in an enumeration)
Example	
AMOUNT_OK (Specified as value between $5,000 and $25,000)	public static double getAmount(AMOUNTS name) { switch (name) { case AMOUNT_INVALID: return ComponentAdapter.AmountArray[INVALID]; case AMOUNT_OK: return ComponentAdapter.AmountArray[OK]; case AMOUNT_NOK: return ComponentAdapter.AmountArray[NOK]; default: return ComponentAdapter.AmountArray[ERROR]; } }
Linear scripting MBT approach	
Function calls with concrete data values	Implement function in test automation library
Example	
enterValue(ctrlAmount, "10,000.00");	int enterValue(clsGuiElement ctrField, string strValue) { /* Get the GUI element by name*/ ... *(some code)* /* Set value */ ... *(some more code)* }

---

[8]"Click" is a predefined function provided by Selenium WebDrive to manage application GUI events.

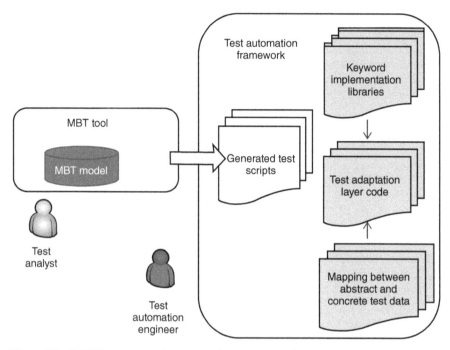

Figure 9.8   MBT for test execution automation – reuse of existing keyword implementations.

test script aborts before reaching them. Therefore, we have to pay particular attention to the preconditions.

In MBT, we no longer edit single test scripts but entire diagrams. Therefore, we have to provide the pre- and postconditions in the MBT model. How we can do this depends on the selected MBT tool. One possible solution involves tagging specific model elements or even entire test cases as pre- or postconditions. Then, the MBT test generator computes a so-called postamble for each generated tests to ensure the postcondition at the end of each test run.

9.2.4   Benefits of Model-based Test Automation

A major advantage of model-based test automation is the separation of concerns. On one hand, the test analyst writes the MBT model. On the other hand, the test automation engineer or the developer of the system under test may implement the keywords. Thus, everybody concentrates on his or her core competency. Testers design tests and programmers, who usually hate testing, write code.

If your company already applies keyword-driven testing, you may reuse existing automated keyword implementations in your test adaptation layer code (see Figure 9.8).

Globally, model-based test automation associated with good software engineering practices leads to the following benefits:

- MBT models serve for model-driven development of the underlying test libraries invoked by the scripts in the test environment.
- It is easier to keep the action words and their implementation consistent, thus making the development of the test library more efficient.
- The MBT model provides the test automation engineer with a clear and less ambiguous understanding of the action word's meaning and technical interfaces, thus reducing errors in the test library implementation.

In a way, we encounter the same test automation practices with MBT and without MBT. However, MBT helps us to structure the keywords, to separate abstract and concrete test data values and let us automatically generate test scripts from the MBT model.

9.3   ADAPTING MBT ARTIFACTS DUE TO CHANGES

9.3.1   How Changes Impact MBT Artifacts

In the beginning of this chapter, we discussed different test automation approaches and the related maintenance effort. In this section, we have a closer look at the impact of changes on MBT artifacts.

We cannot close our eyes on the necessity of changes. Late requirements should no longer be a nightmare. Instead, we should prepare ourselves (and our processes) to deal with them. "Welcome changing requirements" is one of the basic principles of agile software development.[9]

In MBT, changes may affect the MBT model, the test adaptation layer (specification and code, if existing), and/or the test selection criteria. We distinguish three main causes for changes (see Figure 9.9) with different impact:

- Functional evolution

    Functional evolution results in changing requirements, a new version of the system under test and possibly changes in its environment. In the case of behavioral tests, business rules change or process workflows evolve according to the modified requirements. Functional evolutions may affect all MBT artifacts: the MBT model, the test selection criteria, and the adaptation layer. In particular, you have to check (and probably update) all input data, expected results, and the detailed description of test actions.

- Technical evolution

    Unlike functional evolution, technical evolution does not change the functional behavior of the system under test, but may influence the detailed test

---

[9]In 2001, a group of software developers wrote the "Agile Manifesto" in which they agreed on four main values and twelve basic principles regarding agile development. The second principle reads "Welcome changing requirements, even late in development. Agile processes harness change for the customer's competitive advantage." (http://www.agilemanifesto.org).

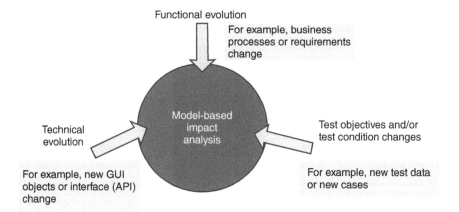

Figure 9.9   Three dimensions of changes.

actions. Examples are changing graphical objects or interface functions, as well as any change in the technical layer used to stimulate or to observe the SUT. Ideally, those changes merely influence the detailed description of the test actions and the test adaptation layer. However, technical evolutions may require MBT model updates, too. It all depends on the level of abstraction of the MBT model and the specific kind of change.

- Test objectives and/or test condition change

    If the test objectives change, our generated test cases are no longer appropriate. In the worst case, even the modeling language is no longer a good choice. You may end up writing another MBT model using a different modeling language to cover a new test objective. In addition, the change may influence the choice of test selection criteria. Changes in the test conditions, that is, the verified items or events will definitely affect the MBT model and the test adaptation layer.

For manual test execution, changes may affect the adaptation layer specification, if it exists, but we do not have any implemented test source code.

9.3.2   How MBT Tools Supports Adaptation Due to Changes?

Fortunately, many MBT tools provide features to support automated impact analysis regarding changes:

- When updating a requirement, you may easily find the model elements impacted by the change thanks to the traceability between those elements and the requirement.
- If interfaces change, you can trace this change to the test description and the test adaptation layer (specification and code). Thus, you get a clear idea what should be updated.

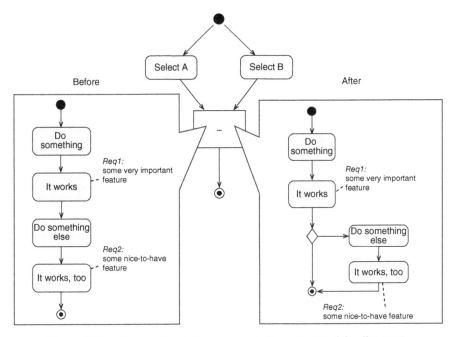

Figure 9.10   Change of a subdiagram seen in its context (activity diagrams).

- With appropriate tool support, you may simulate previously generated tests in the MBT model to verify, whether which of them are still valid and which of them require an update (new test generation).
- Most MBT modeling tools support refactoring. For example, if the name of a button changes, you may search for this name to identify the action that requires update. Once the change has been performed, it is automatically reported into all generated tests by the test case generator.

However, accepting late changes is always synonymous to taking additional risks.

9.3.3   Adapting the MBT Model in Practice

A simple change in the MBT model may have much more impact at test generation level than expected. For example, new edges in a diagram strongly influence test case generation in the case of coverage-based test selection. Figure 9.10 illustrates this effect with a very simple example. Initially, we had only one path through the diagram; suddenly we have two. Even worse, our modified diagram is only a small part of the entire model. Before the change, we had two test cases, now we have the choice between four combinations. In the worst case, we end up with two modified test cases. Figure 9.11 shows the updated test procedure specification including the change tracking of Microsoft Word.

Test case 1

#	Type	Action/expected result
1	TestStep	Select A
2	TestStep	Do something
3	VP	It works
4	~~TestStep~~	~~Do something else~~
5	~~VP~~	~~It works, too~~

(a)

Test case 2

#	Type	Action/expected result
1	TestStep	Select B
2	TestStep	Do something
3	VP	It works
4	~~TestStep~~	~~Do something else~~
5	~~VP~~	~~It works, too~~

(b)

Figure 9.11   Change bars in Microsoft Word.

The impact of changes on test case generation is not specific to the test execution phase, but at this moment, it starts to hurt. Imagine that we already executed Test Case 1. Suddenly, we changed both of them. Do we have to repeat Test Case 1? Definitely not, but how do we know? Therefore, never delete a model you generated test cases from, especially if execution results exist. Place the model under configuration management and keep it logically together with the generated artifacts. At least, you will be able to compare with older versions and understand, what happened when.

Again, tool support is helpful. Unfortunately, change tracking is the weak point of many modeling tools. In fact, it is not so easy to determine what a change is. Moving a node to improve the layout does not affect the model content. Adding an element or changing their order definitely does. What about deleting an element and adding it again, because it was wrong to delete it? For the tool, it is a completely new element. For humans, it is the undesired side effect of a missing "Undo" button.

It is easier to compare the output of the test case generators. Some tools offer change-tracking features. Otherwise, you can still compare the generate test specification or test script with a comparison tool. However, if the tool selects the test cases from the variety of possible paths, be prepared for surprises. Depending on

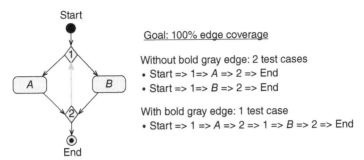

Figure 9.12 content:

Goal: 100% edge coverage

Without bold gray edge: 2 test cases
• Start => 1=> A => 2 => End
• Start => 1=> B => 2 => End

With bold gray edge: 1 test case
• Start => 1 => A => 2 => 1 => B => 2 => End

Figure 9.12   Impact of one edge (indicated by the bold gray line) on test case selection.

the algorithm, one additional edge may complete change the selection as illustrated in Figure 9.12.

Therefore, MBT models, as well as any other MBT artifacts, should be subject to controlled change management. Analyze impact and options, decide in a change management board, control the change activities, and review the results.

10

INTRODUCING MBT IN YOUR COMPANY

This chapter covers the learning objectives of syllabus Chapter 5 "Evaluating and deploying an MBT approach."

10.1 FIVE STEPS TO MBT ADOPTION

Introducing model-based testing (MBT) into an existing test process is comparable to any other organizational change project. MBT can also be compared with a new product or technology that has to be adopted by the consumers. Marketing theory on product adoption distinguishes five phases of product adoption: awareness, interest, evaluation, trial, and adoption.

To initiate organizational changes, there must be some suffering combined with the conviction that the new methodology or tool might improve the situation. Awareness of the pain points and of the improvement potential is very important. It is the main motivation for the test team to accept the idea of changing the existing process. However, it is also a common pitfall. Unrealistic expectations seriously jeopardize the success of a change project. Therefore, make up your mind about what you want to achieve with MBT. As Michel de Montaigne said: "No wind serves him who addresses his voyage to no certain port" [47]. Ask yourself: "Why do I want to use MBT?"

Model-Based Testing Essentials–Guide to the ISTQB® Certified Model-Based Tester Foundation Level,
First Edition. Anne Kramer and Bruno Legeard.
© 2016 John Wiley & Sons, Inc. Published 2016 by John Wiley & Sons, Inc.

☐ Do you want to improve your test coverage, leading to more effective testing?

☐ Do you want to spare time and/or money by using MBT?

☐ Do you struggle with the complexity of the system or of the testing task?

☐ Do you wish to improve the communication between stakeholders?

☐ Do you wish to start test design earlier to be able to provide feedback to requirements engineering?

Your expectations determine the monitoring metrics you should define to measure success.

MBT helps us in testing systems of such complexity we would never be able to manage in the "traditional" document-based approach, but new opportunities raise new expectations. If you buy a larger vehicle for your family your will end up taking more baggage on vacation. There will never be enough space in the rear trunk. The same is true for MBT. The method delivers far better and complete tests, but also more of them. The model clearly indicates what we should test. We can no longer close our eyes on test cases. Similar to the trunk, the budget for testing will always be too small.

Models definitely help starting the test design earlier. However, if you do not have any tester to work on them, testing will nevertheless be late. Last, but not least, you still need skilled and committed testers to obtain good tests, regardless of the methodology they use.

By reading this book, you reached already the second phase of a classic product adoption process, called "interest" in marketing. You try to gather more information about MBT by reading books or attending conferences. The ISTQB MBT certification scheme is a good starting point, since it presents main MBT principles and existing MBT approaches. Once you are sufficiently convinced by the idea of MBT, you should start a serious evaluation, analyzing the applicability of those principles and approaches in the context of your own testing projects. This includes process as well as tooling aspects. How does the approach fit into your process? What do you have to change? What tool support do you require? Which of the existing MBT tools provides the required capabilities and what are their limitations? Download trial versions of those tools and establish a concept, how to use it in the current or in a newly defined workflow.

The evaluation phase ends with a decision against or in favor of MBT. You now have acquired a clear idea of how much tailoring is required. Next comes the trial phase with a pilot project. The pilot project should be small to medium size and, obviously, not be the most critical project of your company. To assess the improvements obtained by introducing MBT, you have to define measurable key performance indicators (KPIs). We deal with this subject in more detail in Section 10.4. During the trial phase, you will probably also perform some fine-tuning of the process and the tailoring.

If the final assessment is positive, the last phase starts in which the MBT process is rolled out in the entire department or organization. New users will require training and time. They have to change their attitudes and habits and we should never underestimate human resistance against change.

The key question for the testing team remains: Why should we change to MBT? People usually have mixed feelings about changes in their working environment. Somehow, we all feel that being good at work is essential for our job security. Any change makes people wonder whether they will be as good as before. Testers lacking modeling experience may be scared of the unknown: the modeling language, the tool, or the task itself.

As a manager, do not underestimate these fears. We know from Maslow's hierarchy of needs [48] (see Figure 10.1) how bad doubts regarding job security are for motivation. Financial security is located quite low in Figure 10.1, indicating how fundamental it is. Only direct threads such as hunger and thirst are more destabilizing. Thus, a positive attitude and an atmosphere of security are necessary for any change project to be successful.

As a tester, do not worry too much. It should not be too difficult to learn working with the tools. Just make sure, "learnability" is one of the tool evaluation criteria. For the modeling itself, you have seen sufficient examples in this book to know there is no magic involved. Ask for training and become an ISTQB Certified Model-Based Tester.

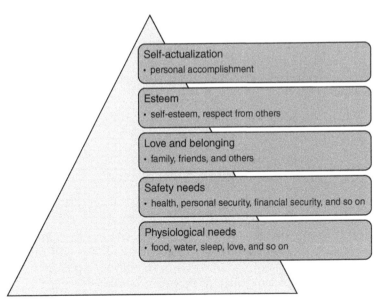

Figure 10.1 Maslow's hierarchy of needs [48].

> *Affective learning objectives*
>
> *Syllabi like the ISTQB MBT usually focus on cognitive learning objectives. Following Bloom's taxonomy of educational goals [49], they define learning objectives on different cognitive levels. However, cognitive skills are only one dimension out of three. The other two skill domains are affective and psychomotor.*
> *Bloom distinguished five affective levels:*
>
> 1. *Receiving – You just listen and (hopefully) remember, what has been said.*
> 2. *Responding – You are sufficiently interested to ask questions.*
> 3. *Valuing – You consider the information received as being important.*
> 4. *Organizing – You start thinking of your own, putting information together, and trying to organize them in your head.*
> 5. *Characterizing – You are so convinced of the idea that you start to act accordingly.*
>
> *By buying this book, you already reached level 3 on your own. Now, it is our aim to bring you to level 5. If you perform MBT trainings for your test team, keep those affective levels in mind.*
>
> *(Anne Kramer)*

10.2 RETURN-ON-INVEST CONSIDERATIONS

If you wish to start with MBT in your organization, you will need a sponsor within your company. However, before you ask for budget, you should be prepared to estimate return-on-investment (ROI), that is, the financial ratio of savings versus costs on a long-term scale:

$$\text{ROI} = \frac{\text{Savings}}{\text{Total Costs}_{\text{MBT}}} - 1$$

$$= \frac{\text{Running Costs}_{\text{trad.}} - \text{Running Costs}_{\text{MBT}} + \text{Other Savings}}{\text{Initial Costs}_{\text{MBT}} + \text{Running Costs}_{\text{MBT}}} - 1$$

Knowing ROI, you are also able to predict the break-even point when the savings counterbalance the initial and running costs ($\text{ROI} = 0$).

Enumerating the monetary costs of introducing and running an MBT process is the easier part of the ROI exercise. We discuss the cost factors of MBT in detail in Section 10.6. Determining the savings is more difficult, especially if we look at indirect benefits due to quality improvements, for example, regarding requirements specification and test design. We have to find a way to measure the positive impact of MBT on the overall development process. Otherwise, our ROI considerations are biased and we lack good arguments to convince sponsors. We present some useful metrics and KPIs in Section 10.4.

10.2.1 Savings on Running Costs

10.2.1.1 Early Fault Detection The earlier you discover a bug in your system or an inappropriate feature of your product, the cheaper it is to fix. Therefore, early testing is one out of seven principles you learn about in the ISTQB Certified Tester – Foundation Level course. MBT makes early test design possible. This is one of its most important advantages. You do not have to know about the detailed realization of, for example, the user interface to model workflows. The high-level model will uncover inconsistent or missing product requirements.

To measure this effect in financial terms: (1) track the issues you detect during the MBT modeling phase; (2) ask your experts in which phase you would have discovered the flaw in a classic test design approach; (3) use Barry Boehm's exponential cost curve with the factor of 100 between fixing a bug during the design phase and fixing a bug after delivery [50].

10.2.1.2 Automated Test Case Generation Most reports on MBT case studies state that MBT requires some initial investment for the first test iterations, but pays off rapidly during the next iterations (e.g., see Ref. [11]). In fact, using a test case generator considerably facilitates the maintenance of existing test cases. We change one single location in the MBT model and the test case generator then reports this change into all the derived test cases.

At closer look, the running costs split up into two parts[1]:

$$\text{Running Costs} = \text{Running Costs}_{\text{TC creation}} + (n-1) \cdot \text{Running Costs}_{\text{TC maintenance}}$$

Even if the effort for the initial test case creation with MBT exceeds the effort following a traditional approach, the savings in subsequent iterations prevail on a short-term scale.

During our own studies, we observed about 75% effort reduction in the maintenance phase. For long living traditional projects, the maintenance efforts easily sum up to 400% or more of the initial effort. For those projects, using a test case generator is particularly interesting.

Other case studies (including some of our own) report up to 30% savings even during the first iteration. Those savings are not related to test case implementation, but to initial test case design. While the test case generator improves the efficiency of test implementation, it is the graphical visualization of complex dependencies, which spares effort and, thus, money during test design.

Several factors that influence the percentage of savings are as follows:

1. The complexity of the system under test
    The more complex the system under test is, the more advantageous it is to use models to describe them. In the extreme, we arrive at a point where it is no longer possible to manage the complexity without models. For complex

---

[1]TC stands for "Test Case" and n is the number of iterations.

systems, the running costs for creating the first version of the test cases in an MBT approach are far less than in a document-based approach.

$$\left(\text{Running Costs}_{\text{TC creation}}\right)_{\text{MBT}} \ll \left(\text{Running Costs}_{\text{TC creation}}\right)_{\text{trad.}}$$

2. The tester's knowledge of the domain

If the tester has not yet acquired the necessary domain knowledge, he will have to ask many questions. MBT models are a perfect communication basis and allow regular crosschecks of the tester's understanding on a regular basis. The effect might be less pronounced than in the previous point, but still we expect:

$$\left(\text{Running Costs}_{\text{TC creation}}\right)_{\text{MBT}} < \left(\text{Running Costs}_{\text{TC creation}}\right)_{\text{trad.}}$$

3. The targeted degree of automated test execution

If we wish to generate automated test scripts from the MBT model, it has to be more precise than for generating of manual test instructions. Consequently, we have to spend more time in the modeling activity. This is the reason why most case studies report an increased effort during the first iteration:

$$\left(\text{Running Costs}_{\text{TC creation}}\right)_{\text{MBT}} > \left(\text{Running Costs}_{\text{TC creation}}\right)_{\text{trad.}}$$

In a fully automated approach, more iterations are required to counterbalance the increased effort for the first iterations. However, as

$$\left(\text{Running Costs}_{\text{TC maintenance}}\right)_{\text{MBT}} \ll \left(\text{Running Costs}_{\text{TC maintenance}}\right)_{\text{trad.}}$$

the point of break-even is reached soon.

Maintaining MBT models

In my first project using model-based testing, we had to test workflows using a well-known Enterprise Resource Planning (ERP) system. The customer did not really care about the test design approach. He was just concerned with the resulting test cases, which had to be in MS Excel respecting the company's template.

A few weeks before final delivery, the customer changed the template header. At that moment, we were truly glad to work with a test case generator. All we had to do was to change the definition of the export function and to regenerate all test cases. The effort for this was definitely lower than for manual rework.

However, maintaining models can become laborious, too. Model-based testing is an iterative process. We write the model, generate the test cases, adapt the model, generate again etc. etc. Consider this in your project plan! Usually, we tend to underestimate the number of iterations required to finalize the tests.

(Anne Kramer)

10.2.1.3 Test Selection In principle, the effort for test execution should not depend on the test design approach. However, MBT test selection criteria and MBT tool support enable us to choose the minimum set of test cases that fits the test objectives. As a result, the number of test cases to execute can be smaller in an MBT approach than in a traditional approach, but the effect is difficult to quantify. Especially for complex systems and without a test case generator, we will probably not even realize we are missing tests, which are important for our test goal. Still, we should not overlook the potential reduction in the number of test cases due to test management support provided by MBT.

10.2.1.4 Reuse of MBT Models The possibility of reusing existing models from other development activities (e.g., requirements elicitation or system design) is the most prominent saving argument, but it is not a good one. You will not save money due to reuse of a model from system design, but due to the possibility to reuse MBT models or parts of it from previous projects. Even within the context of one single project, the reuse of subdiagrams considerably reduces the effort for test design and implementation. Similar to a programmer, who avoids redundancies in the source code, a good MBT model author will create a subdiagram whenever the same test procedure is needed twice. If the subdiagram changes, all test cases derived from the models will be updated automatically.

To predict the savings expected from MBT model reuse, we need empirical values from the past. If you document the findings during test specification reviews, you may count the number of changes having an impact on several test cases. A defect database can also provide quantitative data on test cases failed due to unprocessed changes. Unfortunately, it is probably quite difficult to find those specific defects among the large quantity of defects due to other causes. Alternatively, you may exploit your tester's experience. In that case, use classic effort estimation techniques to increase the confidence level of the estimation.

10.2.2 Other Savings

The positive impact of MBT on test quality is tangible, but difficult to express in financial terms. You may consider it as a reduction of the risk reserve fund.

MBT models help us to keep the overview and to discuss the tests with other stakeholders. They support test case reviews and, thus, improve the consistency and the overall quality of the test design. By applying precise test selection criteria, you at least know how bad or good your test coverage is. In case of doubt, we are able to identify the high-priority tests from the MBT model and, again, reduce the risks of going completely wrong with our product.

In safety-critical domains, documenting the traceability between requirements and test cases is mandatory. Writing a traceability matrix manually is time-consuming and error-prone. If the MBT tool generates this matrix automatically, we do not only spare time, but also obtain important, up-to-date information on requirements coverage.

Last, but not least, the saved effort mentioned in the previous section sums up to improved time-to-time and let us earn money earlier.

Pragmatic versus dogmatic modeling for MBT

In any MBT approach, the model plays an important role. But, what is exactly the status of the MBT model compared to the tests you generate from the model? In other words, what is more important: the model or the test you are delivering?

You certainly know the answer. The first class citizen is the set of tests you produce, how good they are and how cheap it was to obtain them. The model is just a good support, but nothing else.

This is what I call pragmatic modeling for MBT, as opposed to dogmatic modeling. The model should never be an obstacle between you and your delivery. It should not be the "sacred cow" it can be. This is why reusing existing system design models (with their constraints) or applying strict UML modeling rules is not our first concern (and may be sometimes counter-productive).

When using MBT, keep the testing goal in mind and do not let other considerations distract you too much. Then, you will automatically apply a pragmatic MBT approach.

(Bruno Legeard)

10.3 PRIORITIZE YOUR ORGANIZATIONAL OBJECTIVES

For a moment, let us step back again and consider the organizational objectives for MBT introduction again. Was it "better tests" or "cheaper tests," "managing complexity," "improved communication," or "earlier test design"? Depending on your objectives, some aspects of MBT are more or less important. It is important to prioritize the organizational objectives to know, which characteristics of the MBT approach matters most.

10.3.1 Improved Quality

To obtain better tests, the first step involves improving the test design itself. In addition, you should reduce human errors as far as possible. Train your testers in test design techniques. Remember: MBT does not replace those techniques, but extends them (see Chapter 7). Establish traceability between model elements and requirements, because it becomes easier to verify whether the tests really cover the content of the requirements, if you can literally "see" the relationship. Moreover, tool-supported traceability analysis enables you to verify the requirements coverage. Automated test case generation helps to avoid human errors. If the model is wrong, all generated test cases will be wrong, too, but the probability to detect the error is high. If the model changes, the chance of overlooking test cases that have to be changed is very low with automated test case generation.

Regarding the characteristics of the MBT approach supporting improvement of test quality, the ISTQB MBT syllabus provides some recommendations on what is to be focused:

- Independent MBT models

    Separate models for system design and MBT activities improve the independence of the tester's activities from development activities. The MBT model will verify implicit assumptions and describe "mean" scenarios to push the system under test to its limits. We call this the "tester's mindset."

- Focused MBT models with different abstraction levels

    Different MBT models with different levels of abstraction help to keep the tests focused on the different test levels defined in the test plan. The rules for writing those MBT models have to be clear and should be defined or referenced in the test plan.

- Automated generation of test artifacts

    A high degree of process automation helps avoiding human errors. We discussed the advantages of automated test case generation earlier, but the same argument holds for test data generation, test execution, and other process activities (e.g., generating the traceability matrix).

- Well-defined test selection criteria

    The chosen test selection criteria strongly influence the test quality. Therefore, it is important to define specific criteria for each test level in the test plan.

With those recommendations in mind, you will be able to improve the test coverage and, thus, the overall quality of your tests.

10.3.2   Improved Efficiency

To reduce the overall effort of testing activities, we have to reduce the running costs of the test process. Therefore, the MBT approach should focus on the aspects discussed in Section 10.2: reuse of MBT models, early fault detection, automated test case generation and execution, and dedicated test selection.

Process automation is essential. For requirements-based testing, this also requires traceability between requirements and model elements. Otherwise, you will neither be able to apply requirements coverage test selection nor generate a traceability matrix.

The reuse of MBT diagrams requires some organization. Be prepared to write and manage many small models. From the beginning itself, think of some structure on how to organize them because, otherwise, you will soon get lost. It is useful to establish a model library to anchor the idea of reuse in the MBT process.

10.3.3   Managing Complexity

For complex systems, MBT implements the "divide and conquer" principle. Structuring your MBT model(s) hierarchically and working at the appropriate level of abstraction are the key success factors for managing complexity. Particular attention should be paid to modeling guidelines and training on the one hand and to iterative MBT model development with regular reviews on the other hand.

In an MBT approach with automated test execution, keep the test script implementation apart from the MBT model design by using a keyword-driven approach (see Chapter 9).

10.3.4   Improved Communication

To improve communication between stakeholders, using models is already the first step. However, even graphical MBT models can be difficult to understand, if the model is not on a suitable abstraction level. The model has to describe the fact the stakeholder knows about and its level of detail has to correspond to the stakeholder's mindset. Business analysts do not want to discuss detailed state diagrams with test instruction, but they feel comfortable with high-level, workflow-oriented models. However, if you target automated test execution, you may also find it helpful to have other diagrams or textual models that describe the tests rather than the system under test. One approach does not exclude the other. The MBT model may have different facets, each of them being appropriate for the given objective.

It is important to establish a common understanding of the MBT approach. Stakeholders should know about the three different subjects of an MBT model (system, environment, and test) to feel comfortable with them. The MBT models should be easy to use and stay as pragmatic as possible.

Traceability helps focusing the stakeholders on the relevant requirements. During MBT model review, all reviewers know the topic and scope of the review. Tool support for traceability also plays a role in improving communication. If a requirement changes, we are able to analyze the impact of the modification in the MBT model and in the generated test cases just by following the links. In a high-end MBT approach, it is even possible to trace back from test execution results to the model element, for which the test failed.

10.3.5   Early Test Design

Ironically, we are able to specify those tests first, which are usually executed last, that is, system and user acceptance tests. We will not be able to automate those tests unless we know about precise implementation details, but anyway, the degree of automated tests with respect to manual tests decreases with test level [51]. This makes the task easier. MBT models used to generate test cases for manual execution may be less precise.

While MBT supports early test design on a technical level, it does not help on organizational level. Since all developers are occupied with design and coding, you have to allocate at least one dedicated test analyst from the beginning. This influences the project plan, because you need more persons in parallel for your development team. Even worse, they will constantly talk to each other. The test analyst will repeatedly ask the business analyst to review the business aspects of the model. Thus, your effort in planning should include some additional time for communication. Even if this is true for all early test design approaches, it does not harm to point the issue out repeatedly. Lack of resources for early testing tasks is a common problem and it will hamper any MBT approach, if not solved.

To summarize this entire section, keep in mind that MBT is not a Swiss army knife. If you try to achieve all improvements at once, you will probably fail. The knife is good, but if you open all tools simultaneously, there is a big chance of cutting yourself. Again, introducing MBT in a company should start with a clear prioritization of the organizational objectives to achieve.

10.4 HOW TO MEASURE PROGRESS AND SUCCESS?

To know whether the introduction of MBT was successful or not, there has to be a clearly defined goal and the means to measure, whether it has been reached or not. Therefore, it is good project management practice to define so-called KPIs, which are based on metrics, which are in turn based on measures. Let us briefly clarify how we understand those terms.

A measure is a value of some quantity, which is relevant to the organization. Examples are the number of test cases, the effort required for a specific activity or the number of diagrams in an MBT model. The measure itself is neither good nor bad. It is a fact.

A metric is usually a ratio of measures. Examples are effort per month, test cases per requirement, or number of diagrams per MBT model. Any measure sampled in time is a metric. For a metric, we can define a goal and compare the metric to it. This allows us to judge the facts and to monitor trends.

KPIs are metrics of particular importance for performance management. While a company may collect many metrics, it should concentrate on few KPIs to measure performance and improvements.

Which metric is a good KPI in your context depends on your organizational objectives. In this section, we present some metrics, but the list is not exhaustive.

Once the MBT approach has been deployed, it is also important to measure the progress of the MBT activities. In this section, we therefore present metrics to measure the success of MBT introduction as well as metrics to measure progress during operation, based on the measures given in Figure 10.2.

10.4.1 Measuring Success

10.4.1.1 Metrics Based on the Number of Defects The number of defects detected per test case has never been a good metric to measure the effectiveness of testing, because it strongly depends on the maturity of the system under test. Without additional validity checks, it is not a good indicator for the success of MBT introduction. If done correctly, that is, if the modeling activities start as early as possible to have an impact on early development phases, you will find even less defects during test execution than in a traditional approach.

Nevertheless, it is possible to use metrics based on the number of defects. For example, we may compare the number of defects found in a certain time period using an MBT approach to the number of defects found during the same period in a document-based approach, if (and only if) the maturity of the system under test is

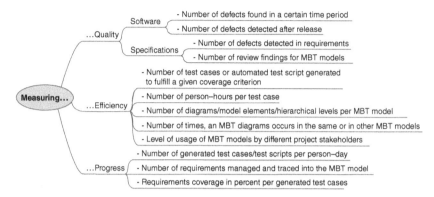

Figure 10.2   Some possible measures for metrics in the MBT context.

comparable. During an MBT evaluation phase, it is sometimes possible to monitor those figures for exactly the same system under test. If not, the system under test should pass a predefined quality goal (e.g., unit tests).

Useful metrics based on the number of defects are the number of defects detected in requirements during MBT modeling activities and the number of defects detected after release. The first one measures the effect of MBT on test quality through early test design. The second is an indicator regarding the quality of test coverage.

It is also possible to compare the number of review findings for MBT models with the number of review findings for an equivalent document-based test specification. This metric measures improvements in communication and/or better management of complexity.

10.4.1.2   Metrics Based on the Number of Test Cases   Most case studies report improvements regarding the number of person-hours or person-days per test case. They compare the figures obtained with an MBT approach (usually the pilot project) to figures from previous or parallel projects using the traditional approach. This metric measures the efficiency gain in terms of productivity [13].

The number of test cases or automated test script generated to fulfill a given coverage criterion measures the gain in efficiency for test execution. Fewer test cases take less time for execution. However, the number of test cases is only comparable if the tests are of comparable length (e.g., having comparable number of test steps). If not, we should replace the number of test cases by pages of test specification and the number of automated test scripts by lines of code.

10.4.1.3   Metrics Based on the Number of MBT Model Elements   The number of diagrams, of model elements and of hierarchical levels per MBT model measures the complexity of the MBT model. If used for the same system under test, it indicates the understandability of the MBT model itself. If used in the context of different products, but written by testers with comparable modeling experience, it measures the complexity of the system under test.

The number of times an MBT diagram occurs in the same or in other MBT models measures the reusability of modeling artifacts. This metric relates to improvements in efficiency, just as the number of person-hours spent on MBT model review compared with the number of hours spent for reviewing an equivalent document-based test specification.

It is also interesting to monitor the level of usage of MBT models by different project stakeholders. How often does the MBT model serve in discussions between testers and business analysts or developers? How many times does the MBT model appear as figure in a document such as the test plan or training slides? Unfortunately, this metric requires data that are not easily available.

10.4.2 Measuring Progress

All metrics presented up to now measure success. The ISTQB MBT syllabus proposes two more metrics based on the number of test cases: the number of generated test cases per person-day and the number of generated test scripts for automated execution per person-day (if applicable). Those metrics rather measure the progress of MBT modeling and test generation activities. However, be careful with those metrics. They can create undesired side effects (see box "Unintended side effects of KPIs").

Unintended side effects of KPIs

KPIs are an effective method to steer organizations, but they may backfire and create wrong incentives. People adapt their way of working to optimize the KPI, if their personal appraisal depends on it. This may have unintended consequences. It is easy to increase the generated number of tests per person-day just by changing the test selection criteria. However, more tests will take more time for test execution, which might be the contrary of what you wanted to achieve.

Likewise, it is easy to increase the number of defects found per test case by creating duplicates or by creating defects for minor findings, which had not been documented before. If undocumented defects are a problem, the KPI is good. Otherwise, you should keep an eye on this unintended side effect.

Other metrics to measure the progress of MBT modeling activities are the number of requirements managed and traced into the MBT model or the requirements coverage in percent per generated test cases. The second one relates to the first one, since you have to link the requirement to a model element to make it appear in the generated test cases. If the coverage percentage is still small, there is still much work left for test design.

10.5 DEPLOYING MBT

MBT never stands alone. We write test cases to check requirements, and those requirements are possibly stored in a database. We generate test cases to execute them afterward, possibly using a test automation tool for execution and a test management tool to keep track of the results. Last, but not least, we have to set up some configuration management for our MBT models.

Section 10.7 addresses the topic of tool integration in more details. In this section, we concentrate on good practices regarding deployment of an MBT process.

10.5.1 Configuration Management

In a document-based approach to testing, configuration management comprises versioning and archiving of artifacts such as the test concept, the test cases including test data values and the source code of automated test scripts. If done correctly, it is possible to trace back which test case has been executed at a given point of time with which test data and which source code.

In an MBT approach, we have additional artifacts to consider in configuration management. For example, it is important to establish a link between the generated test cases or automated test scripts and the version of our MBT model. In addition, we have to know the test selection criteria and other parameters used to generate the tests. Otherwise, we will not be able to generate the same set of tests again, later. Another important information to archive is the reason why the MBT model is written the way it is. This reason relates to the test objectives, which should be documented in the test concept. The test objectives also influence the choice of test selection criteria. Finally, the test adaptation layer (specification and code) should not be forgotten in case of automated test execution.

A good MBT process integrates those additional configuration management items in the existing configuration management process. It is a good practice to create a baseline over all the items of the development process, whenever the project reaches a milestone. In other words, we label the current revision of those items. This enables us to identify later which version was the valid one at the milestone.

If several testers work in parallel with one MBT model, configuration management can become tricky. Some modeling tools allow configuration management for parts of the model (e.g., diagrams), but who controls the common diagrams intended for reuse? There is no universal answer to this question. You just have to think about configuration management for MBT-specific artifacts *before* you start working with MBT models. Your configuration management plan has to take inputs and outputs of the MBT process into account.

10.5.2 Continuous Integration

The idea of continuous integration is to create a software build automatically each time a developer commits a piece of software (to the code repository) and to test the new build automatically. The build server is configured in a way that it automatically calls the testing tools to check the new integration. Usually, those tests are automated component and integration tests.

Continuous integration is good practice in software development. With an MBT approach, it is possible to integrate MBT tools, or at least test scripts generated from a model.

Regression tests are a good example. In most cases, we will define some specific test selection criteria for regression testing, generate the test scripts, and store them into a specific folder. The build server then knows where to find the regression test scripts and executes them as part of the continuous integration process. If the model changes, your MBT process has to ensure that the regression tests are updated as required.

One common issue in continuous integration is the execution time of some category of tests. For example, your regression test scripts may be too long to execute (say 30 min or more) on each commit. In that case, you may configure your continuous integration tool and schedule the execution of MBT tests at night, or twice a day.

10.5.3   Requirement Engineering and Backlog Management

In the previous sections, we discussed about requirement traceability. In agile development processes, the classic requirements are replaced by user stories or backlog items, that is, product features planned for the current iteration. Whatever the wording is, the idea with respect to MBT is the same. The tested features and requirements should be referenced in the MBT model to establish traceability.

Therefore, we need some kind of interface between the requirements management tool or the backlog management tool on one hand and the MBT modeling tool on the other hand. Again, configuration management plays an important role. It must be possible to identify which backlog item was tested with which test cases, and which MBT model version was used to generate test cases for which test objective [13].

Integrating MBT into an agile development process also affects the sprint planning and the definition of done. For each iteration, tasks are required for writing and updating the MBT model. At the end of the sprint, successful execution of the generated test cases will probably be part of the definition of done. In addition, it is a good idea to include some review of the MBT model in the agile process and to plan refactoring activities.

To summarize this section on MBT deployment, the integration of MBT into existing development processes should be as seamless as possible. MBT should not create additional workload to testers, but make their daily work easier. Otherwise, the approach will not be accepted, and the MBT deployment inevitably fails.

10.6   INITIAL AND RUNNING COSTS OF MBT

In this section, we present various cost factors in their order of occurrence, starting from the initial costs of evaluation and deployment to running costs of a well-established MBT process.

10.6.1   Costs for Introducing an MBT Process

Introducing MBT in an organization starts by a pilot project to evaluate both the method and the tools with respect to the benefits you expect. We deal with tool evaluation in the next section. In that way, the principles of MBT tool evaluation and introduction are the same as for any other testing tool. The Certified Tester Foundation Level syllabus provides guidance on this topic [6].

During the MBT evaluation phase, you should consider the following important topics:

- Assess the maturity of the existing test process. Identify the pain points, that is, the aspects that should be improved first. This step determines your organizational objectives.

- Specify your requirements for both the tool and the process from a user perspective. As always with user requirements, the requirements specification should not contain solutions.

- Perform a market survey (usually some Internet search) to get an overview of which MBT solutions are available on the market and which possibly target your application domain. Assess the available information against your requirements. This assessment does not have to be very detailed. Just get an overview of whether the tool covers the required use cases or not.

- Identify at least two promising candidates for closer evaluation. Contact the vendors and install the trial versions. Perform a detailed assessment of the tool's capacities against your requirements. Do not forget to assess the vendor, its support, and other nonfunctional requirements such as learnability or usability.

- Rate the evaluation candidate according to an objective scheme. This can be the degree of fulfillment of the requirements. Compute the overall rating and decide on the winner.

- Evaluate training needs and possibly even recruiting needs.

- Estimate the expected ROI. If you decide to continue, define the KPIs you wish to improve.

- Last, but not least, define the MBT process and perform a pilot for proof of concept. Measure the previously defined KPIs and assess the pilot's success.

The evaluation and introduction of MBT is very important. Its costs must not be underestimated, but it is well-invested money. The costs only partly relate to tool evaluation. The rest is spent for getting a clear idea about the direction to go and the objectives to achieve.

During deployment of the MBT process, you have to train the team, buy the tool(s), define the MBT process in detail, eliminate "growing pains" detected during the pilot, and perform the required tailoring to integrate MBT into requirement management, test management, continuous integration, configuration management, reporting, and other existing processes.

During this phase, the modeling activity starts. We have to set up the modeling guidelines and create the first version of the MBT model. This first MBT model may be simply a copy of an existing model from system design or a transformation of existing textual test cases into an MBT model.

It is also necessary to create training slides or at least some documented guidelines to qualify testers. In some cases, coaching may be required.

10.6.2 Costs for Operating an MBT Process

The costs for evaluation and deployment are initial costs, whereas the costs for operating the process are what we called "running costs" before. The ISTQB MBT syllabus provides the trainees with a complete list of initial and running costs, classified by testing activity [13] (see Table 10.1).

TABLE 10.1   Initial and Running Costs, as Specified in Ref. [13]

Activities creating initial costs for the organization

- Evaluate the approach
  - check existing resources and knowledge
  - evaluate methods and tools
- Define the MBT process that fits your need
  - define and implement methods and processes
  - integrate both MBT tool(s) and process with requirements, test, and defect management and possibly with continuous integration
  - integrate and automate the MBT reporting
  - establish configuration management for archiving MBT artifacts
- Implement the MBT process in your organization
  - create general modeling and process guidelines
  - communicate the new approach
  - train the test team members
  - perform coaching, if required
  - buy tool licenses

Activities creating initial costs for the project

- Implement the MBT process in the project
  - create project-specific modeling and process guidelines (if required)
- Getting started (required each time a new system shall be tested)
  - create the initial model and/or
  - transform existing artifacts (e.g., from textual test cases to MBT models) and/or
  - migrate existing models

Activities creating running costs for the organization

- Keep the MBT tools running
  - pay tool licenses (for some license models)
  - pay maintenance contract
- Keep the MBT process running
  - train/coach new team members

(continued overleaf)

TABLE 10.1 *(Continued)*

Activities creating running costs for the project

- Plan and control the MBT process
  - ○ plan the development/enrichment/derivation of MBT models
  - ○ continuously check MBT model quality
- Perform analysis and design
  - ○ analyze test basis with respect to MBT testability
  - ○ write MBT models
  - ○ refactor MBT models
  - ○ verify and validate MBT models
- Implement and execute model-based tests
  - ○ choose and document suitable test selection criteria
  - ○ implement test adaptation layer
  - ○ generate executable test cases
  - ○ execute and document test cases (manually or automatically)
- Evaluate exit criteria and report on MBT activities
  - ○ ensure traceability of defects
  - ○ document test completion criteria
  - ○ document evaluation of test results (MBT and non-MBT) in a common report
- Perform test closure activities
  - ○ archive MBT artifacts
  - ○ document new knowledge with respect to MBT
  - ○ possibly: hand over MBT artifacts and processes to maintenance

Some tool vendors "rent" their tools, instead of selling them. In that case, licensing contributes to the running costs rather than to the initial costs. Similarly, training and coaching of new testers may cause running costs. For better reusability of MBT models, it is important to set up some knowledge base and to archive the MBT models in a way that other testers will be able to find them again after some time. Most running costs, however, relate to specific MBT activities – that is, modeling activities, test case selection, test execution, and documentation of the results.

The activities listed in Table 10.1 do not represent extra expenses caused by the new approach. They are just a different way to reach the ultimate goal, that is, a well-tested product. In a traditional approach, we have other activities, creating other costs. If you are still in doubt about the financial advantages of MBT, refer to the ROI considerations in Section 10.2.

10.7   INTEGRATING THE TOOLS

One key aspect of preparing MBT deployment is the integration of the new tool into your existing process. Figure 10.3 shows a typical MBT tool chain. It illustrates both

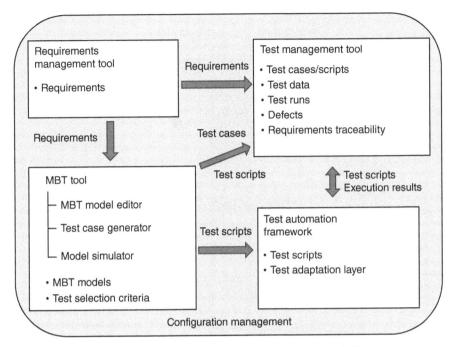

Figure 10.3   A typical tool chain embedding MBT [13].

the data flow between the various tools as well as the artifacts kept under version control.

MBT tools are much more than test generators. They are part of a larger tool chain within the application lifecycle management (ALM). The MBT tool links everything together: requirements to models, models to test cases, requirements to test cases, and possibly test cases to test scripts.

Figure 10.4 shows an overall picture of MBT in the context of ALM.

It is very important to check whether the MBT tools interface well with other tools and processes. Here are some questions you should ask during tool evaluation:

• MBT tools

Does the MBT tool provide support for iterative model development, review, and validation? Is it possible to check the syntactic and semantic quality of the MBT model, for example, using a model checker or a model simulator? Does the test case generator understand the modeling language you wish to use? Does it support the test selection criteria you intend to apply?

• Test automation framework

Does the test case generator create its output automatically in the format the test automation framework expects, or will you have to do some manual postprocessing? Is it possible to use keywords? If the tool provides support for online execution during test case generation, does it log results in a way that is appropriate for your needs?

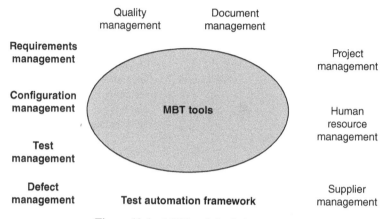

Figure 10.4 MBT tools in their context.

- Requirements management

  Is there a possibility to link requirements to model elements? If "yes," can you visualize these links to facilitate the review of the MBT model? What happens, if a requirement changes? Is there an automatism to pass on changes from the requirements management tool to the MBT tool? Does the MBT tool support automated generation of a traceability matrix?

- Configuration management

  Is there sufficient support for model configuration management? What about other information such as test selection criteria, test objectives, or the test adaptation layer? How can you archive and version them? Does the MBT tool support baselines of all those MBT artifacts within one action?

- Test Management

  If you use a test management tool, can you import the generated test cases? What happens, if the model changes? Can the tool tell you which test cases have changed and which have not? Is there a possibility to define preconditions for test cases (e.g., required test equipment) in the model? Can you obtain a list of these preconditions and of the test cases depending on them? How does the MBT tool interface with test run management and is there a possibility to mirror the test execution results back into the MBT model?

- Defect management

  If a test case fails (either because of a bug in the system or due to an error in the model), is there an easy way to identify the part of the model that is concerned? Can you reference model elements in your defect report, for example, if the MBT model turns out to be incorrect?

- Quality management

  If you have already established test design techniques in your company (e.g., decision tables), are they supported by the tool(s)?

- Document management

  Can you integrate the MBT models, the selection criteria, and generation results into your test documentation?

- Project management

  Does the tool support effort estimation or assignments of tasks? How good is the tool support regarding project-driven selection criteria?

- Human resource management

  How difficult is it to work with the tool? Which kind of training is required? Does it provide native language support?

- Supplier management

  Does the tool supplier provide support? Is it possible to attend online trainings to learn, how to work with the MBT tool?

This list is neither exhaustive nor does it always apply to your project context. If you do not have automated tests, the tool's integration capacity to existing test automation frameworks is irrelevant. The key message is that there are other topics to consider apart from license costs.

11

CASE STUDIES

In this chapter, we present three case studies to give you an impression how model-based testing (MBT) looks like in real-life projects. All three case studies are based on true projects, even if we adapted them slightly for pedagogic reasons and to preserve confidentiality.

The MBT approaches presented here differ a lot from each other. The first case study is dedicated to enterprise IT software testing. It illustrates how MBT models help communicating with stakeholders (e.g., business analysts). We show the concept of the approach without going much into detail regarding the technical realization. The second case study presents an MBT approach for tool validation in a safety critical domain. It focuses more on the modeling experience, on modeling guidelines, and on the iterative definition of test selection criteria. In the end, we generate test cases for manual test execution. The third case study illustrates an MBT approach targeting automated test execution to verify a communication interface. It shows the different activities that lead from the test basis to the generated automated test scripts including technical details how to obtain coverage.

11.1 ENTERPRISE IT MODEL-BASED TESTING – ORANGEHRM CASE STUDY

This case study is dedicated to *enterprise IT software* testing. By enterprise software we mean information systems dedicated to implement business processes and

Model-Based Testing Essentials – Guide to the ISTQB® Certified Model-Based Tester Foundation Level,
First Edition. Anne Kramer and Bruno Legeard.

business rules. Business software is found in all types of organizations and targets all industries, as well as organizations of all sizes. It includes function-specific solutions (such as accounting, customer relationship management, supply chain, human resource management) and industry-specific solutions (banking, manufacturing, retail, healthcare, etc.).

From a testing point of view, these systems have several key characteristics:

- They are generally both data-intensive and process-driven systems.
- They are generally a mix of bespoke and packaged applications.
- They may be large-scale systems with thousands of requirements and dozens of applications, connected together to implement hundreds of business processes.

MBT is well adapted to these key characteristics of enterprise software using models of business workflows and rules. The corresponding MBT models are behavioral models, possibly combined with structural models to model test data. In addition, MBT tools allow automated generation of complete tests suites for manual *and* automated test execution. Last, but not least, MBT integrates well into the quality assurance tool chain, which is usually established for such large systems.

11.1.1 System Under Test and Test Objectives

11.1.1.1 OrangeHRM In this section, we present an example of MBT for a modular application (OrangeHRM) in the domain of human resource management (HRM), which had been configured to the specific needs of our customer. Our task was to validate this configuration and the implementation of related business processes. This case study is close to a real-life project conducted for a similar system under test. It illustrates well how drawing MBT business process models supports the cooperation between test analysts and business analysts, and helps managing the complexity of the testing task.

OrangeHRM is an open source HRM software (see http://www.orangehrm.com/), which supports a large number of processes such as project timekeeping, recruitment, training, and performance appraisals. Being highly customable, it allows the implementation of specific business processes and business rules.

11.1.1.2 Test Scope Figure 11.1 shows a subset of a use case diagram for *OrangeHRM*. In reality, we covered a larger number of use cases, but for simplicity, this case study focuses only on the recruitment process. We consider three main user types who work with *OrangeHRM*:

- Administrator (short: Admin)
    The administrator is responsible for the management of all company data, in general, and for the management of new employee data, in particular.
- Interviewer (Employee Self Service, ESS)
    ESS stands for Employee Self-Service users. They are regular company employees. In the recruitment process, ESS users participate in interviews with job candidates.

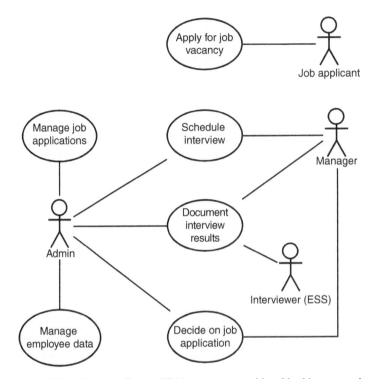

Figure 11.1　The main OrangeHRM use cases considered in this case study.

- Manager
  Managers are ESS users with subordinates (other ESS users) reporting to him/her. In the recruitment process, they are the decision makers.

The fourth user type in Figure 11.1, the Job Applicant, designates anyone with an Internet access. It is simply any person who wants to apply for a job vacancy.

Writing a use case diagram similar to the one in Figure 11.1 is the first step to manage the complexity of large systems. We do not derive test cases from those use case diagrams, but they help us defining the scope of our tests. Use cases describe how potential users interact with the system under test in order to achieve a specific goal. They correspond to the business scenarios "the system is built for," which are exactly the scenarios we wish to test.

11.1.1.3　General Test Objectives　Our main goal was to perform end-to-end tests having a well-defined degree of coverage:

- full requirements coverage (based on existing specifications);
- full coverage of main nominal business scenarios and significant alternative scenarios (based on prioritization performed by business analysts);
- coverage of data equivalence partitions.

Some test data values were predefined and already available in a test database. This included company information, a list of employees and roles, as well as project information. Other data were created especially for the generated tests – in particular, job descriptions and job applications.

11.1.2 Characteristics of the MBT Approach

Figure 11.2 shows the MBT approach used for this project.

During the entire project, the test analyst worked closely with the business analyst to develop the business process models for testing and the decision tables used for test generation (step 1) based on already existing requirements. We used the graphical and business process-oriented modeling language business process modeling notation (BPMN) to support the collaborative work between the test analyst (who is a

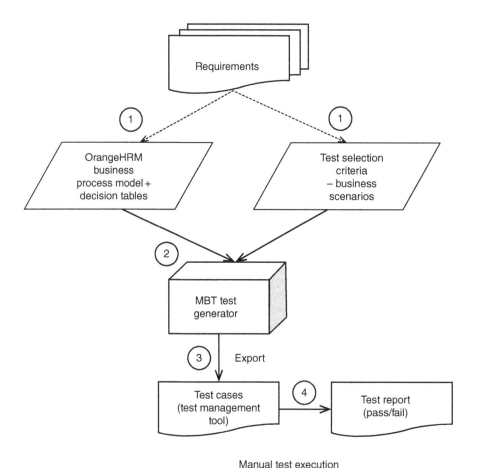

Figure 11.2   MBT process for OrangeHRM.

modeling expert) and the business analyst (who is the domain expert). They shared their understanding and discussed the implementation of the requirements based on the graphical models and, thus, agreed how to test the workflows. Decision tables complemented the graphical models. They formalize business rules and determine the cases to be tested.

The test selection criteria were based on path coverage in the business process models and coverage of the rules in the decision tables.

For test execution, the test analyst generated the test cases using a commercially available MBT tool (step 2) and exported them in a test management tool (step 3). Finally, a tester executed the test cases manually and documented the results directly in the test management tool (step 4). For test reporting, we used built-in features of the test management tool.

11.1.3   Modeling for End-to-End Testing

In this case study, we consider the entire workflow from the creation of a job description by the administrator to the creation of the new employee account.

11.1.3.1   *Requirements and Business Processes*   Figure 11.3 shows an excerpt of the requirements for the OrangeHRM *Recruitment* module. Each requirement has a unique name used for referencing the requirement (e.g., "Vacancy creation") and a short description. The entire requirement tree forms our test basis used to formalize the business workflows in our MBT model.

Figure 11.4 presents the top-level diagram of our MBT model for the *Recruitment* process.

The process starts with the creation of a new (or an update of an existing) job vacancy. A job vacancy consists of a title and a number of open positions. Each position has a name, a job description, and a contact person.

Second, a candidate applies for one of those proposed job positions. Third, the company processes the received job application (performing interviews etc.). If the candidate is accepted, the recruitment is finalized. Bold rectangles in Figure 11.4 represent subdiagrams describing the subprocesses in more detail.

▲ ▷ Requirements	
▲ ▷ Recruitement	
▲ ▷ Access Rights	
◈ REQ: Vacancy creation	Only administrator role may access to vacancy creation
◈ REQ: Candidate Interview	Only administrator and vacancy manager may schedule an interview
◈ REQ: Interview Results	Administrator, vacancy manager and interview may indicate interview results
◈ REQ: Job offering decision	Only administrator and vacancy manager can offer or reject a job after interviews
▲ ▷ Vacancies	
◈ REQ: Vacancy definition	Vacancy is defined by a job title, a name, a hiring manager and a number of open positions
◈ REQ: Apply to a Job	Anyone can access and fill the form to apply for a job. Name, email and resume must be given to validate.
▲ ▷ Interviews	
◈ REQ: Interview Scheduling	An interview has to be scheduled before offering a job, and after first application validation
▲ ▷ Hiring Completion	
◈ REQ: New user creation	For new hires, a user must be created in HR.
◈ REQ: Job Vacancy update	At the end of completion, the corresponding job vacancy must be updated

Figure 11.3   Requirements for the recruitment module (excerpt).

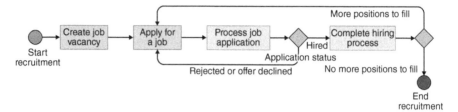

Figure 11.4   Top-level diagram of the recruitment process MBT model.

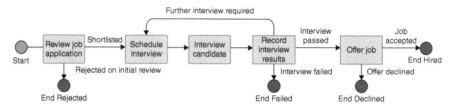

Figure 11.5   MBT model for subprocess "Process Job Application."

Figure 11.6   MBT model for subprocess "Complete Hiring Process."

Please notice that there is only one "End" event in Figure 11.4. For simplicity, we do not consider the possibility that the company cancels the job vacancy or fails to recruit anyone, here. Of course, we could have added additional exit points (as we did in the next figure), but for the tests we consider the process as completed only when all positions for a given job vacancy have been filled (the happy ending process).

Figure 11.5 shows a subdiagram of our MBT model. The subprocess "Process Job Application" starts with the reception of an application and has four possible ends. The company may reject the application before or after an interview with the candidate (*End Rejected* and *End Failed*). If the company is willing to hire the job applicant, the candidate may still decline or accept the offer (*End Declined* and *End Hired*).[1]

The subprocess "Complete Hiring Process" shown in Figure 11.6 is strictly sequential. The order of tasks such as *Access Employee Pages* and *Update Job Vacancy* is deliberate. The former verifies that the new employee is now recognized by the system, which was part of the requirements.

11.1.3.2   Test Data   During the MBT modeling activity, we had to decide whether to work with abstract or concrete data values in the MBT model. The decision depends

---

[1]Alternatively, we could have worked with one end node only and stored the outcome (Rejected, Failed, Declined, or Hired) in a variable for later use.

on the variability we want to obtain for our tests and the level of abstraction we want to keep during modeling.

We decided to work with abstract data for multiple reasons:

- Abstract data are more stable than concrete data values. They are only affected by functional modifications (such as new or modified business rules), but not by test environment characteristics.
- We can start writing the MBT model early, because we do not have to know the corresponding concrete data values in the beginning of the modeling phase.
- We can instantiate the abstract data later with multiple sets of concrete data values, allowing multiple test executions of the same test cases with several data sets.

However, using abstract data was not a dogmatic rule for us. Sometimes, it was easier to work with concrete data in the MBT model, because the mapping between abstract and concrete data was one-to-one, anyway. Moreover, there are situations in which concrete data are absolutely necessary, especially for numerical computation.

Some data are defined in the beginning and used during the whole process similar to a variable. Tasks may change their values or use them for decisions. Those data strongly influence the path through the MBT model and, thus, test generation. For example, the task "Create Job Vacancy" defines the number of open positions for the job. Later, the task "Update Job Vacancy" (subprocess "Complete Hiring Process") decreases this number by one. The test case generator has to know the number of remaining open positions order to decide, which direction to take at the last gateway of the main process ("More positions to fill" or "No more position to fill").

11.1.3.3   Decision Tables for Business Rules   The previous diagrams show the general workflow. However, for requirements verification we have to add more information on test steps and expected results. Technically, we wrote decision tables describing the business rules and associated each rule with a particular task or gateway in the process. The rules define:

- which data to use;
- what decision is made depending on the data;
- which requirements and detailed test criteria are satisfied by applying a rule;
- which actions have to be executed by the tester when effectively performing the task (either manual or automated).

If we consider the "Record Interview Results" task, we want to test the following four scenarios:

- Consider the interview as passed.
- Schedule a second interview.
- Reject the candidate given the results of the interview.
- Try to set the interview results as nonauthorized user.

TABLE 11.1 Decision Table Associated with Task "Record Interview Result"

User	accessType	Actions	Result	Requirements
ADMIN MANAGER INTERVIEWER	ACCESSIBLE	login(user) checkCandidate (candidateName, accessType) selectInterviewResults (candidateName, ACCEPT) logout()	Interview passed	Interview Results
MANAGER	ACCESSIBLE	login(user) checkCandidate (candidateName, accessType) selectNewInterview() logout()	Further interview required	Interview Results
MANAGER	ACCESSIBLE	login(user) checkCandidate (candidateName, accessType) selectInterviewResults (candidateName, REJECT) logout()	Interview failed	Interview Results
N_AUT_USER	NO_ACCESS	login(user) checkCandidate (candidateName, accessType) logout()	Task not done	Interview Results

The first bullet corresponds to the main scenario, that is, the "happy path," the second and third bullets describe alternative scenarios, and the forth bullet is an error scenario. As unauthorized user, you will not be able to execute the task. Note, that the outcome of the subprocess "Record Interview Results" determines the value of the interview "result" and, thus, the subsequent path through Figure 11.5.

Table 11.1 shows the decision table associated with the task "Record Interview Results." The different lines in the "Actions" column correspond to elementary building blocks (*login*, *checkCandidate*, *selectInterviewResult*, etc.). In our terminology, we call them "Test actions." Test actions are the lowest level of detail we consider in our business process models. In other words, they do not have any subdiagrams. Instead, their content is described in an attribute.

The parameters *user*, *candidateName*, *accessType*, and *result* are all abstract data, but there is a difference between them. The values of *accessType* and *result* depend on the business rule we select for the generated test case. If we take the first row in Table 11.1, *accessType* is set to ACCESSIBLE and *result* to ACCEPT. Behind, we have a data mapping, which assigns *accessType = True* and *result = "Interview Passed"*.

For the variable *user*, the selected business role restricts the possible values (e.g., to MANAGER), but the concrete representation depends on the configuration of *OrangeHRM*. This is very important. We did not want to define the specific user name (neither in the business process model nor in the decision tables) to avoid any dependence between the MBT model (composed of the business process model and the decision tables) and the user database of the system under test. Therefore, we kept the mapping between abstract and concrete user names in a separate table (see Table 11.2).

The selected business rule determines the column in Table 11.2, but the tester is still free to select a concrete value during test execution.

11.1.3.4 Test Actions Even if "login(user)" looks like a function call, it is just a parameterized building block. At this moment in the modeling process, we can still decide whether to generate test cases for manual or for automated test execution. It all depends on the detailed test description (actions, expected results) we put in the attribute of the building block. In our case, we associated test descriptions for manual test execution (see Table 11.3), but we could as well add pieces of scripts for test automation using the same business logic.

11.1.4 Test Generation

For end-to-end testing of the complete recruitment process, we used a feature of our test management tool, which allows us to group tests in test suites. Each test suite corresponds to a set of generated test cases. Each test case corresponds to an elementary building block. This was extremely important both for early test design and for maintenance. Having limited knowledge of the detailed steps in the beginning, we were

TABLE 11.2 Mapping Between Abstract and Concrete Data Values

N_AUT_USER	MANAGER	ADMIN	INTERVIEWER	candidateName
Bill Taway	Big boss Old boss New boss	Admin1 Admin2	Joe Carpenter	John Doe Ed Hake Marge Inn Phil. Free

TABLE 11.3 Test Description of *selectInterviewResult*

Action	Expected Result
Select candidate named {candidateName}	The candidate details are shown
Select action **Mark {result}**	A new screen with title **Mark {result}** is displayed
click button **Mark {result}**	The View Action History screen is shown with the correct performed action

still able to write the business process model. Once we had sufficient information, we just adapted the building block. Whenever the building block changed, the test suites referring to this block changed accordingly without generating additional effort.

We generated the test suites using scenario-based test selection criteria. In fact, the MBT tool takes the business process (or subprocess) together with an initial state (the initial values of the variable process data) and applies a set of test selection criteria to produce a set of test procedure specifications.

Technically, we had the choice between generating shorter test suites to test the subprocesses "Process Job Application" and "Complete Hiring" independently and generating longer test suites testing the entire recruitment process in a flow (following the complete path including the subprocesses). In this case study, we show the longer one, but keep in mind that it is only an excerpt of the entire project. For other modules, the possibility to single out independent subprocesses helped us to keep the tests manageable.

In this case study, scenario-based test selection criteria describe the relevant tasks, gateways or connectors we want to go through, and possibly specific business rules we want to test. Depending on the definition of the test selection criterion, one or multiple test cases will be generated. An example related to the "Record Interview Results" task described earlier could be (in prose) "for the Recruitment process test suite, traverse the task 'Record Interview Results' with accessType equal to ACCESSIBLE." This selection criterion explicitly excludes the error scenario and leads to the generation of five paths:

- one with result "Interview Failed,"
- one with outcome "Further Interview Required" and
- three with outcome "Interview Passed" (one for each user type ADMIN, MANAGER, and INTERVIEWER).

Depending on the targeted test intensity, we may further reduce the number of paths to three tests (Interview Failed, Further Interview Required, and Interview Passed) by adding another test selection criterion "traverse the tasks with user "MANAGER."

Once test suites and test cases have been generated, we are ready to transfer them into the final test repository. We published the generated tests in a test management tool, respecting the tool-proprietary format. As the test suite also defines the test case names and hierarchy (using a feature of our MBT tool), we automatically created the project folder hierarchy of the test repository.

Figure 11.7 shows a generated test case for *OrangeHRM* after publication in the test management tool. Some steps are still parameterized (e.g., *login as* <<<user>>>), whereas other steps contain concrete data values (*Mark Interview Passed*).

If you compare Figure 11.7 with Table 11.1, you will observe that the test action *checkCandidate* does not show up in the generated test case. It does not contain any test description for the manual tester, but some internal checks processed by the test case generator.

Details | ▪ Design Steps | ▪ Parameters | Test Configurations | Attachments | ▪ Req Coverage | Linked Defects | Dep

Step Name	Description	Expected Result
Step 1	login as <<<user>>>	Welcome screen is shown
Step 2	Select candidate named <<<candidatename>>>	The candidate details are shown
Step 3	Select action **Mark Interview Passed**	A new screen with title **Mark Interview Passed** is displayed
Step 4	click button **Mark Interview Passed**	The View Action History screen is shown with the correct performed action
Step 5	logout	Welcome screen is shown

Figure 11.7   Details of a generated test case after publication into the test management tool.

11.1.5 Test Execution

Test execution was straightforward. The manual testers documented the results directly in the test management tool. Figure 11.8 shows an executed test suite, that is, a list of generated test cases in the test management tool including their test execution status. The test suite corresponds to the path straight through the MBT model in Figure 11.4 without any loop (only one open position, first candidate hired after first interview).

The tasks "Interview Candidate" and "Offer Job" in Figure 11.5 do not appear as test case in the generated test suite. We have modeled them because they are important for process understanding, but they do not require any interaction with the system under test (OrangeHRM). Thus, they are beyond scope.

🔍 Select Tests   ▷ Run ▾   🗔 Run Test Set   ✖ ⟳ ▽▾ ⬚ 🔲 ◨ ⏵ 🔳 ✉▾ 🗔

Details | **Execution Grid** | Execution Flow | Automation | Attachments | Linked Defects | History

Name	Test: Test...	Type	Status	Iterat
[1]Create Job Vacancy - 1 position	Create Jo...	MANUAL	Passed	
[1]Apply for a Job - Success	Apply for a...	MANUAL	Passed	
[1]Review Job Application - Success	Review Jo...	MANUAL	Passed	
[1]Schedule Interview	Schedule I...	MANUAL	Passed	
[1]Record Interview Results - Interview P...	Record Int...	MANUAL	Passed	
[1]Offer Job - Accepted	Offer Job -...	MANUAL	Passed	
[1]Hire Candidate	Hire Candi...	MANUAL	Passed	
[1]Complete Employee Details	Complete...	MANUAL	Not Compl...	
[1]Create User	Create User	MANUAL	No Run	
[1]Access Employee Pages	Access E...	MANUAL	No Run	
[1]Update Job Vacancy	Update Jo...	MANUAL	No Run	

Figure 11.8   Set of executed tests for OrangeHRM as displayed in the test management tool.

11.1.6   Discussion and Conclusion for OrangeHRM Case Study

In total, we wrote more than 35 business process models and 55 decision tables as MBT model for *OrangeHRM* application. More than 480 test cases have been generated and are maintained using the MBT process. The MBT model seriously helped us to keep the overview and to see the dependencies between tests.

The most important benefit of using models in this project was the strong commitment of the business analyst in the test project. They seriously contributed to the development of the business process models and the related decision tables. The graphical representation of the processes and the structured decision tables strongly helped us to get into details. At the end of the day, the MBT approach strengthened the generated tests and ensured the alignment between test repository and business needs.

11.2   MBT FOR PROCESS-SUPPORTING SW – TOOL VALIDATION CASE STUDY

In this case study, we focus on model-based system validation. More precisely, we see an example of model-based tool validation. Tool validation is a hot topic in all safety critical domains. The international standard on "Functional safety of electrical/electronic/programmable electronic safety-related systems," IEC 61508 requires in part 3, Section 7.4.4.6 for each tool that directly or indirectly influences the executable code of our system under test, that "evidence shall be available that the tool conforms to its specification or documentation" [52].

Obviously, a compiler directly influences the executable code of our product. The influence of testing tools is more indirect. Still, we pretty much rely on process-supporting software. The "bible" for software development in the avionics domains, RTCA/DO 178C puts it more clearly: "Qualification of a tool is needed when processes (...) are (...) automated by the use of a software tool without its output being verified (...)" [53]. Thus, whenever we are no longer able to check the results manually, tool validation (or "tool qualification," as it is also called) is required. The aim is to ensure that a malfunctioning in process-supporting software will not affect the quality of the product we try to develop.

The MBT approach presented in this section is very pragmatic. The aim was not to obtain test cases for automated test execution, but to understand and document the process, in general, and the role process-supporting software plays, in particular. Our generated test cases are concrete. Instead of using decision tables, we described all test steps and verification activities in our MBT model.

In this case study, we do not explain technical details, but try to illustrate how the different activities presented in previous chapters look like during daily work.

11.2.1   System Under Test and Test Objectives

11.2.1.1   HP ALM Defect Tracking Alias "BuxExterminator" This case study is based on a series of projects in the medical domain, during which we validated test management and defect tracking features of Hewlett-Packard Application

Lifecycle Management (HP ALM), an application lifecycle management tool sold by Hewlett-Packard. However, it is difficult to present MBT of a test management tool without confusing everybody. You never know whether "test cases" mean the tests you write or the test cases you manipulate during test execution. Therefore, we restrict the case study to the defect-tracking module of HP ALM. To make it even easier, we do not talk about the "HP ALM defect-tracking module," but call our tool the "BugExterminator" (short: BugEx). Anyway, the models in this case study are not one-to-one the original MBT models from the real project(s), but they are quite close to the truth and apt to convey the idea of MBT used for tool validation.

Admittedly, the influence of a bug tracker on product quality is rather low, but the example is universal. We all have process-supporting software and we have no idea how it was developed. Unlike for our own products, we usually do not have well-defined requirements for process-supporting software. Still, in safety-critical domains, we are obliged to prove that the system is apt for usage and that it does not have any negative influence on the quality of our product.

11.2.1.2   Test Scope   Unlike in the previous case study, we did not have any specification to validate the BugEx application against. Instead, determining the test scope was the first step of our activities. We had to document the intended use of BugEx. What are the business scenarios relevant for validation, or, speaking UML, what are the use cases? Thus, Figure 11.9 was the first diagram we drew.

When we showed the picture to the stakeholders, discussions started. In fact, Figure 11.9 is far from being complete. What happens before the first defect is created in the system? Does the Change Control Board never change its opinion? How does the tool know who is the Quality Manager?

Back in the office, we added the use cases "Modify defect," "Maintain SW," and "Manage users/user groups." For the last two use cases, we also needed an additional actor, that is, the "Administrator." In an even more precise version, we finally split "Maintain SW" and "Manage users/user groups" into several use cases, corresponding to the bullets in the attached notes. Figure 11.10 shows the result. It describes the scope of our validation activities. Therefore, we included those figures in our validation test plan.

Figure 11.10 illustrates two important facts. First, the use case bubbles alone are insufficient to document the intended use. It is always helpful to add additional text. In the example, this text is included in the figure as comments. On one hand, this has the advantage of keeping the entire information together. On the other hand, you rapidly run into layout problems. In addition, you spend quite a lot of time correcting typos and other minor errors in the diagram, because of the large amount of text it contains.

Second, a use case diagram cannot provide more than an overview. We still do not know exactly what defect attributes are used or how the defect solving process looks like. For this, we need diagrams with more details about the behavior of the system.

11.2.1.3   General Test Objectives   Our major test goal was to validate the defect life cycle. Therefore, we decided to model the different states a defect takes from NEW to CLOSED. In addition, we had to test the access restrictions implemented

The *BugExterminator* use cases

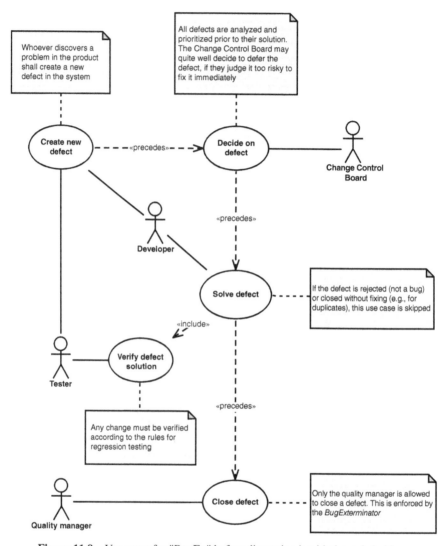

Figure 11.9   Use cases for "BugEx" before discussing it with the stakeholders.

for different user groups. Those access restrictions resulted from a criticality analysis of the tool, which we performed in parallel to the use case analysis.

Regulatory compliance is not the only motivation for performing a tool validation. The second reason is self-protection. You want to be sure that you can rely on your tools. Still, tool validation does not directly add value to a company's product. There-fore, it shall be as efficient, but also as effective as possible. MBT is the ideal way out of this dilemma. Using a test case generator and appropriate test selection criteria, you can obtain a well-defined degree of coverage with a minimum of tests.

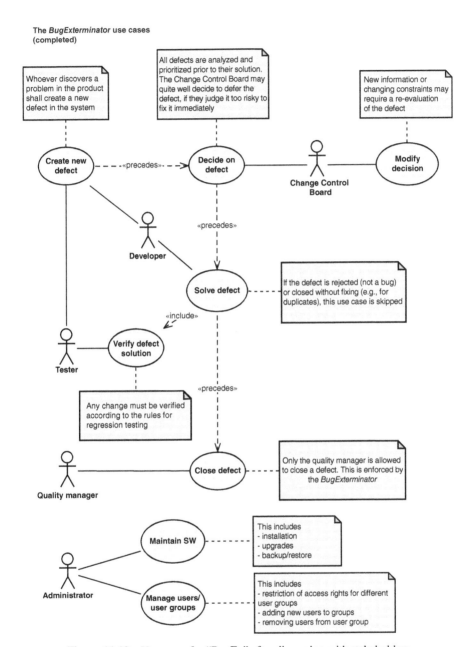

Figure 11.10 Use cases for "BugEx" after discussion with stakeholders.

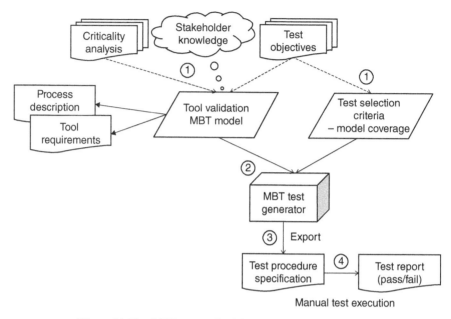

Figure 11.11   MBT approach of the tool validation case study.

11.2.2   Characteristics of the MBT Approach

Figure 11.11 shows the MBT approach presented in this case study. Having no formalized requirements specification to test against, the only input for the MBT model were the requirements derived from a previously performed criticality analysis, the test objectives, and all information obtained during stakeholder interviews. The test objectives also determined the test selection criteria (step 1). Several iterations were necessary to obtain all required information. The two use case diagrams in Section 11.2.1.2 illustrate well how the MBT model helped to pin down the implicit process requirements.

Whenever a diagram was formally correct and sufficiently stable, we generated some test cases (step 2). Technically, we export the MBT model as XMI from the modeling tool and import it into *MBTsuite*, the test case generator of sepp.med GmbH.[2] During the first iterations, we neither formally reviewed nor executed the tests. We just checked the correctness of the MBT model and of the generated output. In addition, we discussed the test selection criteria and refined them in some cases.

To be able to read the generated test cases, we exported them either in an MS Word document or in a test management tool (step 3). While we discussed the MBT model with the stakeholders, we finally reviewed the generated test cases. Last, but not least, we executed the tests manually and reported the results either in MS Word (for one project) or in the test management tool (for the other project).

[2]www.mbtsuite.com.

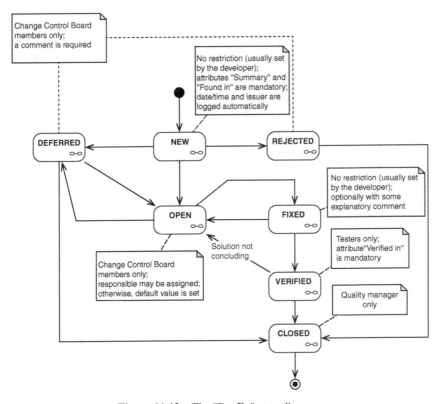

Figure 11.12   The "BugEx" state diagram.

Figure 11.12 shows the topmost level of the MBT model we used for test case generation. It describes the defect states and possible transitions between those states. Each note summarizes briefly the aspects to test for the corresponding state.

If you are an unconditional supporter of UML, please take a deep breath before looking at the figure! Technically, it is an activity diagram drawn using Sparx System Enterprise Architect. Logically, it is a state diagram with a note attached to each state. The reason for this apparent mixture is pragmatic. "OPEN" is shorter than "Set defect to state OPEN," which improves the readability of the diagram and facilitates the layout. Anyway, we do not need the specific model elements of state diagrams for our test objectives, but we want to describe the test procedure on lower hierarchical levels. This explains why we chose to write activity diagrams.

11.2.3   Documenting the Requirements

As stated before, we did not have any documented requirements for BugEx, but it was not difficult to derive them from Figure 11.12. Here they are … (By the way: CCB stands for "Change Control Board.")

- REQ_ID 101: defect states

  BugEx shall provide a state machine for defect that reflects the defect life cycle. The following states and transitions shall be available: NEW, REJECTED, OPEN, DEFERRED, FIXED, VERIFIED, and CLOSED. Transitions shall be possible as described in Figure 11.12.

- REQ_ID 102: restricted state transitions depending on role

  BugEx shall provide the possibility of restricting state transitions in a way that only members of a specific user group may set the state. In particular, the following transitions shall be restricted:

  - NEW => REJECTED, OPEN, or DEFERRED: only users in group CCB_MEMBER;

  - FIXED => VERIFIED: only users in group TESTER;

  - DEFERRED, VERIFIED, or REJECTED => CLOSED: only users in group QUALITY_MGR.

- REQ_ID 103: tool-supported process checks

  BugEx shall enforce the process through implemented checks including:

  - mandatory attributes "Summary" and "Found in" at defect creation;

  - mandatory comments for state DEFERRED and REJECTED;

  - mandatory attribute "Verified in" for state VERIFIED.

- REQ_ID 104: assignment of responsible

  BugEx shall provide the possibility of assigning a defect responsible. If this is not done when setting the defect state to OPEN, a previously configured default responsible shall be set.

- REQ_ID 105: automatic logging at creation

  BugEx shall automatically log the defect creation date and time, as well as the defect issuer at defect creation.

- REQ_ID 106: text fields for further explanations

  BugEx shall provide the possibility of entering additional text for further information, in particular about defect fixing.

Till now, we did nothing else than model-based requirement engineering. If you already have a requirements specification as basis for product development written in natural language, it is a good idea to start the MBT modeling activity by translating this specification into a model.

11.2.4   MBT Modeling for Tool Validation

11.2.4.1   Modeling the Test Procedure Specification   The next step was to model the detailed test procedure specification. We described the actions and checks a tester has to perform manually for each state in Figure 11.12.

Technically, we did this in subdiagrams,[3] following some particular rules we defined in our project-specific modeling guidelines (see Section 11.2.4.3).

---

[3]In this section, subdiagrams are indicated by the infinity sign instead of rectangular boxes.

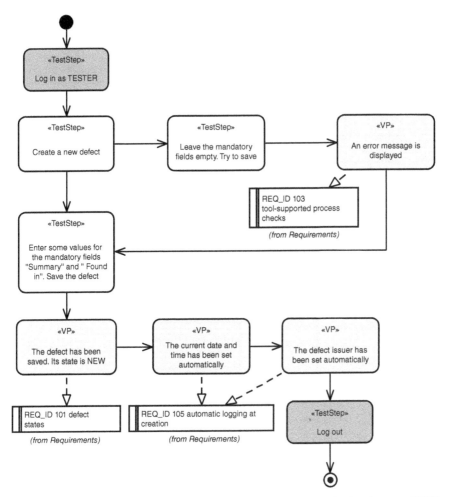

Figure 11.13 Actions (TestStep) and checks (verification point, VP) for the state NEW (activity diagram).

Figure 11.13 shows the subdiagram for the state NEW, Figure 11.14 for the state OPEN. For better readability, we distinguish between test steps (in white) and verifications points (VP, in light gray). Verification points (VPs) describe the expected result. They check the requirements indicated by the dashed arrows. To test the role-based restrictions, we have to log in with different roles. The test steps for login and logout are highlighted in dark gray. The color scheme is a completely arbitrary decision, which is a good one, as long as it fosters understanding and a bad one, if it confuses the model reader. For us it was a good one, because those test steps required a second tester.

Figure 11.14 contains very important information on the level of detail we wish to limit the test to. In principle, we could test the role-based restriction for all user

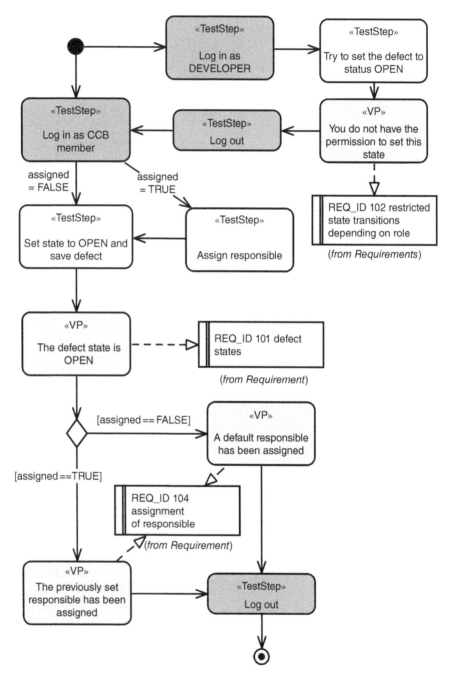

Figure 11.14   Actions (TestStep) and checks (verification point, VP) for the state OPEN.

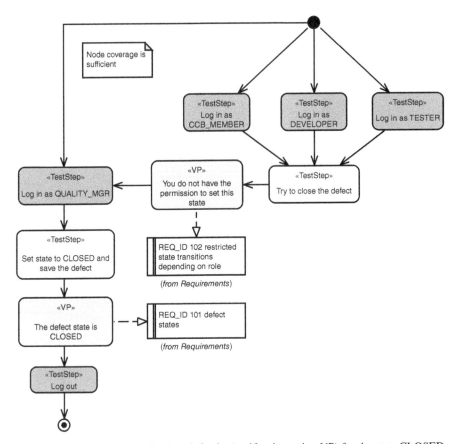

Figure 11.15 Actions (TestStep) and checks (verification point, VP) for the state CLOSED.

groups. However, during test design we decided that it is sufficient to check the restricted state transition with a user from the DEVELOPER group only. This is reasonable because we have many developers, but only a few testers and just one quality manager. In addition, developers are probably most tempted by the idea of rapidly fixing a bug.

For defect closing we may decide differently and check the role-based restriction for all user groups (see Figure 11.15), mainly because there is no further process check after defect closing. In other words, nobody would realize if an unauthorized person closes the defect. This example illustrates how the tester's mindset reflects itself in the model.

11.2.4.2 Check and Discuss It is high time to check the model. For example, we forgot to set the variable "attrib_set" to TRUE (indicated by the speech bubble) in Figure 11.16. As a result, our test case generator runs into an infinite loop.

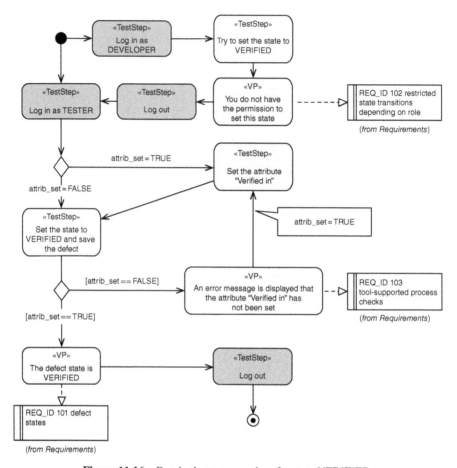

Figure 11.16   Bug in the test procedure for state VERIFIED.

In addition, you may have inconsistent diagrams (e.g., missing arrows), which can be easily detected by the test case generator.

However, the formal correctness is only one quality aspect of a model. Checking the model content early is even more important.

Figure 11.17 shows the test procedure for the state FIXED. When elaborating this diagram, we started wondering about the missing attribute "Fixed in." BugEx forces the user to enter "Found in" (Figure 11.13) and "Verified in" (Figure 11.16), but does not even display a warning if "Fixed in" is missing. During discussions with the users, the quality manager, and the tool administrator, we finally discovered another mandatory attribute missing in our MBT model (the defect priority) and a hidden feature (the automatic logging of the tester's name).

11.2.4.3   Modeling Guidelines   As stated in Section 6.4, modeling guidelines are essential for MBT projects. To be honest, we should have presented them in the

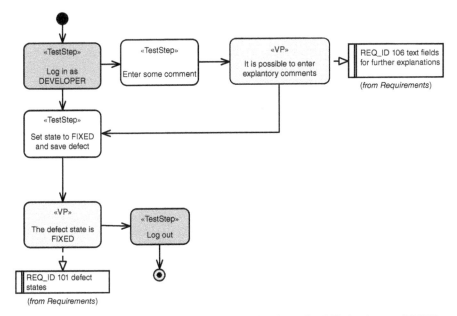

Figure 11.17   Actions (TestStep) and checks (verification point, VP) for the state FIXED.

beginning of this case study. Here they are, followed by some explanations on how they show up in the defect tracking system example of this section:

- On the highest level, we have a use case diagram, describing the business scenarios. If this diagram exists already for requirements elicitation or system design, it may be reused.

  Not having any system design documentation at all, we modeled the use case for *BugEx* in Figure 11.10.

- It is recommended to follow the structure suggested by the use cases for work-flow modeling.

  For *BugEx*, we disrespected this rule, because it was more convenient to base test design on bug states (Figure 11.12).

- The structure of the MBT model shall be hierarchical with the test procedure specification located on the lowest level(s).

  In our example, we have an activity diagram per defect state.

- We distinguish test steps and verification points. Test steps describe actions to perform to trigger the system under test. Verification points describe the expected reaction of the system the tester shall verify. Technically, both elements are actions of a UML activity diagram.

  The *BugEx* activity diagrams contain test steps (TestStep) and verification points (VPs).

- It is mandatory to link a verification point to the requirement it checks. Test steps shall never reference a requirement.

All activity diagrams for *BugEx* respect this rule.

- Test steps related to login and logout require special preparation by the tool administrator. Therefore, they are highlighted in the MBT model in dark gray. Verification points are colored in light gray.

  All activity diagrams for *BugEx* respect this rule.

- Variables are set in the attribute "Name" of an edge; logical expressions defined in the attribute "Guard." It is not possible to set variables or interpret logical expressions in nodes.

  In Figure 11.14, we use the variable "assigned," which is set ("=") first and interpreted ("==") afterward.

- Any annotation of the diagrams that improves understanding is welcome. In particular, it is mandatory to comment the diagram, if specific test case selection criteria apply.

  The defect state diagram in Figure 11.12 is rather well commented. For the activity diagrams, we could have done better. At least, we find information on the selection criterion in Figure 11.15.

11.2.5   Test Generation

We designed the BugEx MBT model to generate test cases including test scripts for manual execution. Without a test case generator, we would probably start discussing which of the following test cases is important and which may be left out:

- "standard workflow": NEW => OPEN => FIXED => VERIFIED => CLOSED
- "not a bug": NEW => REJECTED => CLOSED
- "minor bug never fixed": NEW => DEFERRED => CLOSED
- "long-running issue": NEW => OPEN => DEFERRED => OPEN => FIXED => OPEN => FIXED => VERIFIED => OPEN => FIXED => VERIFIED => CLOSED
- "checked-in too early": NEW => OPEN => FIXED => OPEN => FIXED => VERIFIED => CLOSED
- "badly implemented solution": NEW => OPEN => FIXED => VERIFIED => OPEN => FIXED => VERIFIED => CLOSED.

With a test case generator, we do not discuss generated test cases, but test selection criteria. Our three main test objectives are as follows:

1. Validate the defect life cycle.
2. Validate the access right restrictions in BugEx.
3. Provide objective evidence that the tool works as intended (with least effort).

Based on the first objective, we decided to test each transition in the defect state diagram at least once. This corresponds to the model coverage criterion called "edge coverage" in Section 8.1.2.

However, this does not necessarily imply that we have to apply edge coverage to all subdiagrams. In the state REJECTED, do we really have to check the direct login as CCB_MEMBER without passing via the test of the role-based restriction? The pragmatic answer is "No, we don't." It should be sufficient to prove everything works fine once logged in as CCB_MEMBER. The same argument holds for the direct login as QUALITY_MGR in the CLOSED subdiagram. Thus, we reduce our selection criterion for these two subdiagrams to "node coverage" and skip the large angular edge in Figure 11.15.

For better understandability of this case study, we annotated this decision directly in the diagram. In reality, we wrote a section on test case generation setting in our validation test plan.

11.2.6   Test Execution

The next step was straightforward. We exported the generated test cases to MS Word, executed them, and documented the results in a validation test report. Table 11.4 shows an example of a generated test case.

11.2.7   Discussion and Conclusion

The defect management workflow was only one out of eight workflows we validated during our project. Altogether, it took us 6 weeks with one person to analyze and document the existing process, to perform the criticality analysis, and to document the derived requirements. The major difficulty encountered was the fact that parts of the process were still undefined in the beginning and some of them changed during the analysis phase. Therefore, those six weeks included a large portion of process consulting. In product development, we call this activity "early requirements validation."

The modeling activity was performed within 8 days. Deriving the test cases took another 2 weeks, all reviews, corrections, and a change of document templates included. We generated 73 test cases documented on approximately 150 pages using our test case generator. Finally, test execution was performed in 4 days.

The module called BugEx in this case study represented less than 15% of the requirements, but one-third of the generated test cases. This was due to its complexity, the large number of possible transitions, and the different access rights we had to test. It was definitely the part of the system, where MBT helped most.

Some weeks later, our customer successfully passed an audit showing the tool validation documentation.

Exercise 18   Do you feel ready to model the test of the state DEFERRED? Please try, following the examples given in this section. Cover the requirements REQ_ID 101, 102, and 103 defined in Section 11.2.3.

TABLE 11.4   Test Procedure Specification for Test Case "Not a Bug"

#	Type	Action/Expected Result	Actual Result	
1	TestStep	Log in as TESTER	passed □	failed □
2	TestStep	Create a new defect	passed □	failed □
3	TestStep	Leave the mandatory fields empty. Try to save	passed □	failed □
4	VP	An error message is displayed	passed □	failed □
5	TestStep	Enter some values for the mandatory fields "Summary" and "Found in." Save the defect	passed □	failed □
6	VP	The defect has been saved. Its state is NEW	passed □	failed □
7	VP	The current date and time has been set automatically	passed □	failed □
8	VP	The defect issuer has been set automatically	passed □	failed □
9	TestStep	Log out	passed □	failed □
10	TestStep	Log in as TESTER	passed □	failed □
11	TestStep	Try to reject the defect	passed □	failed □
12	VP	You do not have the permission to reject the defect	passed □	failed □
13	TestStep	Log out	passed □	failed □
14	TestStep	Log in as CCB_MEMBER	passed □	failed □
15	TestStep	Set the defect to REJECTED without entering a comment	passed □	failed □
16	VP	It is not possible to reject a defect without comment	passed □	failed □
17	TestStep	Enter a comment, set the state to REJECTED and save the defect	passed □	failed □
18	VP	The defect state is REJECTED	passed □	failed □
19	TestStep	Log out	passed □	failed □
20	TestStep	Log in as CCB_MEMBER	passed □	failed □
21	TestStep	Try to close the defect	passed □	failed □
22	VP	You do not have the permission to set this state	passed □	failed □
23	TestStep	Log out	passed □	failed □
24	TestStep	Log in as QUALITY_MGR	passed □	failed □
25	TestStep	Set state to CLOSED and save the defect	passed □	failed □
26	VP	The defect state is CLOSED	passed □	failed □
27	TestStep	Log out	passed □	failed □

11.3   MBT FOR SECURITY COMPONENTS – PKCS#11 CASE STUDY

Security components, such as Hardware Security Modules (HSM), store cryptographic keys, and perform cryptographic operations, for example, signing data
(messages, authentication information, documents, etc.). To ensure safe and secure

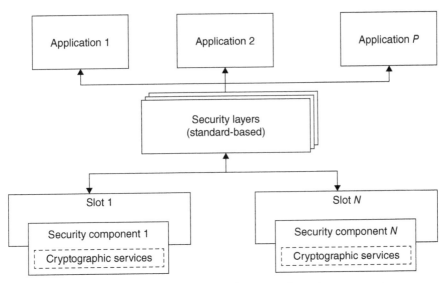

Figure 11.18 General high-level environment of security components.

communication their interfaces undergo well-defined standards. Examples of such standards are PKCS#11[4] [54] and FORTEZZA [55].

Figure 11.18 illustrates on a high level the relationship between the security component offering cryptographic services on one hand, and third-party applications on the other hand. Access to the security components is possible through an API defined by the chosen standard. In addition, other security layers might regulate the communication between the API and the third party applications.

Although it is often assumed that the cryptographic algorithms are correctly implemented since they are used by or are part of services provided by the component, misuse of the cryptographic algorithms in the API and noncompliance to the standard may lead to a number of vulnerability issues. To ensure security, the cryptographic components should be thoroughly tested to assess their compliance to the standards.

In this section, we give an overview of an MBT approach applied in the context of MBT of security components. More specifically, we performed testing security functions of a specific implementation (called SoftHSM[5]) of the PKCS#11 standard.

Bearing in mind the security-critical nature of the components, our approach had two targets. On one hand, we wanted to ensure the API's compliance to the specification. On the other hand, we searched to uncover potentially dangerous behavior resulting from the interactions of the API with the cryptographic component.

11.3.1 System Under Test and Test Objectives

Typical security components are, among others, HSM, smartcards, and USB. They are used by various security applications to verify and, thus, prove the identity of a person.

---

[4]PKCS is a group of public-key cryptography standards devised and published by RSA Security Inc.
[5]www.opendnssec.org/softhsm/.

Examples are secure authentication on bank accounts, monetary transactions and electronic signature of documents. These devices offer cryptographic functions, but they also store user-sensitive information such as cryptographic keys or certificates.

The MBT approach we used assesses the compliance of the component under test to the standard and uses the standard itself as entry point to define the testing perimeter and testing objectives. In other words, the standard will be the reference to create the MBT model used for test generation.

In this subsection, we introduce the specification used to create the MBT model (PKCS#11), the system under test (SoftHSM) and the test objectives to be covered (identified from the specifications).

11.3.1.1 PKCS#11 Specification

In 2004, RSA Public Key Cryptography Standards (PKCS) first proposed the PKCS#11 standard to promote interoperability and security of cryptographic tokens [54]. The standard defines an interface called *Cryptoki*, which is an API for cryptographic hardware, such as HSM or smartcards. PKCS#11 has been widely adopted by the industry. It is the common standard for communication with cryptographic tokens, even though the tokens offer other security layers as well.

Our study focuses on the PKCS#11 v2.20 specification, because this was the current revision of PKCS#11 at that point in time.[6]

Any software calling a security component through the *Cryptoki* API first initiates the communication with the token before calling any other function. Then, it opens a session and logs the user. Only then, we are able to call cryptographic functions such as signing a message.

Whenever an internal function is called by the token's API passing a reference to a specific object (for instance a key used for signing a message), the token first checks the object's permissions. Permissions are attributes that might be represented as Boolean flags signaling the properties of an object. If the flag is true, the object has the permission that allows it to be used for that function. For example, the CKA_SIGN flag of a cryptographic key indicates whether a key can be used for signing a message.

In addition, the interface itself performs further controls of access to functions and objects. In general, the user must login to the application before he can perform cryptographic functions. To guarantee security, Cryptoki implicitly or explicitly defines security properties that must hold. An example of such property is "a signature verification operation must have been initialized."

11.3.1.2 SoftHSM – A Virtual HSM

The system under test in this case study was SoftHSM, a virtual cryptographic store.[7] SoftHSM is a software implementation of a cryptographic store accessible through the PKCS#11 interface. It is developed as part of the OPENDNSSEC project, which goal is to offer an open source solution to manage the security of domain names on the Internet.

[6]Currently, PKCS #11 v2.40 is available on www.oasis-open.org [last accessed May 2015].
[7]https://www.opendnssec.org/.

More specifically, we used SoftHSM version 2.0.0b2, which implements PKCS#11 v2.40. However, there is no functional difference between these two versions of the PKCS#11 specification.

We chose this virtual token because it is representative for any HSM and implements most PKCS#11 functions. In fact, the ultimate goal of this case study was to set up a test harness[8] for verifying compliance to the PKCS#11 specification of any cryptographic token.

11.3.1.3   Test Scope and Test Objectives   For better understandability, we limited the scope to a subset of PKCS#11. Anyway, industrial security tokens classically support only subparts of PKCS#11. The chosen subset is self-contained, realistic, and sufficient to illustrate the main aspects of the specification.

For our study, we chose 24 functions most commonly present in industry tokens, such as session, token, key, and user management functions, as well as cryptographic functions for signing messages and verifying signatures. The complete list is as follows:

C_Initialize, C_Finalize, C_GetFunctionList, C_OpenSession, C_CloseSession,

C_CloseAllSessions, C_InitToken, C_Login, C_Logout, C_InitPIN, C_SetPIN,

C_CreateObject, C_DigestInit, C_Digest, C_DigestUpdate, C_DigestFinal,

C_SignInit, C_Sign, C_SignUpdate, C_SignFinal, C_VerifyInit, C_Verify,

C_VerifyUpdate, C_VerifyFinal

Based on the PKCS#11 specifications, we manually identified the requirements for each of those 24 functions and clustered them by function in a so-called test objective charter (TOC). Table 11.5 shows an extract of our TOC for PKCS#11 for two functions used to sign a data ("C_SignInit" used to initiate the signature and "C_Sign" used to sign the data).

For each function, we define one or several test objectives. Each test objective is composed of a high-level requirement denoted as @REQ and its refinement denoted as @AIM. @REQ is the function name, and @AIM is a text describing an expected behavior of the function. In the example in Table 11.5, the two high-level requirements "C_SignInit" and "C_Sign" have a common test objective, which requires initialization of the communication with Cryptoki by a calling "C_Initialized" successfully.

In total, we obtained 193 elementary test objectives for the considered subset of PKCS#11.

Our MBT model traces these test objectives by linking each requirement/behavior in the function with the corresponding @REQ and @AIM, thus ensuring the bidirectional traceability between the requirements and the generated tests.

---

[8]A test harness is a test environment comprising stubs and drivers needed to conduct a test [1].

TABLE 11.5   Test Objective Charter Example for PKCS#11

@REQ	Description	@AIM		
C_SignInit	C_SignInit initializes a signature operation	CRYPTOKI_NOT_ INITIALIZED The Cryptoki library has not been initialized by a call to C_Initialize	USER_NOT_ LOGGED_IN The normal user is not logged in	OK The initialization of the signing operation succeeded
C_Sign	C_Sign signs data in a single part	CRYPTOKI_NOT_ INITIALIZED The Cryptoki library has not been initialized by a call to C_Initialize	OPERATION_NOT_ INITIALIZED The signing operation has not been initialized by a call to C_SignInit	OK The signing operation succeeded

11.3.2   Characteristics of the MBT Approach Used on PKCS#11

Figure 11.19 shows the MBT approach presented in this case study. PKCS#11 specifications and project test objectives serve as input to develop the MBT model and to define test selection criteria (step 1). The MBT model contained static and dynamic views of the system. Using automated test generation based on model-coverage test selection criteria, we generated (step 2) and published (step 3) our test scripts using CertifyIt, the MBT tool of Smartesting.[9]

The scripts in combination with a test adaptation layer link each step from the abstract test to a concrete command of the SUT. They automate the test execution (step 4). Finally, after test execution, test results and metrics are collected and feedback is sent to the user.

All four steps were performed iteratively and incrementally, performing the entire process in each iteration.

The core idea of our MBT approach is to link requirements and test objective information to model elements and, then, to use the test generation tool's feature to cover them during automated test generation. Thus, we applied coverage-based test selection relying on the test objectives that the tester initially derived from the specification (see Table 11.5). More specifically, the test generation is guided by requirements-based test selection criteria. The test generation engine searches those paths that maximize the coverage of model elements (in our case requirements).

The MBT modeling approach uses a subset of UML. Each MBT model in our case study comprises two types of diagrams: class diagrams and object diagrams. Each diagram type has a specific role in the test generation process. The class diagram describes the system's structure, namely the set of classes that represents the static view of the system: its entities including their attributes, operations that model the

[9]www.smartesting.com.

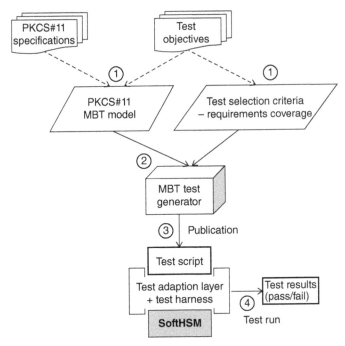

Figure 11.19   MBT process used in the PKCS#11 case study.

API of the SUT and observations that serve as oracles. For instance, an observation returns the current state of the user's connection to a website. The static view of the class diagram is instantiated by object diagrams. The object diagrams provide the test input data (i.e., the objects) that will be used as parameters for the operations in the generated tests.

In addition to the static view, we describe the dynamic view of the system or its behaviors by Object Constraint Language (OCL) constraints written as pre-/postcondition.[10] Technically, those OCL constraints are contained in the operations of a class in a class diagram. The test generation engine sees those behavior objects as test targets. The operations can have several behaviors, identified by the presence of the conditional operator if–then–else. The precondition is the union of the operation's precondition and the conditions of a path that is necessary to traverse for reaching the behavior's postcondition. The postcondition corresponds to the behavior described by the action in the "then" or "else" clause of the conditional operator.

Finally, each behavior is identified by a set of tags (as initially defined in the test objective charter – TOC), which refers to a requirement covered by the behavior. For each requirement, two types of tags exist: @REQ – a high-level requirement – and @AIM – its refinement, both followed by an identifier. Using a feature of our MBT tool, we created a new tag called "*CKR*," which refers to the expected return value

---

[10]Please refer to Ref. [46] for more details on OCL constraint in MBT.

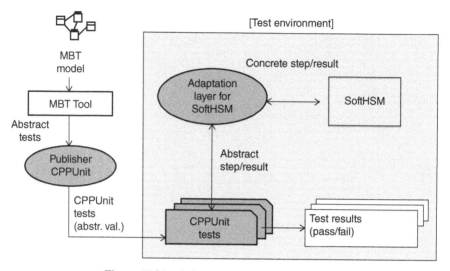

Figure 11.20 SoftHSM 2.0.0b2 test environment.

of a function as defined by the specification. A specific type of operations, called observations, defines the test oracle. Using those special operations, the tester can define the system points or variables to observe, for instance, a function return code. Based on these observations, the test generation tool automatically generates the test oracle[11] for each test step.

11.3.3   SoftHSM Test Environment

Figure 11.20 depicts the SoftHSM test environment, which is a Linux Virtual Box containing

- the SoftHSM version 2.0.0b2 installed on a virtual machine,
- the adaptation layer for SoftHSM, and
- the generated abstract tests exported in C++.

After test execution, the test results (pass/fail) are collected by the MBT tool in an XML format.

We created a Virtual Machine with Ubuntu 32 bits and 2G of RAM. On the machine, we installed SoftHSM version 2.0.0.b2 and the libraries SoftHSM depends on, such as Botan and OpenSSL. For more details on the SoftHSM installation, please refer to the OPENDNSSEC project wiki-page.[12]

On the Virtual Machine, we included the generated concrete tests, the test adaptation layer and test execution script.

---

[11] Test oracle is a source to determine expected results to compare with the actual result of the software under test.

[12] https://wiki.opendnssec.org/display/SoftHSMDOCS/SoftHSM+Documentation+v2.0.

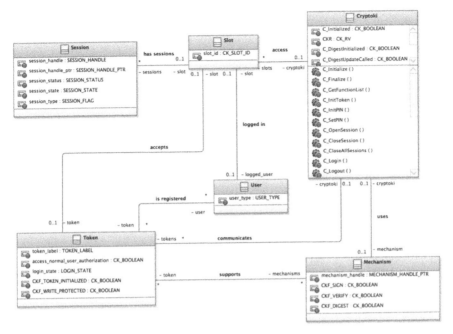

Figure 11.21   PKCS#11 MBT model – simplified class diagram.

11.3.4   MBT Modeling for PKCS#11

The MBT model for PKCS#11 focuses on the test objectives we defined in the TOC. A class diagram represents the static view of the Cryptoki API. Figure 11.21 provides a simplified view of the MBT model. The class diagram contains six classes: *Cryptoki*, *User*, *Token*, *Slot*, *Session*, and *Mechanism*.

The model represents the API *Cryptoki* that offers an interface to a *User* for communicating with cryptographic tokens, modeled by the class *Token*. Each token is connected to the system through a *Slot*. Once the user has been connected to a *Session*, *Cryptoki* offers cryptographic operations, such as signing a message (*C_Sign*) or verifying a message signature (*C_Verify*). The cryptographic operations use different cryptographic algorithms represented by the class *Mechanism*.

The dynamic view of the Cryptoki API is modeled using OCL postconditions added to the description of the Cryptoki functions. An OCL postcondition captures the test objectives for each function given in the TOC. In addition, we annotate each behavior in the postcondition using the tagging system with @REQ and @AIM.

For example, the signing function "*C_SignInit*" has three test objectives:

- the Cryptoki API has not been initialized – CRYPTOKI_NOT_INITIALIZED,
- the normal user has not been logged in – USER_NOT_LOGGED_IN, and
- successful execution of the signing initialization function – OK,

```
/**@REQ:C_SignInit*/
if (self.C_Initialized=CK_BOOLEAN::CK_FALSE) then
  self.CKR = CK_RV::CKR_CRYPTOKI_NOT_INITIALIZED
  /**@AIM:CRYPTOKI_NOT_INITIALIZED*/
else if (session.slot.logged_user.oclIsUndefined()) then
  self.CKR = CK_RV::CKR_USER_NOT_LOGGED_IN
  /**@AIM:USER_NOT_LOGGED_IN*/
else
  self.CKR = CK_RV::CKR_OK
  /**@AIM:OK*/
endif
endif
```

Figure 11.22   OCL postcondition for C_SignInit.

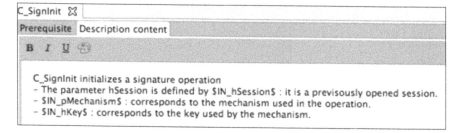

Figure 11.23   Example of function description, C_SignInit.

represented as OCL postcondition in Figure 11.22. As shown in the figure, the @AIM tags in the postcondition correspond one-to-one to the definition in the test objective charter. Thus, the test generation tool is able to export a report documenting the coverage of each test objective by the generated tests.

As depicted in Figure 11.23, we provide further test description for the function (in this example "*C_SignInit*"). This allows us to export the test cases in a readable format as HTML and guides the test automation engineer during his work to implement the test adaptation layer, when concretizing the tests.

11.3.5   Test Generation

The test generation activities involve creating an object diagram to define the initial state for test generation, and then to define the test selection criteria to be used to drive test generation.

The object diagram contains the input data based on the principle of equivalence partitions, represented as instances (objects). For example, the two instances of cryptographic keys in Figure 11.24 correspond to the two equivalence partitions we want to test. *KEY_ID1* represents a typical cryptographic key that can be used for signing and verifying messages, while *KEY_ID2* represents another key that cannot be used for signing and verification, and when used in such context, the function should fail.

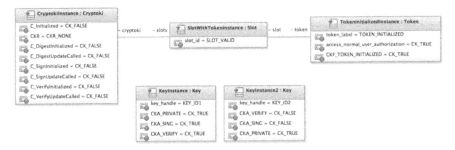

Figure 11.24 Excerpt of the PKCS#11 initial state definition.

The complete set of instances in Figure 11.24 defines the initial state of our system (CryptokiInstance) with a slot (SlotWithTokenInstance) having a connected token (TokenInitialized) and a set of cryptographic keys (KeyInstance and KeyInstance2) used for signing/verifying messages.

In the next step, we state the test selection criteria to guide automated test generation. In our case, this is an automated process. Based on the @REQ and @AIM tags in the MBT model, the test generation tool extracts a set of model elements to be covered during automated test generation, first. Then, it generates a set of test cases according to the coverage criteria specified as input.

Figure 11.25 shows a snapshot of the generated test cases. To the left, the tool lists the generated tests per covered requirement. To the right, we see the test case details with the list of test steps and the generated test oracle of each test step (upper frame to the right). In addition, it is possible to visualize the test targets (set of tags) of the test case (lower frame to the right) and the selected test step (marked in bold).

As explained before, the tester defines the test oracle manually in a specific type of operations called observations. The observation corresponds to the system point to observe for any API function called. In our case, we defined an observation

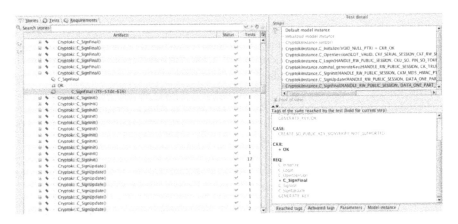

Figure 11.25 Test case view.

Steps	Actions	Requirements, aims, and custom tags	
Step 1 (*CryptokiInstance*)	*C_Initialize* C_Initialize initializes the Cryptoki library	REQ AIM CKR	C_Initialize C_Initialize/OK OK
Step 2 (*CryptokiInstance*)	*C_OpenSession* C_OpenSession opens a session between an application and a token in a particular slot.	REQ AIM CKR	C_OpenSession C_OpenSession/OK OK
Step 3 (*CryptokiInstance*)	*C_Login* C_Login logs a user into a token.	REQ AIM CKR	C_Login C_Login/CKU_USER_RW C_Login/OK OK
Step 4 (*CryptokiInstance*)	*C_SignInit* C_SignInit initializes a signature operation - $$IN_hKey corresponds to the key use for the mechanism.	REQ AIM CKR	C_SignInit C_SignInit/OK OK

Figure 11.26   HTML export of generated test case.

"*checkResult*," which observes the return code of each Cryptoki function with respect to the activated requirement.

Figure 11.26 illustrates the generated test after HTML export. The test represented in the figure verifies the behavior of signing a message with success using the "*C_Sign*" function, where CryptokiInstance is the instance of the Cryptoki class. As you can see in the first two columns, the test initializes the communication with Cryptoki, first (test step 1). Then, it opens a public session with SoftHSM (test step 2) and logs the normal user (test step 3) before initializing the signing operation (test step 4). Once the signing operation has been initialized, it calls the signing operation (test step 5). All test steps are positive tests, that is, we expect them to be successful.

As discussed previously, each test case has a set of associated tags for which it will ensure the coverage. The test case export establishes the mapping between each step and the covered requirements (right column in Figure 11.26) or, more precisely, the test objective tagged by @REQ and @AIM initially defined in the test objective charter. Please notice the newly introduced tag "CKR," which is specific for PKCS#11. It allows us to trace the return value of the Cryptoki API functions, as defined in the specification.

For the considered scope of PKCS#11, the tool extracted 193 model elements to be covered (i.e., expected behavior) and generated 173 tests in approximately 12 min to cover all test objectives. Each test covers one or more test objectives triggered by different test steps. For instance, the test shown in Figure 11.26 covers five test objectives (called AIM – one per step and two in step 3). The test generator will not produce separate tests for the previously reached test objectives (test steps 1, 2, 3, and 4), but will consider the test objectives from steps 1, 2, 3, and 4 as covered by this test, too (in addition to the test objective C_Sign/OK, for which the test case has been generated).

```
CryptokiInstance.C_SignInit(SESSION, CKM_MECH, KEY_ID1)
                → CryptokiInstance.checkResult()
                = CKR_CRYPTOKI_NOT_INITIALIZED
```

Figure 11.27   Simple abstract test case for PKCS#11.

The generated tests are abstract test cases. To execute them on the system they have to be further adapted. We discuss the test adaptation and execution activities on the SoftHSM v2 project in the following section.

For this case study, we extended the MBT tool and created a C++ exporter, which publishes tests into C++ using the CCPUNIT library.

11.3.6   Test Adaption and Test Execution

To illustrate the test adaptation activities, let us consider the following simple test case given in Figure 11.27. The test consists of a single test step that calls the function for initializing the data signature with three parameters: a session handle (SESSION), the signing mechanism to use (CKM_MECH), and a key handle (KEY_ID1). CKM_MECH is important, because Cryptoki authorizes the usage of various cryptographic mechanisms.

The second line in Figure 11.27 shows the test oracle derived from the operation of type "observation" in the MBT model. The observation in our example is "*checkResult*". The expected result of the test is an error (CKR_CRYPTOKI_ NOT_INITIALIZED), since no call of the Cryptoki function "*C_Initialize*" has been effected prior to "*C_SignInit*".

Figure 11.27 shows the test case once it has been generated. To execute this test, we have to export the abstract test case into a test script, which can be compiled and executed on SoftHSM. In our case, we published all test cases using the C++ exporter specially developed for this project.

Figure 11.28 shows the export of our simple test case in Figure 11.27. The exporter is generic for PKCS#11 implementations. Thus, we might reuse it for other SoftHSM versions or other tokens, as well.

Next to publishing the test scripts in C++, we created an adaptation layer that utilizes the keywords, such as "*C_SignInit*" or "*KEY_ID1,*" from the MBT model to match the concrete PKCS#11 functions and input parameters.

Figure 11.29 illustrates how the function "*op_adaptor*" concretizes the call to "*C_SignInit*" and its input data. The "*get_real*" functions return the concrete values of the test data in the test harness. For example, "*get_realKEY*" returns the concrete object containing the key, which will be used to sign.

To execute the tests on the test harness, we compile the C++ tests and launch the resulting executable in the batch. To simplify this step, it is also possible to create batch scripts.

Altogether, we generated 173 tests to cover all test objectives for the 24 functions. Around 5% of the executed tests failed and revealed five different issues,

```
#include "AdaptationLayer.h"

class pkcs11_testsuite : public CppUnit::TestFixture
   {
        CPPUNIT_TEST_SUITE(pkcs11_testsuite);
        CPPUNIT_TEST(C_SignInit);
        CPPUNIT_TEST_SUITE_END();

   public:
       void setUp();
       void tearDown();
       void C_Sign();
   };

   //-------------------------------------

 void pkcs11_testsuite::setUp()
  {   . . .   }
 void pkcs11_testsuite::tearDown()
  {   . . .   }
 void pkcs11_testsuite::C_SignInit()
  {

  string arg1[]={"SESSION","CKM_MECH","KEY_ID1"};
  AdaptationLayer::op_adaptor("C_SignInit",arg1);

  string arg2[] = {"CKR_CRYPTOKI_NOT_INITIALIZED"};
  CPPUNIT_ASSERT_MESSAGE("Expected: " + arg2));
  }
```

Figure 11.28   Concrete C++ tests for SoftHSM.

mainly inconsistencies of SoftHSM implementation with the PKCS#11 standard specification. For comparison, the OPENDNSSEC project provides 24 manually created test for SoftHSM and they all pass.

11.3.7   Project Metrics and Discussion

SoftHSM v2 is still in its early development and it was a great opportunity to apply an MBT approach at such early stage of an industrial project. In fact, we were able to see the benefits of applying an MBT approach in terms of improving the software security and quality in very short time.

In terms of project planning, it took us 16 person–days to create the MBT model within the scope defined earlier in this section. More specifically, it took 4 person–days to model the static view of the system (the class diagram) suitable for testing and 12 person–days to model the dynamic view of the system (to describe the behavioral aspects of the MBT model).

```
#include "AdaptationLayer.h"

//RESULT
CK_RV rv  = CKR_OK;

//SESSION
CK_SESSION_HANDLE SESSION;

//KEY
CK_OBJECT_HANDLE KEY_ID1 =
                       CK_VALID_HANDLE;
CK_OBJECT_HANDLE KEY_ID2 =
                       CK_INVALID_HANDLE;

//MECHANISM
CK_MECHANISM CKM_MECH  = {. . .};
. . .

bool AdaptationLayer::op_adaptor(string name, string* params){
. . .
    if (name=="C_SignInit"} {
        rv = C_SignInit(get_realSESSION(params[0]},
                 get_realMECHANISM[params[1]),
                 get_realKEY(params[2])];
              return true;
   }else { . . . }
      return false;
}

CK_OBJECT_HANDLE AdaptationLayer::get_realKEY(string argument) {
    if (argument =="KEY_ID1")   {
      return KEY_ID1;
    } if (argument =="KEY_ID2") {
      return KEY_ID2;
    } else {
      return NULL_PTR;
    }
}
```

Figure 11.29   Excerpt of PKCS11 test adaptation layer.

These metrics exclude the time spent by the tester analyst to acquire the required domain knowledge on cryptography and the PKCS#11 specification itself. This knowledge ramp-up was specific for our case study. If MBT is introduced in a project, the testing teams have the domain knowledge, but no experience with MBT.

The development of the test adaptation layer took more time (one person-month), but we do not consider it as representative. While we did not have the knowledge of the SoftHSM v2 code, experienced testers in the domain have. It is even probable that the adaptation layer already exists prior to MBT introduction. If this is the case, the effort to adapt the existing test adaptation layer to MBT is negligible.

One major advantage we saw in applying the MBT approach on PKCS#11-based APIs is the clear separation between the test generation layer and the test automation layer. This helped a lot managing the change. In fact, project requirements and specifications may evolve within the project's duration. Until today, the SoftHSM v2 requirements specification changed several times, going from PKCS#11 v2.20 to v2.40 [56] with v2.30 in between. The PKCS#11 MBT model provided a single point of maintenance for requirement changes, thus accelerating the update of the test scripts.

Another advantage we saw concerns the exhaustiveness of testing. It is difficult, if not impossible, to test any system exhaustively. However, the possibility to generate tests automatically and in a systematic way (as we did) allowed us to create a test suite covering the defined test objectives. In addition, our MBT tool also generated reports to document the test objective coverage. Thus, we are now able to provide objective evidence of test "exhaustiveness" with respect to the test objectives, which is, for instance, very useful during audits.

For comparison, we also assessed the existing manually designed test suite of SoftHSM v2 with respect to test objective coverage. Technically, we imported the manual tests as test scenarios in the MBT tool and compared them with the automatically generated tests. We concluded that the manual test suite covered barely 45% of the test objectives, which is less than a half of the tested scope. Moreover, these tests did not reveal any error on the SoftHSM v2 (unlike our generated test suite).

11.3.8 Conclusion

This case study presents a successful application of an MBT approach for security components testing. We believe that this approach can be generally applied on a wide range of specifications defining APIs for security components, for example, FORTEZZA.

Within the PKCS#11 context, the created MBT model is compliant for PKCS#11 v2.20, 2.30, and 2.40 specifications and can be reused for testing a large range of security tokens implementing this standard. The only changes to be made concern the test environment, in order to make it compatible with the component under test.

12

CONCLUSIONS

With the new Model-Based Tester certification scheme, the International Software Testing Qualifications Board promotes a testing approach that convinces more and more professional testers. In 2011, members of the German and Swiss testing boards (together with other authors) conducted a survey on "Software test in practice" among German, Swiss, and Austrian software companies [57]. In this survey, 15% of the 1,600 participants reported model-based test design using graphical models. A more recent survey conducted in 2014 in the automotive domain adjusts this figure upwards (at least in this particular context). More than 38% of the participants apply model-based testing (MBT) techniques for automotive embedded software development [58]. The rather high percentage certainly includes the use of models for hardware-in-the-loop tests, but it illustrates a clear trend toward test design on a higher abstraction level.

In the 2014 MBT User Survey, we asked for the initial expectations and how satisfied the participants were with MBT. Figure 12.1 shows the number of answers for each of the five categories we proposed. The white bars to the left represent the number of participants who mentioned the category in their initial expectations. The second bars sum up the positive, the third bars the negative answers. The gray bars to the right represent indecisive participants.

We observe that MBT nearly meets the high expectations regarding cost reduction and improved management of complexity, while it slightly exceeds the expectations regarding early test design. Only two categories of MBT show

Model-Based Testing Essentials–Guide to the ISTQB® Certified Model-Based Tester Foundation Level, First Edition. Anne Kramer and Bruno Legeard.

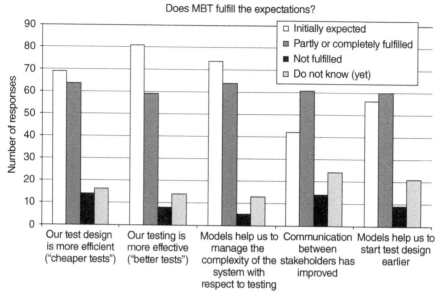

Figure 12.1   Fulfillment of expectations (from 2014 MBT User Survey).

considerable deviations. Curiously, those are exactly the category with most and least expectations. On one hand, 81% of the participants expected an improvement of their test effectiveness, whereas 59% actually reported those improvements. On the other hand, only 42% expected improved communication, but 61% obtained it. One of the participants wrote a comment to this question that gets to the heart of the issue: "Often prerequisites to successfully use models aren't met, so MBT doesn't fully life up to expectations. But early communication with 'others' always works through models."

MBT is not necessarily the solution of all our problems, but it is a tremendous opportunity for improvement. Sixty-four percent of the survey participants rated MBT as moderately to extremely effective (see Figure 12.2). In many situations, we do not really have the choice. The system under test being so complex we are unable to test it without drawing more or less formal models. With MBT, the tests are more complete, or, at least, we know better what is missing.

The main prerequisites for being successful are knowledge of the approach and good practices, modeling skills, and adequate tool support. Reading this book was a first step. By now, you know about the diversity of MBT, how different lifecycles, domain areas, and organizational aspects influence the approach to take; and how MBT models depend on test objectives. Even if we did not present a concise decision table which approach is best for which application area, you should be able to identify the direction to take.

Modeling skills relate to experience. In our survey, we also asked how much time it takes to become a proficient model-based tester. From the answers, we computed

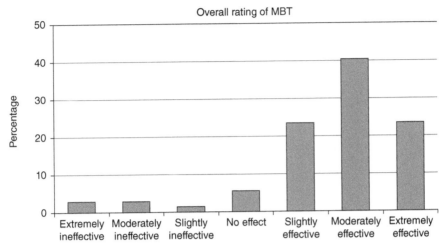

Figure 12.2 Overall rating by MBT practitioners (from 2014 MBT User Survey).

a median[1] of two working weeks (80 h) required to develop the necessary skills. The good modeling practices mentioned in Chapter 6 and the test selection techniques explained in Chapter 8 should help you to avoid common mistakes and pitfalls. However, do not underestimate the modeling task. The quality of the generated tests originates from the MBT model. Writing and maintaining those models requires special care.

Tooling is now mature enough and continues to improve. A variety of open-source and commercial tools exists, which are well adapted to industrial needs. Since tooling plays an important role, you should select them carefully. More generally, it is necessary to adapt the MBT approach to your project's context. There is no universal (and there cannot be any) "one size fits all" MBT solution.

Personally, we became unconditional supporters of the method. Our recommendation is clear: Just do it yourself! It is worth trying!

---

[1] We took the median instead of the average, because it is less sensitive to extreme answers.

A

SOLUTIONS OF EXERCISES

Exercise 1 Each of the following six figures (Figures A.1–A.3) corresponds to three test cases (indicated by the bold arrows), testing the three possible evening activities. In combination, we obtain 18 test cases.

Exercise 2 The model described a test of the Microsoft Windows calculator. The test focuses on the basics operators plus (+), minus (−), times (*), divide (/), and equals (=). Trigonometric and logarithmic functions are beyond scope.

Exercise 3 There is only one transition with trigger "close program," that is, the one from "Deleted" to "End." All deleted e-mails are in the recycle bin, which is purged at the end. The MBT model in Figure 2.9 does not describe any other behavior, which is a flaw we would probably detect during a review. To complete the model, we should draw transitions with trigger "close program" and action "empty recycle bin" from the states "Unread," "Read," and the subdiagram "Processed" to the end node.

Exercise 4 The first test objective relates to verifying a flow of actions. The corresponding MBT model will contain elements such as "Start game," "Complete row," and "Leave gap in row." Thus, the simple graphical modeling language for workflows fits best. It is also possible, but much more complicated, to use the simple graphical modeling language for state diagrams.

Model-Based Testing Essentials–Guide to the ISTQB® Certified Model-Based Tester Foundation Level,
First Edition. Anne Kramer and Bruno Legeard.
© 2016 John Wiley & Sons, Inc. Published 2016 by John Wiley & Sons, Inc.

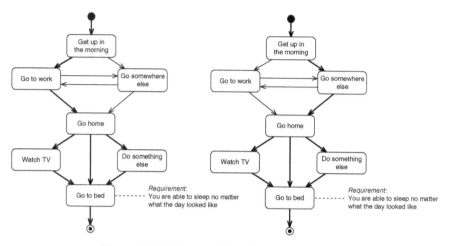

Figure A.1   Solution of Exercise 1 (test cases 1–6).

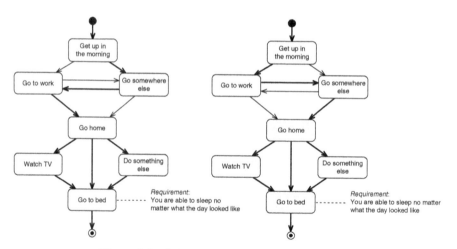

Figure A.2   Solution of Exercise 1 (test cases 7–12).

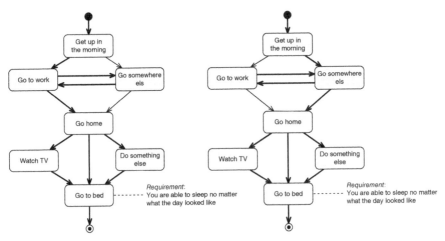

Figure A.3   Solution of Exercise 1 (test cases 13–18).

The second test objective relates to verifying the reaction of the game on user input (arrow keys) and clock pulse. Especially the reaction to the clock pulse is difficult to describe in a workflow modeling language. Instead, the simple graphical modeling language for state diagrams fits well. The corresponding MBT model will contain states such as "Moving," "Rotating," and transitions with trigger "clock interval over" or "move finished."

Exercise 5   The following MBT model (Figure A.4) shows a possible solution of this exercise. Yours will probably be different, but the concept should be the same.

Exercise 6   The following MBT model (Figure A.5) shows a possible solution of this exercise. The user has five options: pressing the arrow keys "left," "right," "up," "down," or any other key (considered as one type). "move(right, 1)" stands for a move of one step to the left, and "rotate(90°, right)" stands for a clockwise rotation of 90°.

Exercise 7   The MBT model in the sample solution of Exercise 5 (Figure A.4) combines two subjects: system and test. For example, the actions "Check: … " describe the test. In addition, the row counter is not important to describe the workflow, but required to guide test generation. The sample solution of Exercise 6 (Figure A.5) is different. It describes the system, but not the test.

None of the two MBT models includes aspects of the environment.

Both MBT models focus on behavioral aspects.

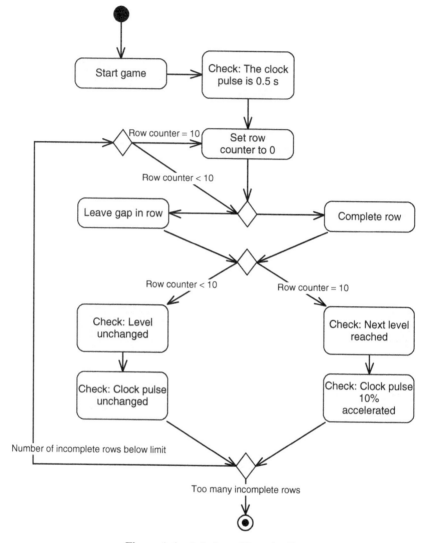

Figure A.4 Solution of Exercise 5.

Exercise 8 It is a rather formal event, because there is a receptionist, and colleagues and deputies are invited in addition to family and friends. Apparently, there will be the possibility of dancing, since the party takes place at a location with a ballroom and live music. Food and drinks are provided by a caterer. The caterer brings his own personal for serving and dishwashing, but they use the location's kitchen. Unfortunately, they forgot the coffee. Finally, the musicians will only get some drinks, but no food.

Exercise 9 The band starts in the state "Playing" and remains in this state until 30 min are over. The condition "timeOver(30 min) EQUAL False" is indicated

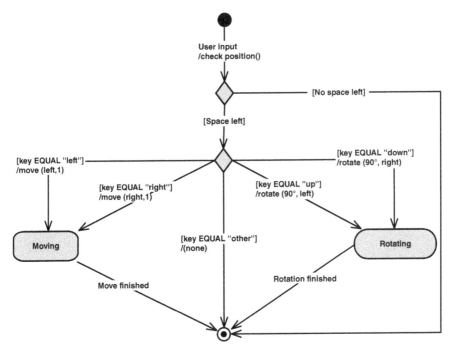

Figure A.5   Solution of Exercise 6.

by the brackets. After 30 min, the condition becomes true and the musician passes into the state "Pausing." This transition initiates two actions: the musicians stop playing and get some beer. Both actions are indicated after the slash ("/"). Once the beer is empty, they eventually restart playing, provided that the pause lasted at least 15 min ("Pause >= 15 min"). Otherwise, they get more beer. If there is no beer left, they immediately quit the party. The time counter reset occurs during the transition from "Pausing" to "Playing."

Exercise 10   We also test the situation that 3D glasses are sold for 2D films. This is not necessarily wrong, but should at least be discussed.

Exercise 11   The answer is "It depends." If it is acceptable to have a place called "canteen" with a drink and chocolate bar dispenser, the requirements coverage criterion as described in Section 8.1.1 is sufficient.

If it is important to check whether it is possible to serve yourself with drinks and meals in different orders, the requirement is not sufficiently precise. We should either split it or fix an additional selection criterion based on the model structure.

Exercise 12   Due to a stupid own goal of team 1, team 2 wins 2:0. However, the game must have been either very short or very dull, because there were only five turnovers.

Exercise 13   The following table shows the three possible test cases for six turnovers and a final score of 4:2 (with the assumptions given in the exercise):

Test Case 1		Test Case 2		Test Case 3	
Step Description	Expected Result	Step Description	Exp. Result	Step Description	Exp. Result
Kickoff		Kickoff		Kickoff	
Team 1 playing		Team 1 playing		Team 1 playing	
Goal	1:0	Goal	1:0	Goal	1:0
Restart		Restart		Restart	
(= turnover)		(= turnover)		(= turnover)	
Team 2 playing		Team 2 playing		Team 2 playing	
Turnover		Goal	1:1	Goal	1:1
Team 1 playing		Restart		Restart	
		(= turnover)		(= turnover)	
Goal	2:0	Team 1 playing		Team 1 playing	
Restart		Goal	2:1	Goal	2:1
(= turnover)					
Team 2 playing		Restart		Restart	
		(= turnover)		(= turnover)	
Goal	2:1	Team 2 playing		Team 2 playing	
Restart		Turnover		Goal	2:2
(= turnover)					
Team 1 playing		Team 1 playing		Restart	
				(= turnover)	
Goal	3:1	Goal	3:1	Team 1 playing	
Restart		Restart		Goal	3:2
(= turnover)		(= turnover)			
Team 2 playing		Team 2 playing		Restart	
				(= turnover)	
Goal	3:2	Goal	3:2	Team 2 playing	
Restart		Restart		Turnover	
(= turnover)		(= turnover)			
Team 1 playing		Team 1 playing		Team 1 playing	
Goal	4:2	Goal	4:2	Goal	4:2
Time over		Time over		Time over	

Version	Engine	Color	Interior	Options
Access A/C	**1.0 VTi 68**	**C1**	**T1**	**Alarm**
Access A/C	1.6 HDi 75	C2	T1	Exterior Pack
Access A/C	1.6 HDi 75	C4	T1	Alarm
Access A/C	1.6 HDi 75	C5	T2	Active City Break
Access A/C	1.6 HDi 75	C3	T3	Alarm
Active	**1.0 VTi 68**	**C2**	**T3**	**Active City Break**
GT line	1.6 HDi 120	C1	T2	Exterior Pack
GT line	1.6 HDi 120	C3	T2	Active City Break
Allure	**1.0 VTi 68**	**C3**	**T2**	**Exterior Pack**
GT line	1.6 HDi 120	C5	T3	Exterior Pack
Access A/C	1.6 HDi 75	C3	T3	Alarm
GT line	1.6 HDi 100	C2	T2	Alarm
Active	**1.0 VTi 68**	**C4**	T1	Alarm
Allure	**1.0 VTi 68**	**C5**	T2	Active City Break
...	...	...	...	...

Figure A.6 Solution of Exercise 16.

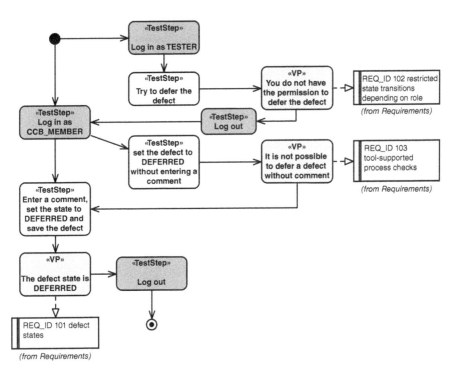

Figure A.7 Solution of Exercise 18.

Exercise 14   You get 7 test cases without loop, 6 more for 1 loop, and another 6 for
the second loop.

Exercise 15   This exercise has several solutions. If we drop only one test case, any of
the remaining test case triplets still ensures 100% transition coverage. If we drop
two test cases, we have to pay attention. The following two test case pairs still
fulfill 100% transition coverage:

(a) • T0 => T1 => T3 => T5 => T2 => T6
    • T0 => T2 => T4 => T5 => T2 => T6
(b) • T0 => T1 => T4 => T5 => T2 => T6
    • T0 => T2 => T3 => T5 => T2 => T6

Exercise 16   The generated tests cover all pairwise combinations of the engine "1.0
VTi 68" with version, color, interior, and extra options (see Figure A.6).

Exercise 17   None of the three exemplary test cases covers the case "risk = HIGH."
The three exemplary test cases for branch coverage do, but you can also invert the
result from APPROVED to Not APPROVED and vice versa.

As a general rule, statement coverage and branch coverage on textual models are
identical, if there is no IF statement without an ELSE branch containing a statement
(just a comment would not do).

Exercise 18   Figure A.7 specifies the test procedure for the defect state DEFERRED.
It is one possible solution of this exercise, but not the only one.

B

TEST YOURSELF

The quiz in this appendix does not replace the sample exam provided by ISTQB. It is only intended to give you the possibility to check your understanding of the topic. You may download the official sample exam document from the ISTQB website: http://www.istqb.org/certification-path-root/model-based-extension.html.

Only one answer per question is correct. If the question ends with … , select the continuation that fits best. You will find the solutions at the end of this appendix.

Good luck!

1) Why do we need new approaches to testing?
   a) Classic test design techniques such as boundary value analysis are incompatible with agile approaches.
   b) New technologies always require new tools and, thus, new approaches to testing.
   c) Testing projects have to cope with increasing industrial demands regarding time-to-market and cost reduction.
   d) By definition, new approaches are better and there is no reason not to use them.

2) The ISTQB standard glossary defines MBT as …
   a) Replacing classic testing techniques by models.
   b) Testing based on or involving models.

Model-Based Testing Essentials–Guide to the ISTQB® Certified Model-Based Tester Foundation Level, First Edition. Anne Kramer and Bruno Legeard.
© 2016 John Wiley & Sons, Inc. Published 2016 by John Wiley & Sons, Inc.

c) Generating test cases for automated test execution from models.

d) Reusing of models from analysis and design phases for testing purposes.

3) Which one of the following statements describes the benefits of model-based testing best?

a) Using MBT increases efficiency and/or effectiveness of your testing activities.

b) Using MBT, the budget required for testing will decrease.

c) Using MBT, you will find more bugs in your product.

d) Using MBT, your developers will become good testers.

4) Which one of the following ideas on MBT is WRONG?

a) MBT works also for manual testing.

b) MBT helps managing complexity in testing.

c) MBT is mainly a question of tooling.

d) MBT improves communication between stakeholders.

5) The work of an MBT tester is not so different from the work of any other tester, but one of the following tasks is specific to MBT. Which one is it?

a) Providing feedback on the requirements specification.

b) Writing workflow-based tests.

c) Reviewing the MBT model.

d) Analyzing test results.

6) There are many ways to use MBT models. Which one of the following is NOT a good idea?

a) Establish traceability between model elements and requirements.

b) Include MBT model diagrams as figures in the requirements specification.

c) Derive test cases from the MBT model.

d) Reference the MBT model in the test plan.

7) MBT is used mostly in …

a) Component testing.

b) Component and integration testing.

c) User acceptance testing.

d) Integration, system, and user acceptance testing.

8) How does MBT foster early requirements validation?

a) The MBT model visualizes complex dependencies and, thus, facilitates discussions between stakeholders having different level of technical knowledge.

b) MBT requires a model-based requirements specification and, thus, forces the requirements engineers to be more precise.

c) The MBT model has to be released together with the requirements specification, which leads to an early start of testing activities.

d) MBT implies the generation of automated test scripts and, thus, ensures a higher coverage of regression testing.

9) MBT models …
   a) Always describe the system under test.
   b) Always describe the test itself.
   c) Usually describe the system and its environment.
   d) May combine system, environment, and test aspects.

10) UML is …
   a) A language for structural models.
   b) A language for behavioral models.
   c) A language for data models.
   d) An integrated language covering various aspects.

11) As a reviewer, you discover flaws in the semantic quality of a behavioral MBT model. What does that mean?
   a) The MBT model does not respect the formal rules of the modeling language.
   b) The MBT model does not describe the correct behavior.
   c) The chosen modeling language does not fit the test objective.
   d) The test case generator cannot interpret the MBT model.

12) You wish to warn a colleague about typical mistakes in MBT model design. What do you say?
   a) Do not use different modeling languages. People will get confused about the models.
   b) Do not use UML. It is too complicated.
   c) Do not put everything into one MBT model. This leads to test case explosion.
   d) Do not apply MBT at all. It is not worth trying.

13) Does it make sense to have test equipment information in the MBT model?
   a) Yes. It helps the test manager to create a test suite with all tests requiring specific equipment.
   b) Yes. Without this information, testers will never be able to specify the tests correctly.
   c) No. It blows up the MBT model without providing helpful information.

d) No. The test case generator will not understand the information and, thus, will not generate any test cases from the MBT model.

14) Which one of the following statements regarding modeling guidelines is correct?
   a) MBT projects with less than five testers do not require any modeling guidelines, because the testers can agree on standards without them.
   b) MBT projects with modeling guidelines are more expensive than MBT projects without modeling guidelines.
   c) MBT projects without modeling guidelines take additional risks, since testers can make the classic mistakes of modeling more easily.
   d) MBT projects that follow the ISTQB MBT syllabus never require modeling guidelines, because they can refer to the syllabus.

15) Your manager dreams of reusing existing models from other development activities, such as requirements elicitation. What do you tell her?
   a) It is only possible to reuse models from system design, but not from the requirements elicitation phase.
   b) Reusing the existing models without any modification is exactly the idea of MBT.
   c) In some specific cases, it is possible to reuse models from other development activities, but this approach has its limits.
   d) MBT has nothing to do with the idea of reusing models from other development activities.

16) Time for test execution is running short. How can MBT help you?
   a) If the MBT model contains information on priorities, you may apply project-driven test case selection to limit the number of generated test cases to those with high priority.
   b) You will not run into this problem, because the automated test case generation in MBT provides you with new test cases within a few seconds by pressing a button.
   c) Test execution is far less important in MBT, because requirements validation takes place even before the first test is performed.
   d) Not at all. MBT does not provide any support for test management in difficult situations.

17) Iterative MBT model development …
   a) Is only useful in agile development processes.
   b) Ensures that the MBT model is correct before you generate the first test case.
   c) Is a way to teach the modeling activity to newcomers.
   d) Should comprise regular reviews of the MBT model and an update of the generated test cases.

18) Test selection criteria …
   a) Are essential to generate test scripts from MBT models.
   b) Simplify the writing of the test adaptation layer.
   c) Are essential to define the test oracle in an MBT model.
   d) Guide the generation or selection of test cases in order to limit the size of a test.

19) Which one of the following statements correctly describes model coverage?
   a) Model coverage measures whether all model elements are covered by a test suite, expressed as Boolean (true/false).
   b) Model coverage measures the degree to which specific model elements are covered by a test suite, expressed as a percentage.
   c) Model coverage measures the number of model elements planned versus the number of model elements executed.
   d) Model coverage measures the degree to which model elements are reused in other diagrams, expressed as a percentage.

20) Coverage-based test selection …
   a) Are the best test selection criteria in MBT.
   b) Are the only test selection criteria in MBT.
   c) Are a group of possible test selection criteria in MBT.
   d) Are one particular test selection criterion in MBT.

21) Test case explosion …
   a) Only happens when the MBT model is badly written.
   b) Is an unavoidable side effect of automated test case generation when using a tool.
   c) May occur when applying some test selection criteria systematically.
   d) Is a myth invented by opponents of MBT.

22) Model-based testing …
   a) Without using a test case generator is nonsense.
   b) Using a test case generator does not require manual postprocessing of the generated test cases.
   c) Using a test case generator always requires manual postprocessing of the generated test cases.
   d) Using a test case generator can be a fully automated process.

23) Which one of the following statements regarding test selection criteria is correct?
   a) It is always sufficient to define one test selection criterion, if the right criterion is selected.

b) It is always necessary to combine test selection criteria to cope with test case explosion.

c) It depends on the test objectives, which test selection criterion/criteria fits best.

d) Test selection criteria always exclude themselves mutually.

24) If the MBT model contains concrete data values …
   a) The generated test cases may or may not be concrete test cases.
   b) The generated test cases are incomplete.
   c) The generated test cases are nevertheless abstract test cases.
   d) The generated test cases are by definition concrete test cases.

25) Online execution in MBT means that …
   a) Test case execution does not require reporting.
   b) Test case generation and execution are combined into one step.
   c) Test case generation is performed after test execution.
   d) Test case generation does not require documentation.

26) Your company combines MBT with keyword-driven testing. Which one of the following statements is correct?
   a) Some projects use MBT, others keyword-driven testing.
   b) The MBT model contains the keywords, but not the concrete instructions.
   c) MBT and keyword-driven testing are synonyms.
   d) The MBT model describes the concrete instructions what to do for each keyword.

27) You convinced your managers that MBT reduces costs. On which aspect should your MBT approach focus on?
   a) Generate as many tests as possible to find as many bugs as possible as soon as possible.
   b) Automate as many process steps as possible to avoid manual errors and to facilitate test case maintenance.
   c) Keep MBT evaluation as short as possible to speed up its introduction in order to profit as soon as possible from its proven benefits.
   d) Limit the case selection to one sharp test selection criterion to avoid executing unnecessary test cases.

28) MBT artifacts include (among others) the MBT model, generated test cases, test selection criteria, and the code of the test adaptation layer. Which of them should be placed under configuration management?
   a) MBT model and test selection criteria.
   b) Generated test cases and test adaptation layer code.

c) MBT model, generated test cases and test adaptation layer code.

d) All of them.

29) Running an MBT process is not free. Which one of the following is NOT a potential cost factor during daily work?

a) Training of MBT users.

b) Writing MBT models.

c) Evaluating MBT tools.

d) Licensing MBT tools.

30) Which one of the following interfaces is typical for MBT?

a) Interface between test case generator and test management tool.

b) Interface between test management tool and requirements management tool.

c) Interface between (offline) test execution tool and test management tool.

d) Interface between defect management tool and test management tool.

Solutions: 1c, 2b, 3a, 4c, 5c, 6b, 7d, 8a, 9d, 10d, 11b, 12c, 13a, 14c, 15c, 16a, 17d, 18d, 19b, 20c, 21c, 22d, 23c, 24a, 25b, 26b, 27b, 28d, 29c, 30a.

C

TAXONOMY OF MBT APPROACHES

Several model-based testing (MBT) taxonomies exist in literature (see, e.g., Refs. [39, 41]), which are more or less exhaustive. The problem lies in the diversity itself. On one hand, a complete taxonomy is necessarily rather complex and difficult to use. On the other hand, a simplified taxonomy excludes parts of the MBT approaches and, thus, cannot be universal.

In this book, we followed a simpler, more down-to-earth classification scheme, leaving out academic approaches not yet established in industrial projects. Figure C.1 shows an overview of the basic MBT characteristics. You can consider it as the table of contents of the ISTQB MBT syllabus for Chapters 2–4 and, thus, of the corresponding chapters in this book.

Some characteristics exclude each other, while others do not. The latter are marked with "and/or." For example, the dimension "Subject" spans a three-dimensional space. Each MBT model describes at least one of those subjects, but may also mix these subjects. The text "ranging from ... to" indicates a continuous scale. Each MBT model is located somewhere between "very detailed" and "very abstract."

Table C 1 provides a mapping between the different categories of the classification scheme and the corresponding sections in this book, in which the content is covered.

Model-Based Testing Essentials–Guide to the ISTQB® Certified Model-Based Tester Foundation Level, First Edition. Anne Kramer and Bruno Legeard.
© 2016 John Wiley & Sons, Inc. Published 2016 by John Wiley & Sons, Inc.

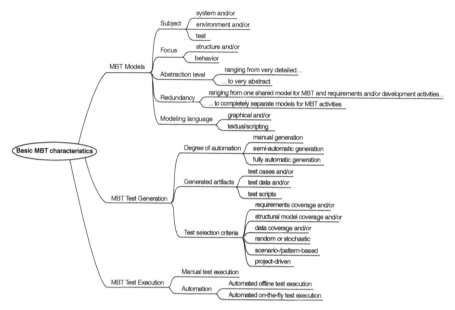

Figure C.1   Taxonomy of basic MBT characteristics.

TABLE C 1   Mapping Between the Classification of Basic MBT Characteristics and the Sections of This Book

Category	Subcategory	Corresponding Section in This Book
MBT models	Subject	Section 4.2.1
	Focus	Section 4.2.2
	Abstraction level	Section 4.1.3
	Redundancy	Section 6.5
	Modeling language	Section 2.2.3 and Chapter 5
MBT test generation	Degree of automation	Section 8.6
	Generated artifacts	Section 3.2.4
	Test selection criteria	Section 8.1
MBT test execution	Manual test execution	Section 9.1.3 and Case study 11.2
	Automation	Section 9.1.3 and Case study 11.3

ABBREVIATIONS

API	Application programming interface
ATDD	Acceptance test-driven development
ATM	Automated teller machine
ALM	Application lifecycle management
BDD	Behavior-driven development
BPMN	Business process modeling notation
CAN	Controller area network
CCB	Change Control Board
CTFL	Certified Tester – Foundation Level
DSL	Domain-specific language
EFG	Event-flow graphs
ERP	Enterprise resource planning
ESS	Employee Self Service
ETSI	European Telecommunications Standards Institute
FSK	"Freiwillige Selbstkontrolle der Filmwirtschaft" (German; "Voluntary Self-Regulation of the Film Industry")
GPS	Global positioning system
GUI	Graphical user interface
HP ALM	Hewlett-Packard Application Lifecycle Management
HR	Human resource
HRM	Human resource management

Model-Based Testing Essentials–Guide to the ISTQB® Certified Model-Based Tester Foundation Level,
First Edition. Anne Kramer and Bruno Legeard.
© 2016 John Wiley & Sons, Inc. Published 2016 by John Wiley & Sons, Inc.

HSM	Hardware security module
ISTQB	International Software Testing Qualifications Board
IT	Information technology
ITU	International Telecommunication Union
KPI	Key performance indicators
MARTE	Modeling and Analysis of Real-time and Embedded Systems
MBT	Model-based testing
MOF	Meta-object facility
MSC	Message sequence charts
OCL	Object Constraint Language
OMG	Object Management Group
PIM	Personnel Information Management (a module of the OrangeHRM application)
PKCS	Public-Key Cryptography Standards
QVT	Query/View/Transformation
REQ	Requirement
ROI	Return on investment
RTCA/DO	Radio Technical Commission for Aeronautics/Document
RUP	Rational unified process
SoC	System on a chip (UML profile)
SUT	System under test
SW	Software
TOC	Test objective charter
TTCN-3	Testing and Test Control Notation Version 3
UML	Unified Modeling Language
UTP	UML testing profile
VP	Verification point
XMI	XML metadata interchange
XML	Extensible Markup Language

TERMS AND DEFINITIONS

ISTQB TERMS

abstract test case	A test case without concrete (implementation level) values for input data and expected results. Logical operators are used: instances of the actual values are not yet defined and/or available (synonyms: high-level test case, logical test case).
concrete test case	A test case with concrete (implementation level) values for input data and expected results. Logical operators from high-level test cases are replaced by actual values that correspond to the objectives of the logical operators (synonym: low-level test case).
coverage item	An entity or property used as a basis for test coverage, for example, equivalence partitions or code statements.
keyword-driven testing	A scripting technique that uses data files to contain not only test data and expected results, but also keywords related to the application being tested. The keywords are interpreted by special supporting scripts that are called by the control script for the test.
MBT model	Any model used in model-based testing.

Model-Based Testing Essentials–Guide to the ISTQB® Certified Model-Based Tester Foundation Level, First Edition. Anne Kramer and Bruno Legeard.
© 2016 John Wiley & Sons, Inc. Published 2016 by John Wiley & Sons, Inc.

model-based testing	Testing based on or involving models.
model coverage	The degree, expressed as a percentage, to which model elements are planned to be or have been exercised by a test suite.
offline MBT	Model-based testing approach whereby test cases are generated into a repository for future execution.
online MBT	Model-based testing approach whereby test cases are generated and executed simultaneously (synonym: on-the-fly MBT).
regression testing	Testing of a previously tested program following modification to ensure that defects have not been introduced or uncovered in unchanged areas of the software, as a result of the changes made. It is performed when the software or its environment is changed.
test automation engineer	A person who is responsible for the design, implementation, and maintenance of a test automation architecture as well as the technical evolution of the resulting test automation solution.
test	A set of one or more test cases.
test adaptation layer	The layer in a test automation architecture that provides the necessary code to adapt test scripts on an abstract level to the various components, configuration, or interfaces of the SUT.
test basis	All documents from which the requirements of a component or system can be inferred. The documentation on which the test cases are based. If a document can be amended only by way of formal amendment procedure, then the test basis is called a frozen test basis.
test case	A set of input values, execution preconditions, expected results, and execution postconditions developed for a particular objective or test condition, such as to exercise a particular program path or to verify compliance with a specific requirement.
test case explosion	The disproportionate growth of the number of test cases with growing size of the test basis, when using a certain test design technique. Test case explosion may also happen when applying the test design technique systematically for the first time.
test condition	An item or event of a component or system that could be verified by one or more test cases, for example, a function, transaction, feature, quality attribute, or structural element.

test data	Data that exist (for example, in a database) before a test is executed, and that affects or is affected by the component or system under test.
test model	A model describing testware that is used for testing a component or a system under test.
test objective	A reason or purpose for designing and executing a test.
test procedure specification	A document specifying a sequence of actions for the execution of a test. Also known as test script or manual test script (synonym: test scenario).
test script	Commonly used to refer to a test procedure specification, especially an automated one.
test selection criteria	The criteria used to guide the generation of test cases or to select test cases in order to limit the size of a test.
test strategy	A high-level description of the test levels to be performed and the testing within those levels for an organization or programme (one or more projects).
traceability	The ability to identify related items in documentation and software, such as requirements with associated tests (in this book, synonymous to "requirements traceability").

OTHER TERMS

action word	Placeholder for scripted code or detailed test descriptions used in keyword-driven testing (synonym: keyword).
MBT process	Short for "test process implementing an MBT approach."
model	A system of assumptions, concepts, and relationships between them allowing to describe (model) in an approximate way a specific aspect of reality [15]. An abstraction of existing reality or a plan for reality to be created [16].
state diagram	Short for "state/transition diagram"
syllabus	Outline of topics covered in a training course with short description.
test analyst	Term used, but not defined by ISTQB. A person who is responsible for the design, implementation, and maintenance of the tests, but on a less technical level than the test automation engineer.

REFERENCES

[1] ISTQB (2015). ISTQB® Standard Glossary of Terms Used in Software Testing, V3.0.1. Available at http://www.istqb.org/downloads/viewcategory/20.html.

[2] Binder, R. V. (2012). 2011 Model-based Testing User Survey: Results and Analysis. Available at http://robertvbinder.com/wp-content/uploads/rvb-pdf/arts/MBT-User-Survey.pdf.

[3] Binder, R. V., Kramer, A., Legeard, B. (2014). 2014 Model-based Testing User Survey: Results. Available at http://model-based-testing.info/wordpress/wp-content/uploads/2014_MBT_User_Survey_Results.pdf.

[4] Binder, R. V., Legeard, B. & Kramer, A. (2014). Model-based Testing: Where Does It Stand?. ACM Queue, 13, 40–48.

[5] Gelperin, D. & Hetzel, B. (1988). The Growth of Software Testing. Communications of the ACM, 31, 687–695.

[6] ISTQB (2011). ISTQB® Certified Tester Foundation Level Syllabus. Available at http://www.istqb.org/downloads/syllabi/foundation-level-syllabus.html.

[7] Kuhn, T. S. (1962). The Structure of Scientific Revolutions. University of Chicago Press, Chicago.

[8] Fulford, R. (1999). Globe and Mail: Robert Fulford's column about the word "paradigm". Available at www.robertfulford.com/Paradigm.html.

[9] Planck, M. (1949). Scientific Autobiography and Other Papers. Philosophical Library, New York, pp. 33, 34.

Model-Based Testing Essentials–Guide to the ISTQB® Certified Model-Based Tester Foundation Level, First Edition. Anne Kramer and Bruno Legeard.
© 2016 John Wiley & Sons, Inc. Published 2016 by John Wiley & Sons, Inc.

[10] Schulze, C., Ganesan, D., Lindvall, M., Cleaveland, R. & Goldman, D. (2014). Assessing model-based testing: an empirical study conducted in industry. In P. Jalote, L. C. Briand & A. van der Hoek (eds.), ICSE Companion, ACM, New York, pp. 135, 144.

[11] Weißleder, S. & Schlingloff, H. (2014). An Evaluation of Model-Based Testing in Embedded Applications. In ICST. IEEE Computer Society, pp. 223, 232.

[12] Gartner, Gartner Hype Cycle. Available at http://www.gartner.com/technology/research/methodologies/hype-cycle.jsp.

[13] ISTQB (2015). ISTQB® Foundation Level – Certified Model-Based Tester Syllabus. Available at http://www.istqb.org/downloads.

[14] IEEE (2008). IEEE 829:2008. Standard for Software Test Documentation.

[15] Requirements Engineering Qualifications Board (2014). Standard glossary of terms used in Requirements Engineering, V1.3. Available at http://reqb.org.

[16] Glinz, M. (2014). A Glossary of Requirements Engineering Terminology, V1.6. Available at http://www.ireb.org/en/downloads.

[17] Stachowiak, H. (1973). Allgemeine Modelltheorie. Springer Verlag, Wien, New York.

[18] Economic Commission for Europe (1968). E/CONF.56/17/Rev.1/Amend.1. Available at http://www.unece.org/fileadmin/DAM/trans/conventn/signalse.pdf.

[19] OMG (2015). OMG® Unified Modeling Language™ (UML®). Available at http://www.omg.org/spec/UML.

[20] ETSI (2011). ETSI ES 202 951 V1.1.1 (2011-07). Requirements for Modeling Notations.

[21] Bach, J. (1999). Risk and Requirements Based Testing, IEEE Computer Journal, 32, 6, 113–114.

[22] ISTQB (2014). ISTQB® Agile Tester - Foundation Level Syllabus, Version 2014. Available at http://www.istqb.org/downloads/viewcategory/52.html.

[23] Crispin, L., Gregory, J. (2009). Agile Testing – A Practical Guide for Testers and Agile Teams. Addison Wesley.

[24] Kafka, F. (1912). Das Urteil. Manuscript, Bodleian Libraries, University of Oxford. Available at http://treasures.bodleian.ox.ac.uk/Das-Urteil.

[25] DeMarco, T. (1979). Structured Analysis and System Specification. Prentice Hall, PTR, Upper Saddle River, NJ.

[26] Kent, S., Evans, A., Rumpe, B. (1999). UML Semantics FAQ, Object-Oriented Technology ECOOP'99 Workshop Reader, Lecture Notes in Computer Science, Volume 1743/1999, p. 793.

[27] International Telecommunication Union (2011). ITU-T Z.120, SERIES Z: Languages and General Software Aspects for Telecommunication Systems, Formal description techniques (FDT) – Message Sequence Chart (MSC), V5.0. Available at http://www.itu.int/rec/T-REC-Z.120-201102-I/en.

[28] OMG (2011). Unified Modeling Language™ (OMG UML), Superstructure, V2.4.1. Available at http://www.omg.org/spec/UML/2.4.1/Superstructure/PDF.

[29] OMG (2013). OMG® Business Process Model and Notation (BPMN). Available at http://www.omg.org/spec/BPMN.

[30] Nguyen, B. N., Robbins, B., Banerjee, I., Memon, A. (2014). GUITAR: An Innovative Tool for Automated Testing of GUI-driven Software. Automated Software Engineering Journal, 21, 1, 65–105.

[31] Myers G. J., Sandler, C. (2004). The Art of Software Testing, 2nd edition. John Wiley & Sons.

[32] Lackner, H., Schlingloff, H. (2012). Modeling for Test Generation – A Comparison. In MBEES 2012 – 8th Dagstuhl-Workshop on Model-Based Development of Embedded Systems, Schloss Dagstuhl, Germany, February 2012.

[33] ETSI (2011). ES 201 873-1 to 10. ETSI Standard, Methods for Testing and Specification (MTS), The Testing and Test Control Notation version 3; Part 1 to 10. Available at http://www.etsi.org/standards.

[34] IBM (2014). IBM Rational Unified Process Datasheet. Available at ftp://public.dhe.ibm.com/software/rational/web/datasheets/RUP_DS.pdf.

[35] Wikiquote. Helmuth von Moltke the Elder. Available at https://en.wikiquote.org/wiki/Helmuth_von_Moltke_the_Elder (Last accessed Oct. 2015).

[36] International Qualifications Board for Business Analysis (2013). IQBBA® Certified Foundation Level Business Analyst Syllabus. Available at http://www.iqbba.org/.

[37] ETSI (2013). ETSI EG 203 130 V1.1.1 (2013-04). Methodology for standardized test specification development, MBT methodology.

[38] Copeland L. (2004). A Practitioner's Guide to Software Test Design. Artech House, Norwood, MA, USA.

[39] Utting, M., Pretschner, A., Legeard, B. (2012). A Taxonomy of Model-based Testing Approaches. Software Testing, Verification and Reliability. 22, 5 (August 2012), 297–312. John Wiley & Sons, Ltd.

[40] Weißleder, S. (2009). Test Models and Coverage Criteria for Automatic Model-Based Test Generation with UML State Machines. PhD thesis, Humboldt-Universität Berlin.

[41] Zander, J., Schieferdecker, I. & Mosterman, P. J. (2011). A taxonomy of model-based testing for embedded systems from multiple industry domains. In J. Zander, I. Schieferdecker & P. J. Mosterman (eds.) Model-Based Testing for Embedded Systems. CRC Press.

[42] ISTQB (2012). ISTQB® Certified Tester Advanced Level – Test Analyst Syllabus. Available at http://www.istqb.org/downloads/viewcategory/46.html.

[43] Dustin, E., Garrett, T., Gauf, B. (2009). Implementing Automated Software Testing: How to Save Time and Lower Costs While Raising Quality. Addison-Wesley Professional.

[44] Graham, D., Fewster, M. (2012). Experiences of test automation. Case Studies of Software Test Automation. Addison-Wesley Professional.

[45] Kanstrén, T., Kekkonen, T. (2013). Distributed online test generation for model-based testing. The 20th Asia-Pacific Software Engineering Conference (APSEC 2013), December 2–5, Bangkok, Thailand.

[46] Utting, M., Legeard, B. (2006). Practical Model-Based Testing: A Tools Approach. Morgan Kaufmann Publishers Inc., San Francisco, CA, USA.

[47] Wikiquote. Michel de Montaigne. Available at http://en.wikiquote.org/wiki/Michel_de_Montaigne (Last accessed Oct. 2015).

[48] Maslow, A.H. (1943). A Theory of Human Motivation. Psychological Review 50 (4) 370–396.

[49] Bloom, B. S., Engelhart, M. D., Furst, E. J., Hill, W. H., Krathwohl, D. R. (1956). Taxonomy of educational objectives: the classification of educational goals. In Handbook I: Cognitive Domain. David McKay Company, New York.

[50] Boehm, B. (1987). Industrial Software Metrics: A Top-Ten List, TRW, Inc. IEEE Software, pp. 84, 85.

[51] Haberl, P., Spillner, A., Vosseberg, K., Winter, M. (2012) Umfrage 2011: Softwaretest in der Praxis (Survey 2011 Software Test in Practice, in German). dpunkt.verlag.

[52] CENELEC (2010). IEC 61508-3:2010. Functional safety of electrical/electronic/ programmable electronic safety-related systems - Part 3: Software requirements.

[53] RTCA DO-178C (2012). Software Considerations in Airborne Systems and Equipment Certification. Available at http://www.rtca.org/store_search.asp.

[54] RSA Laboratories (2004). PKCS #11: Conformance Profile Specification Version 2.20.

[55] Cryptome. FORTEZZA CIPG Application Programming Interface. Available at http:// cryptome.org/jya/fortezza.htm (Last accessed Oct. 2015).

[56] OASIS (2015) PKCS #11 Cryptographic Token Interface Base Specification Version 2.40. In S. Gleeson & C. Zimman (eds.). Available at http://docs.oasis-open.org/pkcs11/ pkcs11-base/v2.40/pkcs11-base-v2.40.html.

[57] University of Bremen and Bremerhaven, Cologne University of Applied Science, ANECON Software Design und Beratung GmbH and the German and Swiss Testing Boards. Umfrage 2011 – Softwaretest in der Praxis (Survey 2011 – software test in practice). Available at http://www.softwaretest-umfrage.de/2011/Broschuere_Softwaretest_ in_der_Praxis.pdf (in German) (Last accessed Oct. 2015).

[58] Altinger, H., Wotawa, F., Schurius, M. (2014). Testing methods used in the automotive industry: results from a survey. In Proceedings of the 2014 Workshop on Joining AcadeMiA and Industry Contributions to Test Automation and Model-Based Testing (JAMAICA 2014). ACM, New York, NY, USA, pp. 1–6.

INDEX

Model-Based Testing Essentials–Guide to the ISTQB® Certified Model-Based Tester Foundation Level,
First Edition. Anne Kramer and Bruno Legeard.
© 2016 John Wiley & Sons, Inc. Published 2016 by John Wiley & Sons, Inc.